A Time of Disastrous Anticipations

This book explores the pervasive anticipation of catastrophe in contemporary society, examining how temporal expectations shape personal and collective experiences and influence our perspectives and responses.

A Time of Disastrous Anticipations highlights the role of anticipation in shaping societal narratives, exploring strategies for redefining responses to catastrophic imaginaries. Through a combination of theoretical insights with practical examples, it offers a comprehensive view of anticipation's impact in contemporary society. The vista of disastrous anticipations reveals that catastrophe is not so much a matter out of place but primarily a matter out of time.

Targeted at scholars, students, and professionals in sociology, disaster studies, and public policy, this book is also valuable for policymakers and practitioners interested in understanding the societal dimension of disaster anticipation.

Reidar Staupe is Associate Professor of Risk Management and Societal Safety at the University of Stavanger in Norway and at UiT The Arctic University of Norway. He is the author of the Routledge title *Disasters and Life in Anticipation of Slow Calamity: Perspectives from the Colombian Andes*. He has also published dozens of articles and chapters on disasters, global public health and development. From 2021 to 2023, he was a Marie Skłodowska-Curie Actions Individual Fellow at Roskilde University, Denmark. His research interests revolve around disaster temporalities and ideas about future catastrophes and prognostications.

Monika Gabriela Bartoszewicz is Associate Professor in Societal Security and Safety at the UiT The Arctic University of Norway, where she leads the *Secure Societies* group. She specializes in nonlinear and cross-sectoral threats to security, especially in the context of political violence and securitized migration. She holds a PhD from St. Andrews University (UK), and her doctoral thesis explored the questions of identity and belonging considered from a security perspective, with a particular focus on the potential terrorist threat posed by European converts to Islam. She has carried out interdisciplinary research in Scotland, England, The Netherlands, Denmark, Kosovo, Poland, the Czech Republic, and Taiwan. She is a European Commission Expert, Rapporteur & Evaluator of Horizon Europe projects, and an associate member of the Centre for Security Research in Edinburgh. Recently appointed as the Arctic Six Chair in Terrorism Studies and the Visiting Research Fellow at the Institute of National Defense and Security Research in Taipei, she focuses now on dystopias and societal collapses.

Routledge Studies in Hazards, Disaster Risk and Climate Change

Series Editor: Ilan Kelman
Professor of Disasters and Health at the Institute for Risk and Disaster Reduction (IRDR) and the Institute for Global Health (IGH), University College London (UCL)

This series provides a forum for original and vibrant research. It offers contributions from each of these communities as well as innovative titles that examine the links between hazards, disasters and climate change, to bring these schools of thought closer together. This series promotes interdisciplinary scholarly work that is empirically and theoretically informed, with titles reflecting the wealth of research being undertaken in these diverse and exciting fields.

Local Adaptation to Climate Change in South India
Challenges and the Future in the Tsunami-hit Coastal Regions
Devendraraj Madhanagopal

Good Practices for Disaster Risk Management of Cultural Heritage
Practices of ITC participants
Edited by Rohit Jigyasu, Kim Dowon and Lata Shakya

Agency in Poverty and War
Consciousness in Rural Human Development
Vivianna Rodriguez Carreon

Religious Responses to Earthquake and Volcanic Eruption Disasters
David Chester, Angus Duncan and John Duncan

Disaster Response by Ceaușescu's Communist Regime in Romania
The 1977 Earthquake
Karin Steinbrueck

A Time of Disastrous Anticipations
Essays on Life in the Shadow of Catastrophe
Edited by Reidar Staupe and Monika Gabriela Bartoszewicz

For more information about this series, please visit: https://www.routledge.com/Routledge-Studies-in-Hazards-Disaster-Risk-and-Climate-Change/book-series/HDC

A Time of Disastrous Anticipations

Essays on Life in the Shadow of Catastrophe

Edited by Reidar Staupe and Monika Gabriela Bartoszewicz

Routledge
Taylor & Francis Group

LONDON AND NEW YORK

Designed cover image: Routledge

First published 2025
by Routledge
4 Park Square, Milton Park, Abingdon, Oxon OX14 4RN

and by Routledge
605 Third Avenue, New York, NY 10158

Routledge is an imprint of the Taylor & Francis Group, an informa business

British Library Cataloguing-in-Publication Data
A catalogue record for this book is available from the British Library

ISBN: 978-1-032-88344-1 (hbk)
ISBN: 978-1-032-88345-8 (pbk)
ISBN: 978-1-003-53731-1 (ebk)

DOI: 10.4324/9781003537311

Typeset in Times New Roman
by Apex CoVantage, LLC

To H, my anticipation.—MGB

Contents

Figures

Tables

Contributors' biographies

Bakke Lie, Leikny. UiT The Arctic University of Norway.
PhD Fellow at the Faculty of Science and Technology, she brings extensive work experience in emergency preparedness, combined with an academic background in human geography, societal security, and risk management, to her current research on local climate change adaptation. Her research interests include concepts of place attachment, philosophy of technology, governance, and decision-making, particularly within the context of climate-induced natural hazards and risk management.

Bartoszewicz, Monika Gabriela. UiT The Arctic University of Norway.
Associate Professor in societal security and safety, where she heads the *Secure Societies* group. She specializes in non-linear and cross-sectoral threats to societal security, especially in the context of political violence, securitised migration, and disastrous futures. She has conducted research and worked in the UK, the Netherlands, Italy, Poland, the Czech Republic, Kosovo, and Taiwan. She is a European Commission Expert, Rapporteur & Evaluator of Horizon Europe projects, and an associate member of the Centre for Security Research in Edinburgh. Recently appointed as the Arctic Six Chair in Terrorism Studies and Visiting Research Fellow at the Institute of National Defense and Security Research in Taipei, she publishes widely on security-related topics, contributing to a knowledge depository on contemporary societal challenges.

Flaherty, Devin. University of Texas at San Antonio, USA.
Assistant Professor in the Department of Anthropology at the University of Texas at San Antonio. She received her PhD in Anthropology in 2018 from the University of California, Los Angeles. Devin's dissertation research and subsequent publications focused on care, ageing, and end of life in St. Croix, US Virgin Islands. In her current work, she is examining care, ageing, and critical approaches to vulnerability and disaster in St. Croix in the long-term wake of Hurricane Maria.

Gil, Piotr. WSB University, Poland.
PhD Fellow at the Faculty of Applied Sciences, Department of Security Sciences. His doctoral research centres on the pivotal role of national identity in shaping

Poland's national security landscape. Piotr's academic interests extend to both national and international security, encompassing ontological and societal security. Additionally, his scholarly pursuits delve into the intricate intersections of national identity, geopolitical spatial dynamics, and temporal imaginations.

Goldberg, David Theo. University of California, Irvine, USA.
Distinguished Professor of Anthropology, Comparative Literature, and Criminology, Law and Society at UC Irvine. Goldberg's work ranges over issues of social, political, and critical theory, race and racism, the future of the university, and digital technology. His numerous books include, most recently, *Dread: Facing Futureless Futures* (Polity, July 2021) and *The War on Critical Race Theory. Or, The Remaking of Racism* (Polity 2023). Earlier in his career, he produced independent films and music videos (some of which aired on MTV) and co-directed the award-winning short film on South Africa, The Island.

Matejova, Miriam. Masaryk University, Czech Republic.
Associate Professor in Political Science at Masaryk University and Fellow at Norman Paterson School of International Affairs, Carleton University. Her research centres on environmental disasters, risk assessment and uncertainty, and environmental movements. She has published in *Global Environmental Politics*, *Environmental Communication*, and the *Australian Journal of International Affairs*. She co-authored *Disaster Security: Using Intelligence and Military Planning for Energy and Environmental Security Risks* (Cambridge University Press) and co-edited *Uncertainty in Global Politics* (Routledge).

Islam Khan, Md Mohaiminul. University of Stavanger, Norway.
Postgraduate in Risk Analysis and Governance at the University of Stavanger and a data analyst for MIR Insight in Portugal, his thesis work is centered on the treatment of uncertainty in innovation projects. His research interests revolve around environmental risks, technology, artificial intelligence, and machine learning, as well as the societal issues that these may pose in the future.

Olofsson, Tobias. Lund University, Sweden.
Postdoctoral Researcher at the Department of Sociology, whose research focuses on the intersection of knowledge production and uncertainty. Before joining Lund University, Olofsson received a PhD in Sociology from Uppsala University, where they defended a thesis investigating how mineral exploration and mining companies use predictions to manage financial, geotechnical, and environmental uncertainty and to persuade stakeholders of the benefits of a mining future.

Schabowska, Barbara. Warsaw University of Business, Poland.
Journalist and culture manager with over two decades of experience in the public cultural sector in Poland. She served as the director of the Adam Mickiewicz Institute from 2019 to 2024, and her expertise encompasses international cooperation, cultural diplomacy, and strategic cultural management. Currently, Barbara is an associate researcher at the Warsaw University of Business. With

a diverse academic background in philosophy, culture, media management, and social science, her research interests span cultural resilience, mental health, societal security, and the geopolitical dynamics of Palestine and the Middle East. She is also a member of the Polish Association of Suicidology.

Staupe, Reidar. University of Stavanger, Norway.
Associate Professor of Risk Management and Societal Safety at the University of Stavanger in Norway and at UiT The Arctic University of Norway. He is the author of the Routledge title *Disasters and Life in Anticipation of Slow Calamity: Perspectives from the Colombian Andes*. He has also published dozens of articles and chapters on disasters, global public health and development. From 2021 to 2023, he was a Marie Skłodowska-Curie Actions Individual Fellow at Roskilde University, Denmark. His research interests revolve around disaster temporalities and ideas about future catastrophes and prognostications.

Stehrenberger, Cécile Stephanie. University of Wuppertal, Germany.
Assistant Professor for Historical Comparative Studies of Science and Technology. After receiving her PhD from the University of Zurich, she has taught at the Universities of Braunschweig and Erfurt and was a visiting scholar at the Institute of Advanced Study in Princeton, the Centre for the Study of Developing Societies in Delhi, and the Center for Advanced Latin American Studies in Guadalajara, Mexico. Her research focuses on the history of disaster science, the entangled history of toxic waste, as well as on studies of anti-disaster activism and gender.

Stephan, Christopher. University of Copenhagen, Denmark.
Postdoctoral Fellow at the Center for Subjectivity Research. While completing doctoral study in anthropology at the University of California, Los Angeles (2019), Christopher conducted ethnographic research projects on embodiment and self-other relations in charismatic Christianity and on empathy and anticipation in architectural designing for healthcare. His current work focuses on narrative, interaction, and social phenomenology.

Usón, Tomás J. Humboldt University of Berlin, Germany.
Postdoctoral Research Associate at the Institute of Geography and the IRI THESys. With a background in sociology, geography, and anthropology, his research interests range from disaster and risk studies to multispecies research, urban studies, science and technology studies, and anthropology of time. Tomás' current research explores the intricate geo-symbiotic interactions between bacteria, heavy metals, and humans in highly polluted environments to contribute novel understandings of health from a multispecies perspective.

Foreword

There is little doubt that the main theme of this book—'disastrous anticipations'—is a topic that is worthy of serious discussion and elaboration. The obsession with doom has a very long history, continues to haunt the human imagination.

Disasters make fascinating stories. They are fortunately infrequent but when they occur, they have a formidable impact on the imagination of the generations that follow. Disasters are often used as the key story of a master narrative through which we understand reality and through which we make sense of human transience. Since they are as bad as things can get, disasters represent a major challenge to values and meanings. That is why, over the centuries, disasters have acquired significant moral connotations. Perceived as Acts of God, a form of divine retribution—disasters are frequently depicted as a form of punishment for human transgression. In previous times, great catastrophes were perceived of the transient quality of human existence and the futility of all purely human ends, and served as a stimulus for religious contemplation. Even in today's secular times, disasters are invested with some hidden meaning. They are rarely perceived as just an accident; disasters appear as events of profound moral significance.

Since the beginning of history, people have been both haunted and intensely interested in disasters. The Bible itself is a rich source of disasters. From the story of Noah and the flood to Divine retribution on Sodom and Gomorrah or the famine that drove Abraham to Egypt, stories of disasters excite the religious imagination. This biblical legacy has been continually reinforced by the apocalyptic tradition that regards disasters as precursors for the day of reckoning. Although we live in a more secular society, the end-of-the-world model continues to influence public perceptions of disaster. Contemporary society possesses a formidable sense of disaster consciousness. The anticipation of doom through global or the extinction of the human species through the emergence of a new ice age or even an asteroid colliding with the earth are some of the many possible scenarios under consideration.

Unlike a religious or philosophical or ideological project, the current *teleology of doom* often assumes the technocratic form of worse-case thinking. We tend to model doom rather than represent it through a religious medium. Hence, the numerous rituals devoted to future proofing human existence. Worse-case thinking runs in parallel with dystopian fantasies regarding the planet, and arguably doom is fast becoming the new normal.

The fascinating essays in this book open up the terrain of doom-consciousness to serious reflection. The editors Monika Gabriela Bartoszewicz and Reidar Staupe should be commended for turning imaginaries of doom and disastrous anticipations into a serious topic of academic inquiry.

Frank Furedi

Preface and acknowledgement

The journey of writing this book began with a simple yet fundamental question: If we anticipate the worst for the future, how do these expectations manifest in our present, and what are their broader implications? While this may initially seem like an abstract dilemma, characteristic of academic preoccupations, divorced from reality, the core of this inquiry is in fact firmly anchored in problems with transcend mere 'hypothetical disasters' and 'socially constructed catastrophes' abstractions to explore the tangible impact of these anticipations on our societal frameworks and policies. This inquiry led us down a path of exploration into the realm of disastrous anticipations, where the future is not just a distant horizon but a force that actively influences our current world. These future-but-present realities touch each and every one of us, if not directly through our lived experiences, then indirectly through the structures of systems, institutions, and technologies, and, most importantly, through the actions and perceptions of others.

In crafting this volume, we were inspired by the idea that anticipation is not merely about predicting what is to come but about understanding the narratives and emotions that drive our perceptions of the future. Whether these anticipations are filled with hope or dread, they reveal more about our present fears and desires than about the future itself.

Every human being carries their own catastrophes within, shaping the dynamic relationship between anticipation and action. This premise allows us to explore how societal fears are navigated and translated into concrete policies and practices. Our contributors offer a diverse range of perspectives, each shedding light on different aspects of this uneasy relationship and reflecting on the ways in which our collective imaginings of the future shape the world we inhabit today.

We are deeply grateful to our colleagues and contributors, whose insights and expertise have enriched this work. Special thanks to Frank Furedi for his support and encouragement and for endorsing this volume with a foreword. This exploration of anticipation would not have been possible without the network we got from our work as editors on volume IV *Living in Anticipation of Disastrous Futures and Everyday Processes of Disaster Risk Creation* of Ilan Kelman's edited multi-volume anthology *Risk Analyses and Actions: A WSPC Reference on Disasters and Dangers*. We are thankful for the encouragement of Ilan for this volume. We are also grateful for the excellent editorial team at Routledge, with special thanks to Faye Leerink and Akansha Bharali for their enthusiasm and support.

We also want to extend our gratitude to our colleagues at UiT The Arctic University of Norway and the 'Secure Societies' research group, as well as colleagues at the University of Stavanger, whose backing helped make this book a reality.

It goes without saying that this volume would not have been possible without the excellent chapters that our collaborators have submitted. Thanks to their hard work, dedication, and brilliance, this volume is boasting fresh and thought-provoking essays on disastrous anticipations.

Last but not least, we wish to acknowledge the unfaltering support of our spouses, who have patiently watched and cheered as we spent long hours in front of the computer editing this volume.

Introduction
A time of disastrous anticipations

Reidar Staupe and Monika Gabriela Bartoszewicz

We live in a time permeated by a deep sense of impending catastrophe, with multiple intersecting crises unfolding on the horizon. This state of affairs has triggered a sense of insecurity and contingency that has been described by social theorists for decades, evoking different terms and frames, ranging from risk society (Beck, 1992), uncertainty in liquid times (Bauman, 2007), ontological security and insecurity (Giddens, 1990), culture and politics of fear (Furedi, 2002), acceleration and dissonance (Rosa, 2020), and more recently, though the notions of dread (Goldberg, 2021), crisis of attention and narrative (Han, 2024), doom (Mann, 2019; Ferguson, 2021), crisis of disillusionment (Reckwitz, 2021), futurelessness (Tutton, 2023), and polycrisis (Henig & Knight, 2023). Whether concretised through climate change, pandemic, financial turmoil, geopolitical unrest, or socio-economic upheaval, the expectation of a disastrous future has taken hold in an increasingly profound way and become woven into the fabric of daily life.

New fields of research have emerged around the study of 'collapsology' (Charbonnier, 2019) on the one hand and 'boredom studies' (Haladyn & Gardiner, 2016; see also the Journal of Boredom Studies) on the other. Is ours just another epoch where the global mood is tainted by dystopian thought? And why, like some authors have questioned, is the current crisis ultimately so 'boring' (Liu et al., 2018; Anderson, 2023; Gardiner et al., 2023)? Are crises not known for their splendour (Charbonnier, 2019)? In this context, scholarship on the historical idea of crisis (e.g., Koselleck, 2006; Roitman, 2013) provides a reminder that crises often look very different when narrated historically compared to how they are experienced by those who find themselves in the midst of it. This collection of essays explores the effects of living in the advent of catastrophe, highlighting how anticipations of disaster influence both personal and collective experience. The volume approaches disaster not simply as a material event or process but also as an imaginary that is embedded in social life and thought.

This volume centers on the concept of things to come—not a pre-selection of specific issues, but ideas that not only orient us in the present but also shape our anticipation of the future. Its timeliness is underscored by several considerations: First, there is an emerging need to deepen our understanding of how disastrous anticipations influence our era. Second, these perspectives are still under-represented in disaster and crisis scholarship. For this reason, the collection introduces fresh

DOI: 10.4324/9781003537311-1

insights, treating disaster, regardless of the level of its occurrence, not as a relic of the past but as a dynamic, unfolding phenomenon. Furthermore, while existing studies often view disastrous anticipations as concrete realities to be prevented, this volume presents them as hybrid phenomena, possessing both material and ideal dimensions (Popke, 2016). Last, by exploring the effects of these anticipations, we aim not only to reveal how disaster imaginaries impact us but also to ignite hope and uncover strategies for coping in a world that often appears overwhelmingly catastrophic. In this light, exploring disaster anticipation provides a lens through which to examine the everyday experience of looming threats and the social strategies developed by individuals and communities to navigate them. For the authors gathered in this volume, waiting for things to happen does not signify an endless present; rather, it transforms into a space for human agency.

Catastrophe is frequently depicted as a sudden break, even when its underlying causes may stretch back centuries. Diverging perspectives between structuralist theories and more functionalist research have fuelled a long-standing debate on whether disasters should be seen as events or as processes. While critical work grounded in structuralism ties many of the major catastrophes in history to processes of disaster risk creation (e.g. Dickinson & Burton, 2022; Wisner et al., 2004; Hewitt, 1983), the emphasis often remains on impacts localised in time and space (Donovan et al., 2023; Hsu, 2019; Matthewman, 2015). By focusing on disastrous anticipations, which we see as a defining aspect of the current global mood, this collection of essays shifts the attention of the field towards the generativity of catastrophic prognoses, raising new questions about disaster scholarship and beyond. This is not to suggest that the future is inherently mastered and controlled by the present, particularly given that a sense of crisis—or perhaps multiple crises—permeates much of social life. However, this volume explores the concept of modernity as a forward-looking narrative of progress that extends into politics as a tool for realizing the myth of preparedness.

This volume shines light on how the idea of future disaster has real impacts in the present, cutting across phenomenology, politics, society, and health. In this context, the anticipation of disaster represents a distinctive emotional and temporal state, one where people adjust their routines and decisions in response to an ever-present sense of what might lie ahead. As Throop (2022, p. 69) writes on the phenomenal presence of looming crises:

> To say that something is looming is to recognize that something, while still yet indefinite in form, is imposing its impending presence upon us. To speak of the type of not yet that defines a looming future, is thus to recognize the saturated and weighed down arrival of a foreboding reality that has already somehow taken form and has, accordingly, already partially penetrated the present, even despite its hazy hovering just beyond our each. Just beyond our reach, looming is, in this respect, not only the yet to come, but in some respect also the already somehow almost here. What's felt to be the inevitable coming into being of what looms fills the horizon of our future possibilities.

What can be read out from the above is that disastrous anticipations directly affect the present. Their looming presence in everyday life becomes almost palpable while at the same time depending on how much attention we pay to them, as they are not directly in front of us, not completely within our grasp. Rather, it exists as an indeterminate hybrid space:

> Inhabiting the indeterminate between, what looms is not yet, however, an object or event. And yet, it is still an object or event-like in its pending actualization. Pressing heavily against the always already receding veil that separates the unfolding present from the indeterminate horizon of the future, what looms is something whose arrival we must await, that we have no choice but to await.
>
> (Throop, 2022, p. 71)

This temporal aspect of disastrous anticipations is essential. Futures seldom unfold in a static way and can always become otherwise. Yet they give rise to an uncanny experience of time, with the lines between past, present, and future blurring (Bryant, 2016). Catastrophes, both actual and ideal, unfold in the social world as much as in the natural world. We live in a time where prognostic forms of knowledge about the future is increasing at an exponential rate, which has been blamed for all kinds of social ills ranging from burnout, stress, a breakdown of the symbolic order, and mental health disorders (Goldberg, 2021; Han, 2024). Even in the absence of visible hazards in everyday life, people find themselves waiting, anticipating, wondering, questioning, and otherwise reacting to news and projections about disastrous futures in ways that infuse everyday routines with an undercurrent of tension and dread.

The propensity to anticipate disaster in contemporary social life goes beyond the individual and cannot be grasped solely through terms like anxiety or depression. It is a cultural force sustained by social and symbolic interactions and collective narratives, creating shared frameworks based on dystopian outlooks. These outlooks are informed by scientific inquirers and daily reports on how close we are to catastrophe, how all the arrows are pointing in the wrong direction, and the discovery of ever-new systems that are on the brink of breakdown. The anticipation of disaster thus becomes a communal reality, one that strengthens social ties while also shaping shared emotional responses; our very identities are built around which issues we are most concerned about. This outlook reflects the complex, often contradictory nature of the times in which we live. The chapters in this volume grapple with these issues from multiple perspectives.

Recent scholarship has described doom and a sense of foreclosed future as an omnipresent affective state that increasingly defines our present moment. It results partially from unfolding ecological and societal crises, with 'the acknowledgment of the likelihood of the futility of efforts to avoid catastrophe' being 'fundamental to contemporary social life' (Mann, 2019, p. 92; cf. Clayton, 2021; Tutton, 2023). Scholars are increasingly asking about the 'conditions under which a form of life—a landscape, community, livelihood—may be considered unviable' (Paprocki,

2022, p. 1). Goldberg (2021, p. 16) observes that 'it is as if dread pandemonically has seeped into every crevice of our ambiguous and ambivalent being today,' that 'we are living in its grip.' Together, these perspectives highlight the urgency of understanding how the anticipation of disaster operates within society and what its effects might be on individual and collective outlooks.

The experience of anticipating disaster is, of course, not limited to the present moment. Historical and cultural records tell us that societies have long wrestled with the spectre of imminent catastrophe (and ideas about the apocalypse). The historical record is also full of examples of societies that were wiped out as a result of calamities (Elborough, 2019; Ferguson, 2021). What might be said to distinguish our own time from the past is the sheer volume and pervasiveness of catastrophic predictions and the continuous prognostication of their continued development—indeed, their worsening, bringing the expected catastrophe ever closer. Information about risks is pervasive and spreads into ever-new issue domains, sectors, contexts, and environments.

In this volume, we invite readers to consider how the anticipation of catastrophe alters the ways people experience and understand the world. Our aim with this collection of chapters is to provide a starting point for questioning and reflecting on the work that disastrous anticipations and catastrophic prognoses do in the social world.

Opening the volume David Theo Goldberg in 'Situating dread' takes the reader on a fascinating journey into the pervasive sense of dread that has emerged globally, examining its roots in historical events such as Brexit, the election of Donald Trump, and the Syrian Civil War, but also the ramping up of 'surveillance capitalism' into the technological tracking of all people at all times. Goldberg identifies dread as a complex affective condition, distinct from fear or anxiety, and explores its manifestation as an unsettling feeling in response to a lack of predictability and an inability to define its specific object. The analysis extends to the political implications of dread, contrasting responses of withdrawal and closure with those of resistance, collective action, and the urgent need for socio-structural transformations to address interconnected challenges. The chapter concludes by emphasising the necessity of reimagining and reconstructing collective values and ways of being to confront the complexities of our shared world.

Building on this conceptual exploration, Christopher Stephan and Devin Flaherty, in 'A phenomenology of anticipation: experience, culture, social distribution, and collectivity,' advance a phenomenological model of anticipatory experience, investigating specifically its applications for disaster studies. The authors offer a rubric of experiential variables for anticipation and argue for how the patterning of these experiences is primed and informed by sociocultural context. From here, the essay develops an approach to the social organisation of anticipation, examining its distribution within communities and proposing a phenomenological model for understanding collective anticipation. The authors conclude by highlighting key variables for disaster researchers to consider and suggest a diachronic perspective to capture the temporal dynamism of anticipatory experiences.

Monika Gabriela Bartoszewicz continues this examination of temporal experiences in 'We are the times: temporal agency of utopian, dystopian, and (post)apocalyptic futures' offering a far-sighted reflection on deep futures and their temporal dimensions, and aiming to understand the implications of diverse temporal orientations and agogics understood as tempo of divergent modalities. The exploration distinguishes between utopian and dystopian frameworks, emphasising the interconnectedness of these seemingly contrasting visions. The chapter also explores the apocalypse, dissecting its implications and highlighting the role of temporality in shaping human hopes, fears, and societal transformations within the interconnected utopian, dystopian, and apocalyptic settings.

The theme of temporality is further explored by Tomás J. Usón and Cécile Stephanie Stehrenberger in 'Disasters as time, time as disasters.' They theorise the conceptualisation of disasters, moving beyond traditional ideas of them as events or processes. Drawing on assemblage thinking, science and technology studies, and the notion of chronopolitics, the chapter suggests viewing disasters as temporising assemblages, emphasising their role in producing certain forms of time and temporal arrangements. The discussion challenges common assumptions about disasters, providing an alternative perspective that considers disasters as complex mechanic devices and enunciative conditions, leading to reflections on their sociopolitical nature and the need to re-evaluate temporal assumptions in disaster studies.

Piotr Gil in 'Surviving (in) time: national history and memory as temporal factors underlying ontological and national security' probes the relationship between temporality, national identity, and the pursuit of national security. Gil emphasises the inescapable influence of the past on present and future visions, particularly in the context of a nation state. The discussion engages ontological security scholarship, which enables a revealing of how the interplay between national history, memory, and politics shapes the understanding of security. The conclusion underscores the multifaceted challenges posed by time, urging a nuanced approach to national identity, memory, and security policies that recognises the complex and sometimes unpredictable nature of temporal dynamics.

Transitioning from a national to a global perspective, Md Mohaiminul Islam Khan and Reidar Staupe in 'The changing mood of the world in times of "polycrisis" and its impact on the post-2015 development spirit' engage the work of Heinz Bude on the 'mood of the world' and related work on Zeitgeist and epochal moods. This chapter brings these concepts into a global development studies context by applying them to an analysis of changes in the post-2015 development spirit. Drawing on close readings of the sustainable development goals (SDGs) literature and flagship reports on SDG progress, the authors argue that we can witness a change in the mood of the world in the SDGs literature after 2020 and particularly after 2022–2023. A major contribution of this essay is to introduce the work of Bude on global moods into a global development context and show the wide applicability of this notion to analyse global issues.

The impact of emotional states on global agendas is taken further by Miriam Matejova, who in 'Misconstrued anticipations? Disaster politics in the age of disinformation' explores the intersection of disasters and disinformation, focusing on public risk perception. Matejova discusses the impact of misinformation, particularly conspiracy theories, on how individuals perceive and respond to disasters, using case studies of the Covid-19 pandemic and the Chernobyl nuclear disaster. The analysis underscores the role of social media in spreading false information during crises and emphasises the importance of effective communication in reducing uncertainty, building trust in political institutions, and countering the influence of conspiracy theories on public behaviour in the post-truth era.

Disaster response is probed further by Tobias Olofsson in 'Entangled disasters: relations and vulnerabilities in the transformation and dissolution of Kiruna and Malmberget.' Olofsson takes a deep dive into the urban transformation and dissolution of cities and villages in Sweden's Malmfälten region, particularly Kiruna and Malmberget, where communities are forced to move due to ground deformations caused by mining activities. He explores the entangled relations, both social and geographical, and the consequences of such transformations on residents, revealing aspects of disasters beyond conventional definitions. The chapter emphasises the importance of considering human-made disasters within the broader spectrum of disasters, highlighting the role of political, economic, and social relations in shaping disastrous processes in the Anthropocene.

The broadened scope is further explored by Barbara Schabowska in 'Cultural resilience in polycrisis: a pathway to suicide prevention' in her reflections on the role of cultural resilience amidst polycrisis. Schabowska's point of departure is the pervasive mental health pandemic, an everyday, quiet disaster that, while less spectacular than a tsunami or earthquake, represents a societal catastrophe of immense proportions and ramifications. The chapter boldly looks into the profound existential void, highlighted by the escalating mental health crisis where the future appears either overwhelming or terrifying, driving individuals to the brink of despair. By interweaving psychology, cultural studies, and philosophy, Schabowska proposes an innovative approach to suicide prevention, viewing culture as a repository of moral wisdom and universal principles, akin to the societal immune system. This perspective unveils a new dimension of culture's role—not only in cultivating a meaningful existence and imbuing our actions with significance but also in overcoming the ennui of catastrophic anticipations, and empowering individuals to face the future, no matter how daunting it may seem, or even to discover any future at all.

Leikny Bakke Lie and Reidar Staupe round the volume. Their chapter titled 'Understanding natural hazard phenomena and risks from the perspective of "instrumental realism": examples from Geiranger and Lyngen, Norway' draws on the instrumental realist perspective developed by philosopher Don Ihde to analyse how technical hazard monitoring instruments mediate the lived experience of imminent catastrophe in Norwegian fjords exposed to fjord tsunami risk. The authors introduce four technology-human-world relations theorised by Don Ihde and other philosophers of technology and reflect on how technologies can be seen as generative of ingenuity, reflexivity, safety, and security, as well as how technologies can be seen as having a transcendentalist worlding power in that they can open previously inaccessible aspects of the world up for human experience. The chapter extends natural hazards and disaster scholarship by shifting the focus to the world-building power of technical instruments and their role in maintaining a sense of looming disaster in areas exposed to considerable disaster risk.

Together, these essays weave a comprehensive narrative that explores the challenge of the inaccessibility of the future, which lies at the fulcrum of anticipation, opening it up and transforming what might otherwise be perceived as an empty space governed solely by contingency and chance. This conceptual lens challenges the traditional organizing principles of possibility and necessity that often define our expectations of the future. Instead, anticipation is structured along the variable of expectations that can span the spectrum from the impossible to the unnecessary, reconciling them both by following multiple trajectories that are neither linear nor reversible. As Delanty insightfully notes, an anticipated catastrophe might signify that there is no future other than the memory of a time that still believed in it (Delanty, 2024, p. 163). After all, only those who do not anticipate any future are truly doomed.

References

Anderson, B. (2023). Boredom and the politics of climate change. *Scottish Geographical Journal*, *139*(1–2), 133–141.

Bauman, Z. (2007). *Liquid times: Living in an age of uncertainty*. Polity Press.

Beck, U. (1992). *Risk society: Towards a new modernity*. Sage.

Bryant, R. (2016). On critical times: Return, repetition, and the uncanny present. *History and Anthropology*, *27*(1), 19–31.

Charbonnier, P. (2019). The splendor and squalor of collapsology. *Revue du Crieur*, (2), 88–95.

Clayton, D. (2021). Historical geography I: Doom, danger, disregard–towards political historical geographies. *Progress in Human Geography*, *45*(6), 1692–1708.

Delanty, G. (2024). Introduction: Social theory and the idea of the future. *European Journal of Social Theory*, *27*(2), 153–173.

Dickinson, T., & Burton, I. (2022). Disaster risk creation: The new vulnerability. In G. Bankoff & D. Hilhorst (Eds.), *Why vulnerability still matters* (pp. 192–205). Routledge.

Donovan, A., Morin, J., & Walshe, R. (2023). Interdisciplinary research in hazards and disaster risk. *Progress in Environmental Geography*, *2*(3), 202–222.

Elborough, T. (2019). *Atlas of vanishing places: The lost worlds as they were and as they are today*. White Lion Publishing.

Ferguson, N. (2021). *Doom: The politics of catastrophe*. Penguin Press.

Furedi, F. (2002). *Culture of fear: Risk-taking and the morality of low expectation*. Continuum.

Gardiner, M. E. (2023). Make the holocene great again! Or, why is climate change boring? *Journal of Boredom Studies*, (1), 1–21.

Giddens, A. (1990). *The consequences of modernity*. Stanford University Press

Goldberg, D. T. (2021). *Dread: Facing futureless futures*. Polity Press.

Haladyn, J. J., & Gardiner, M. E. (2016). Monotonous splendour: An introduction to boredom studies. In M. E. Gardiner & J. J. Haladyn (Eds.), *Boredom studies reader* (pp. 15–30). Routledge.

Han, B. C. (2024). *The crisis of narration*. Polity Press.

Henig, D., & Knight, D. M. (2023). Polycrisis: Prompts for an emerging worldview. *Anthropology Today*, *39*(2), 3–6.

Hewitt, K. (1983). The idea of calamity in a technocratic age. In K. Hewitt (Ed.), *Interpretations of calamity: From the viewpoint of human ecology*. Allen and Unwin.

Hsu, E. L. (2019). Must disasters be rapidly occurring? The case for an expanded temporal typology of disasters. *Time and Society*, *28*(3), 904–921.

Koselleck, R. (2006). Crisis. *Journal of the History of Ideas*, *67*(2), 357–400.

Liu, H. Y., Lauta, K. C., & Maas, M. M. (2018). Governing boring apocalypses: A new typology of existential vulnerabilities and exposures for existential risk research. *Futures*, *102*, 6–19.

Mann, G. (2019). Doom. In Antipode Editorial Collective (Ed.), *Keywords in radical geography: Antipode at 50* (pp. 90–94). Wiley.

Matthewman, S. (2015). *Disasters, risk and revelation: Making sense of our times*. Palgrave Macmillan.

Paprocki, K. (2022). On viability: Climate change and the science of possible futures. *Global Environmental Change*, *73*, 102487.

Popke, J. (2016). Researching the hybrid geographies of climate change: Reflections from the field. *Area*, *48*(1), 2–6.

Reckwitz, A. (2021). *The end of illusions: Politics, economy, and culture in late modernity*. Polity Press.

Roitman, J. (2013). *Anti-crisis*. Duke University Press Books.

Rosa, H. (2020). *The uncontrollability of the world*. Polity Press.

Throop, C. J. (2022). Looming. *Puncta: Journal of Critical Phenomenology*, *5*(2), 67–86.

Tutton, R. (2023). The sociology of futurelessness. *Sociology*, *57*(2), 438–453.

Wisner, B., Blaikie, P., Cannon, T., & Davis, I. (2004). *At risk: Natural hazards, people's vulnerability and disasters*. Routledge.

1 Situating dread

David Theo Goldberg

1. Introduction

A gnawing sense of unsettlement, insecurity, even peril nips at our times, clouding any collective feelings of well-being. The concerns have widened from the statistically unlikely one of being knocked down crossing the road to being caught in a mass shooting at a college, school, or mall. Many worry daily about a stray—or not so stray—bomb dropping on the neighborhood, or a massive flash flood, raging fire, or taps running dry becoming far more readily localized. Of late, the worries have swelled, prompted by supply chain disruption, making even staple food availability less certain, energy delivery threatened, and prices soaring into spheres of mass unaffordability. Why has this materialized, especially now? And how to specify this state or affective condition afflicting the collective sense of being: How, in short, to name the nameless?

This unsettling shift manifested across much, if not all, of global social life in the latter half of 2016 and the opening of 2017. It's not that the sensibility for some can't be dated earlier, that its underlying conditions couldn't be traced back, perhaps even decades. But a confluence of globally significant events manifested in the mid-twenty-teens. Britain had voted narrowly to exit the European Union in mid-2016. Donald Trump was elected to the US presidency five months later. By this time, the Syrian Civil War had surged, with the involvement of numerous other states exacerbating the violence. Refugees surged, and not just the well-publicized streams into Europe. Lebanon, already facing economic meltdown, absorbed nearly a million Syrians, reaching almost 15 percent of its population. Authoritarian regimes, whether consolidating themselves or just manifesting, multiplied, drawing support from each other: Putinism in Russia, Orbanism in Hungary, Modi's growing stress on Hindutva in India, Xi's assertion of power in China, Duterte's grip on the Philippines, even Netanyahu's reach for commandment in Israel-Palestine.

In late 2016 and early 2017, I was waking each morning to a knotted feeling in the pit of the stomach, a sense of unease that only heightened and tightened through the day. Almost all with whom I discussed events were feeling similarly. What was this sensibility, and how to identify it in ways that made most sense of our collectively troubling times?

DOI: 10.4324/9781003537311-2

Early one morning as I swam laps a few months into 2017, it hit me. This abiding and enveloping feeling was best characterized as one of dread. What, then, is this kind of feeling? When I looked to the philosophical literature, I was half-surprised at how little writing had focused explicitly on dread. There was Kierkegaard, to be sure, not only the famous work on fear but an earlier essay on dread. Freud's focus on anxiety splashed throughout his writings is, no doubt, related, but he does little to spell out how dread expresses itself and what its relation to anxiety is. Sartre's writings on nausea can be read as describing what happens to one suffering unrelenting dread, but here too an analyst would have to pull the threads together. Otherwise, a fragment here or there can be uncovered in this or that thinker. But nothing much more sustained.

Why, one might ask? For one, enduring stretches of dread as a social condition—in contrast, say, to a casual everyday use like "I am dreading going to the dentist"—are at most periodic, at times of widespread distress. For another, when afflicting a corner of the world, largely not visible and before social media made corners no longer so readily covered (up) in shadows, concern might not register or even be visible to those taking themselves to be more central players in worldly matters. That shifts in the (re)production of global power and wealth might be the very underlying conditions prompting dread in the shadows would be lost on those pulling levers promising handsome payoffs. Another's dread may be one's ticket to the carnival, the theme music for which drowns out dread's Klimtian scream for help.

Kierkegaard's understanding was prompted by a significantly revealing shift he had observed about his own circumstances in the mid-nineteenth century. For him, dread is a psychic or affective condition produced in the face of Nothing, given God's demise. Dread oozes into one as a realization of absence, an emergent sense that what was taken by so many as a guiding spirit, a deep existential dependence, was in fact ontologically unavailable. Kierkegaardian dread, then, arises from this absence, the growing realization of the impossibility of forgiveness. Redemption from sin is unavailable should God fail to exist. The ancient history of dreadlocks—dating at least to Egypt and perhaps (also) India—suggests a longer entanglement of dread and deity. As with Kierkegaard, this expressed itself as concern over godly abandonment. But it also manifested—as with the Rastafari movement from its earliest spawning in critical rejection of industrialism's discipline and regulation—as the dread of not living up to God's commandments or perceived expectations. Dread here suggests being ill at ease, unsettled, in the face of desanctification and disenchantment, of abandonment of or by religious belief, the hole filled by an instrumentalizing political economy serving narrowing self-interest.

An affect is an intense and shifting emotion. As a consequence, it is one no longer understood because it has become socially disconnected from its predictable set of prompts, or one not yet comprehended because responding to a condition is still unrecognized. Affect accordingly stands in stark contrast to the simplism of sentimentality because unnameable and unnavigable. Dread, along these lines, is less like fear and more analogous to melancholia. One knows pretty much definitively what one fears, just as one knows who one mourns. Like melancholia, by contrast, dread has no exactly defined object. But where for melancholia the object is lost, unrecovered and seemingly unrecoverable, in the case of dread one remains unsure of what exactly its object is, how to define or find it at all.

Dread accordingly follows from a lack of definitive object and singular cause, of predictability, of legibility and discernibility. It arises in the wake of denial or complete absence of principle. Dread emerges when discernibility slips into indiscernibility, the known or thought known becomes obtuse or opaque, and so unknown, as the pandemic experience has brought home. Dread follows not only from lack of information or predictability; it grabs subjects, as in "eco-anxiety" or Covid-19 inscrutability.

It manifests especially where doubt proliferates about what information or evidence would count—about origins or explanation or predictability about a condition and its implications. How do we actually know a catastrophic storm is the effect of climate change? What world-historical transformations or even tomorrow will pandemic impacts bring about? I fear getting infected with Covid-19; I dread the possibility of it lingering long term, on me and the world around me, precisely because of the unknowability of its impacts. Dread, in short, conjures a feeling of anticipatory doom.

Dread is an affective state unmoored from the originating conditions giving rise to it, or not yet recognized or recognizable in the terms currently available to us. In each case, there is a degree of indecipherability. In *Cruel Optimism*, Lauren Berlant raised the relation, in the US context, between affective sensibility and the crush of the material conditions of life. Berlant accordingly opened up a way of thinking more generally about the material conditions of affects and their political economy.

I think of dread, then, as requiring a more sustained analysis of the relation of indecipherability to its underlying material conditions for an affect like this to take hold socially. And to assess in different cases whether the affect depresses, encouraging constraint (serving as a downer) or mobilizes (serving if not as an upper), at least as fuel to do something about it.

The indiscernibility underlying dread's manifesting is a sense that there's something unsettling happening but one cannot quite put one's finger on it. It prompts a condition of being ill at ease, unsettled, in the face of what Kierkegaard identifies as desanctification and disenchantment. At the very least, it registers how the taken-for-granted world has slipped from conception or grasp, less recognized or unrecognizable in the terms at our disposal. Dread manifests as the anxiety to which this uncanniness gives rise, more or less abiding or increasingly so. It is, as Freud put it, the unheimlich condition of things being faced, which are sensed but still obscure, of something social being amiss. I call this an unmatchable tear in the social fabric through or out of which all sorts of noxious social leakages are oozing, seeping out, which one cannot quite name, or identify what is giving rise to it. Dread might arise, take hold of one unexpectedly as a nauseating smell or sound, something not known or (quite) experienced before. So dread registers an insecurity in the face of the altogether unpredictable and indecipherable.

As Kierkegaard indicates, then, dread is a sensibility taking hold exactly in the absence of any larger or higher reliable power, one at least bigger than ourselves, to which to turn either for an account of what is being faced oneself and collectively, or to blame for the condition in which we find ourselves. Dread in effect registers that there is no easy possibility of salvation, of being saved, from the mess into which we have gotten ourselves, alone or in more pressing ways made together by design or default. Every choice for addressing dread's prompts would mean giving something up that has been central to life's stability but perhaps no longer is. Dread, it could be said as a result, sounds a siren of sorts, one's own canary in the coal mine of the social.

Why does dread as a widespread inhabited condition of Being manifest now, and what are its prompts?

By the mid-twenty-teens there were a range of deeper underlying forces less visibly at work in fomenting the unsettlement, perhaps just coming into conscious view. Technological developments were transforming how we lived, related, and interacted. The impacts of climate change were increasingly making themselves felt, the mounting evidence and experience becoming undeniable. The global pandemic exploded in our midst, a symptom of the broader social tensions. A palpable sense that we were descending into a state of civil warring took hold; political systems were no longer so readily able to mediate conflicts conceptually and materially. That everything was being monetized as money itself was being virtualized only ramified the sense of unsettlement. These social developments provided the interrelated sources of this contemporary proliferation of social dread.

*

Over the past two decades, algorithmic culture has increasingly come to colonize all aspects of human life, and perhaps all life more generally. While this has made life more mobile, agile, interactive, instantaneous, and networked, it has also made us more superficially visible, reachable, and even penetrable. If there is one word that captures this tension between agility and speed, on the one hand, and incessant availability and superficiality, on the other, perhaps it is how "facile"—and with it increasingly and pervasively fleeting—virtually everything in life has become.

Algorithmic culture has reshaped our ways of being in the world. The temporality of instantaneity and presentism that this culture produces dematerializes as it embodies time. This dematerialization renders more opaque because of more ephemeral and so ungraspable recurring inequalities resulting from social relations of power between groups socially dominant and subordinate. It effectively erases the terms for recognizing these deepening socioeconomic divides, materially and ideologically. The inequalities in time, as Michael Hanchard points out, are also temporal inequalities; time itself is marked and experienced differentially, whether in racial or gendered or class terms.

All of this is accompanied by a space-time and culture of virtuality, of instantaneity. Inductive reasoning, tending to correlations, not causations, has become central to this contemporary culture, especially commercially. The resultant culture encourages and is reinforced by an activation of the logic of hypothetical imperatives, of if-then thinking in the practices of the everyday. As a result, the allure of the new and a culture of disruption have taken hold, in turn exacerbating hyper-individualization and reductively "personal" as opposed to social or collective responsibilities.

Algorithmic culture is designed to inform and reinforce one's choices, the recognized desires, likes, and preference schemes expressed. It pumps up the volume of the choices it has actually encouraged one to make, generalizing divisions those choices reflect, enact, and reproduce. These in turn become codes for committing oneself to the life and lifestyle they represent. This amounts to a commitment to a way of being in the world, and so to those projecting to one that they are working to maintain that way of being, to advance or better it. Consumptive preference schemes are political-cultural iron cages and socio-solipsistic echo chambers. I am talking to no one but reflections of myself in the social mirror.

Algorithmic fuelings of hyper-self-satisfaction, cycles of satisfaction-dissatisfaction or insatiation, disruption, and renovation are exactly the impulse toward incessant conflict. Here the turn is to "self"-securitization: more alarms, guns, security guards, and technologies. There is a stress on individual security and the reach for regimes of securitization. This entails securing both what one takes to be one's own, and more pressingly, one's way of being in the world.

One can see all this playing out in the ways cultures of "whiteness" become embedded as default into algorithmic codes, in a sense their idiom and vernacular presumption. Where "white" is the default color of coding, assertive masculinity is its gendered expression, and if the HBO Max series "Succession" is any metaphoric indication, success and succession are its obsessions. Success is measured quantitatively by numbers of views, likes, and consequent revenue. The reach for succession—as in the next version or app or available plug-in—is the hyper-fuel keeping it pumping.

These interactive values for which the algorithmic stands imprint the cultures, assumptions, dominant preferences, and frames through which the world is viewed. They color the unseen, taken-for-granted background of all formative experience associated with what has come to be identified with whiteness. Coded bias and digital discrimination assume the status of the given, the social structure of the time of the algorithm. In naturalizing these divides, algorithmic culture encourages that they be seen as part of nature, the givens of everyday life, unchangeable because they are natural and so lawlike. Algorithmic neutrality in the abstract becomes racial, gendered, and classed reproduction in fact. Its operations are now more or less invisible even as the effects are visibly ramped up as though coming out of nowhere, the natural state of the world. As such, the algorithmic is the perfect discriminating machine, racial, gendered, and classed. It traces the spiraling anonymity of evil.

Algorithms are invisible; they operate unseen. They have a shadowy presence. Their power is felt in their effects, in their appification, with their application. The algorithm is made to seem naturalized, invisible until seen or felt in effect. The lag is the labor of discriminatory application. Lacking motive, algorithms actually don't do anything as such. So algorithmic discrimination (racism, gender discrimination) is subject-less discrimination, a "non-done" differentiating, one for which no responsibility is assumed or taken. It is discrimination, the discriminating of which is denied in the doing, in the making. An anonymous discrimination, not just one without intention. Discrimination by automaton. One that purports to be no one's. It is discrimination, freeing itself of all responsibility.

There is widespread admission that explanations cannot be given for more complex algorithmic operations like high-speed and high-volume stock trading, as well as large data pool hiring reviews and selection outcomes. Algorithmic discrimination is like implicit bias, very difficult to get at, identify, and undo. Indeed, to an extent, the former is predicated on the latter among coders. The digital doesn't "know" it is discriminating in ways for the most part coders—in coding—don't. E-discrimination repeatedly occurs with digital facial recognition, hiring review and selection, and bond review algorithms and their applications. Discrimination is written silently into the code, invariably without recognizing that it is being done at the point of inscription and, by extension, application. Charges of bias, racism, gender discrimination, and the like are "algo-neutralized" of charges of racism on the basis of lack of intentionality.

*

Algorithms are also operationalized robotically, as or via robots. The insistence on the "Great Replacement" is at work in its doubled sense, both as labor and as racial projection. In the United States, Europe, and their quickly withering number of colonial legacy countries where whites have remained the majority or retained dominant power, the expression of dread in terms of being "replaced" signals the draining self-assurance that they could walk uncontested into any job, residential areas, and schools while keeping those not "like" them largely out. That this presumption is increasingly challenged both racially and robotically has heightened the unsettlement.

The algorithmic is unseen. It holds robotic—or automotive/automated—power over us. It is, in a sense, outside the law (think here of Foucault's characterization of monstrosity). It violates the (established) law—evades it, mutes it—leaving it with nothing to say. Hence, algorithmic effectivity in getting away with murder, with it all. Where there is algorithmic application, in effect, who or what is responsible? Algorithmic discrimination is discrimination in denial of intentionality, and so the evasion of responsibility: She was shot but no one had a hand on the trigger. He was kneeling on the neck all those minutes, but paying no attention, just following departmental policy and protocols on his phone. The car was driving itself, oops.

The undertaking to anthropomorphize the robotic—all those robots made to look (sort of) human—is the attempt to hide its monstrosity. The point is to ameliorate its violence, its invisible but felt effects, to naturalize the techno-human. If the robot didn't do it, it's because the algorithm did. But algorithms share code with no touch, no feeling, no thoughts of their own, or anybody's for that matter. Algorithmic logic is intelligible unintelligibility, unintelligible intelligibility, seemingly making the unintelligible plausible while plausibility unintelligible. Computer engineers, even those writing the code, cannot tell you exactly how the algorithms produce their real-world outcomes. If completely codified, there is nothing like intentionality or will. The very heart of algorithmic rationality entails that abnormality has become "everyday," monstrosity the "commonplace," unintelligibility and plausible deniability of our operating system. Who's at fault when the driverless car kills someone, the shooterless gun goes on a rampage, the delivery bot runs over a pedestrian's bare foot, or cuts in front of a skateboarder? Can the robot be negligent, purposely or irresponsibly avoiding what it is supposed to do?

The techno-human, like monstrosity more generally, calls law into question. Disruption, the undoing of the given and the predictable, is the very logic, if not the drive, of digital technology. "Ex Machina," the movie, represents the liberation of the machinic while erasing the temporality of the past, its collapse into a techno-human new. Over the past decade, anti-seizure neuro-technology, implanting technology into the brain to warn of impending seizures, has made extraordinary advances. But it has come at the cost of transforming personality (moods, emotions, dispositions), in some cases unrecognizably, and sometimes to the point of suicide. Here the exemplification of techno-determinism is in dramatic tension with the sense of human self-making. Dread is the realization of techno-futures turning our futures futureless.

*

Underlying these contemporary shifts is the emergence over the past decade of a novel phase in the development and expression of capitalism, perhaps the groundwork of persistent and pervasive dread. From the mid-1970s on, neoliberalism took increasing hold of global political economy. The driving characteristics of neoliberalization include a deregulation of economic flows and markets, accompanied by the push to financialize—to monetize—all value. As money and markets are relatively deregulated (consider the corruptive challenges relatively unregulated cyber-currency markets have caused), the welfarist or caretaking functions of the state have been delimited: less funding for public resources of the commons, such as hospitals, schools, and universities. Securitizing state functions have ramped up coterminously: more resources for the military, policing, and surveillance. The point is to maximize securitization on the ground. Responsibility is personalized so that one is increasingly on one's own—responsible—to make something of oneself, to care for self and family. The stress is on the "Man of Enterprise," as Foucault calls "him," through ceaseless self-making and capitalizing on the proliferation of opportunities economic liberation is supposed to engender. And this logic of the enterprising subject, the one who disrupts through ceaseless self-(re)invention, the self-making man, entails no limit on self-fabrication.

It should come as little surprise, then, that neoliberalization has been driven by a temporality and cultural or ideological practice of immediation. The instantaneous, the new, the disrupting are celebrated. Event-capitalism was the natural outgrowth of these developments. Spectacular events kept bringing large numbers of people together: festivals, concerts, large stadium sporting events, megachurch services and mega-ship cruises, even political rallies, and the like. The spiraling spectacularity of opening ceremonies for the Olympics and World Cup are perhaps the über exemplifications of this trend. In gathering large numbers of people in crowded sites of heightened excitement, wallets are opened and money spent, as much on memorabilia of the eventfulness as on the event itself. Everything, from parking, tickets, food and drink, to sports jerseys, CDs, photos, and even anniversary reminders, is on offer to ensure participants keep purchasing. (Contrast all of this to the mud-filled, on-the-ground experience at Woodstock in 1969.) The eventfulness is made to stretch into ceaseless consumptive opportunity and so endless flows of capital generation and profitability.

Information is increasingly and more quickly collected to determine what is most likely to appeal and what new experiences can be added as revenue generation to future events. Nothing is forgotten; everything is data-based. The road to info-power was paved with these glittering experiences, fueling the collapse of fantasy and fancy.

All this came to a screeching halt with pandemic onset. Large events were the ground zero of viral circulation. Cruise ships, megachurch services, screaming concerts and sports stadiums were the collective cauldron of disease. The boasted freedom to consume brought life to lockdown. Live events, from music to cinema, were replaced by streaming services. Algorithmically enabled tracking through one's electronic devices, which had ramped up over the preceding half-decade to enable the streamlining of delivery on demand, now quickly got turned into track-and-trace. China led the way in Wuhan. Surveillance was outpaced by tracking; its political economy was at once supplemented and overrun by tracking capitalism. Tracking capitalism is a capitalism that tracks—everyone and everything. Losing any possibility of an afterlife could only end in dread, the affect accompanying the refusal to realize end-times staring one in the face. The impending immediacy of lurking environmental disasters only ramped up the sense that any future was looking increasingly bleak and futureless.

Surveillance proceeds by monitoring the content people are communicating. Tracking plots movements and networks. Surveillance reads off threat, danger, and performance from the content of communication and interaction. Tracking reads likely future behavior from people's activity, from their "metadata,"—via prediction algorithms—from relational data about movements, networks, and lines rather than the content of communication. The flows of products are digitally monitored, their demand determining their desirability. In turn, digital users and consumers are tracked to establish their digitally monitored profiles. They, or really we, are then further inundated with materials—news, information, consumer products—that the profile determines to add up to their or our preferences. The profile reinforces and is reinforced by the data.

Tracking updates the Benthamite panopticon made critically popular by Foucault. The panopticon, recall, establishes a watchtower at the center of a prison courtyard from which guards can peer into all the surrounding prison cells without themselves being seen. Indeed, all it takes for discipline to be universally enforced in the prison population (or for school kids) is for the prisoners to think there may be a guard (or school staff) watching them at every moment, whether or not there is in fact one. The sense of discipline is self-internalized. I won't act out because there is a chance I am being watched. I become the self-watching, policing myself.

With tracking technology, all can be technologically tracked, at all times. The technological tracker becomes more deeply and literally internalized: carbohydrates and protein imbibed, number of footsteps taken, sugar monitored, insulin reminder if not inserted, and so on, 24/7. The all-seeing "guard" never turns off, never goes to sleep, never changes guard. It operates as a universal technopticon, across all time and space. Indeed, its info-loop feedback of information one has "liked" serves as a constant reminder of the inescapable: every click and call is the alarm ringing in the ear. Dread becomes its tune, its dire dirge.

The technopticon is the virtualization and pervasion of the opti-political, the all-"seeing" techno-eye without an eye, an invisible visibility that not only surrounds but effectively plumbs our respective interiorities: we know you better than you know yourself, from your desires to your interests, your quirks and gestures to your rhythms and dream states. The technopticon, in fact, knows you completely because it is investing in you, shaping and massaging your preference schemes. It knows your interiority by making it a tabula rasa, on which it writes and rewrites its—and now your—operating code.

"Amelia" claims to be the world's first digital employee, a robotic human look-alike of the stereotyped office assistant: blond, blue-eyed, well coifed, manicured, made-up, and suited. Responding unerringly and irresistibly—without resistance or back talk or behind the back smirk—to every demand. Amelia, the sales pitch has it, is made through machine learning technology to be like, to be us. It immediately learns office idiom and practice, picking it up from existing human office workers with the literal bat of an eye, only to threaten the "Great Replacement" as soon as the tasks are mastered. It is in fact us who are being made more Amelia-like. Machines like us are us, liking, and like machines. We are desiring machines, ambiguity intended. Amelia is made of us because we are effectively turned into Amelia. In desiring Amelia, we are desiring ourselves. Narcissism is the operating code of the algorithm.

The technopticon, then, primes dread's self-habituating operating system. All are tracked, mostly invisibly, anonymously. Tracking capitalism offers an affectation of certainty in the face of dis-ease. Employee tracking in the United States rose 10 percent from April to June 2020 as a result of pandemic work-from-home requirements. It has kept rising since. Companies are increasingly deploying sensors attached to workers' brains to determine their fatigue on the job, attention to the task at hand, or checking out while at work. It remains to be seen whether next-gen "Amelias" and "Armands" make homework irrelevant, just as we are getting used to it. Robots may suffer viral infections, but they don't cough and spread it to the human population. It is ironic that in a world in which everything is at least trackable, thanks to our voluminous digital footprint, the ultimate sources of the tracking are much less readily so. The algorithmic makes the tracking, if not invisible, more opaque, more readily overlooked.

Dread, the anxiety caught up in sensing a concern while not knowing its sources given the abiding anonymity, intensifies in the opacity of transmission, the more or less absolute anonymity of misinformational circulation. Dread hides the repressible, the uncomfortable effects from (self-)view. It's as if the effects are "natural," produced by unseen forces beyond discernibility or control. Algorithms are the new natural law. The conditions producing climate change and global warming, for example, are more or less invisible and so indiscernible too: the effects seep across borders, through cracks, into the normalcy of our lives, the new normal abnormal. What has come to be diagnosed (even in medical and psychological handbooks) now as eco-anxiety seeps and spreads across borders and boundaries. Dread oozes into and, in turn, is secreted by us, a seeping anonymity of evil.

So, algorithmic culture unsettles without being able to pinpoint the source of the unsettlement. The affordances provided by the algorithmic cover over the sources of the unease, in part because the sources of the benefits are also the grounds of the unsettlement and disruption.

*

Coming atop the globally creeping unsettlement of the Covid-19 pandemic itself, the disease intensifies a more general and pervasive dis-ease: lockdown, lack of work, a-sociality, geopolitically and nationally weaponizing the source and the treatments. The very virtualization of interaction and communication—not the face-to-face, but the face-less-facing—has become the pandemic's face, the new normal. Virtualizing the face-to-face effectively anonymizes interaction: Who is speaking, where are they coming from? It turns the face-to-face interaction into an avatar-like state of facelessness. Lockdowns, quarantines, and the anonymity of masked and faceless social interactions. Time and space are collapsed, the immediate made to rule, techno-mediation obscured by the "being-in-the-moment." (It is perhaps not unrelated that "the Event"—eventfulness—has become so central to both experience and its theorization.) Universalized (quasi-)quarantine makes the experience of (self-)quarantining feel like the new normal. And the invisibility of the pandemic—its leakage and seepage, not knowing where it is, when it will hit, who it will hit or more severely affect—proliferates the dread, the unease, the indecipherability. Dread as the everyday of everyone, the given, effectively invisibilizes the intense dreadfulness of abjection.

In both the pandemic and climate cases, it is as if "nature," the world, is getting back at "us" for our inattentiveness and disrespect, our extractive exploitation. But as many have now pointed out, there is no extrication of the human from nature, of the "world" from "us." We are the world, as the globally embracing song once too easily put it. So, the world screwing us, as we have the world, is in fact us having screwed ourselves all along. As Kierkegaard commented, there is no distance, no appeal to a higher order, no disentanglement. And so, definitively, no redemption, only the prospect of dread in the face of decisions about living, dying, and their conditions of (dignified) possibility.

*

There is a tradition, almost as long as that characterized in European philosophical history, of attending to an ecology of suspicion. This has stretched from the Greek

Cynics through Hobbes to Schmitt, and now to the anti-thinking radical rightists of those today like Alain de Benoist in France and Steve Bannon in the United States, not to mention Génération identitaire (though these latter-day references hardly qualify as philosophy so much as a style of reasoning). Suspicion has juiced the fuel prompting the turn to autocratic rule and a willingness to pursue civil war in the interests of instituting and institutionalizing it.

Suspicion places in question a thought, idea, or even evidence because trust in its source has been undermined. If the suspicion is sustained, it works, either by default or design, to dismiss the claimant and claim. It threatens or undoes trust and, once socially weaponized, tugs at, if not pulls apart, the social seams. Pervasive dysfunction and dread are the likely outcomes of suspicion turned socially tormenting, with civil war the endgame.

War is the inevitable outcome of this logic. This, namely, is the war, the conflict, between contrasting or contesting modes of being in the world. Civil war is no longer the end of politics but its normalized expression. Dread is the affect most readily associated with this generalized disposition of warring, where everything is made a contestation, an intrusion, and its resistance. Dread is the affect for and of this time precisely because—in contrast to fear—dread is never clear about its exact object of concern. As one is presented with proliferating technologies of self-control—appified measurements of heart rates, steps taken, calories consumed—dread is the driving sense of anxiety lurking in losing control of large swathes of one's life while never quite knowing exactly what one has overlooked. Algorithmic culture is the ghost haunting the operating system that produces it.

Civil warring, we tend to think, consists of those in a society seeking physically to expel or eliminate the contesting party, government, or rebel. Elimination may include, but is not reducible to extermination, in the extreme cases. Elimination more readily proceeds by removal, both by expanding detention or imprisonment and by physical displacement through expulsion or refugeedom. Civil war, rather than the limit case of warring, should be thought of as contesting ways of being in the world, of the contestants seeking to establish or sustain their way of social being at the risk of death to themselves. Civil warring is less a case of Hegel's lordship-bondage dialectic than it is a war to the social death—exclusion from rights claims and social benefits, removal from social register and space—of the other to institute or maintain one's insistent way of being in the world. One may fear extermination or expulsion, palpable outcomes, evidence for the possibility of which is mounting before one's eyes. In this sense, Russia's invasion of Ukraine to reinstate the empire is both war and civil war. It is, one could say, war as civil war, an invasion seeking both to expand its borders and impose its way of being upon an unwanting population it purports to take as its own.

Dread is the condition of the consequential political and social unsettlement, the anxiety of irreconcilability, of losing even the possibility of a socially self-sustaining or appealing way of life. Dread expresses the irresolvable tension between the apocalyptic promise of afterlife tomorrow and the worldlessness of perpetual flight from global abandonment and ever-present death now. Generally characterized, the warring contrast has tended to be between closed, bounded, walled states—Russia, in the instance at hand—and the insistence on an openness to counter - or differentiated thought, expression, and ways of being.

*

Out of this contesting politics associated with dread and counter-dread, two contrasting sorts of refusal tend to be expressed: One is that of my country or no country. The other is that of an open country, all the ensuing tensions and contestations played out for all. In short, a politics of digging in, the refusal of engagement outside of the narrowing circle not just of the national but the ordained and agreeable, is at odds with a politics of digging out, refusing the narrowing and pinched closures, while insisting on being open to worlds different than the homogeneous on most if not all registers. In the United States, Florida contrasted with California. Globally, Russia or Hungary contrasted with New Zealand.

For Kierkegaard, dread takes hold with the impossibility of awe, with the evaporation of awe's ultimate source. To one side of indifference, a feeling of being overwhelmed manifests. Here dread tends to reproduce the politics of despair, of compounding violence or political and cultural standoffs in its wake. In such cases, dread extends apartness and stresses the logic of enforced separation and ultimately civil war. It takes as given the refusals of engagement, the projected torments, despair, and loathing directed at the non-recognizable and presumed non-belonging. All deeply predicated on holding futureless futures at bay, while in fact bringing them about.

To the other side of indifference, however, dread can also imply that one cares. That care can take hold, even as the abiding sense of dread makes it difficult to get out of bed in the morning, suggests a more complex landscape of concern. Ukrainian resistance at risk of annihilation, like those preceding it elsewhere, is currently the most pressing example. But what was witnessed in the wake of George Floyd's public execution is something akin to Herbert Marcuse's *The Great Refusal*. A global taking to the streets. El-Tahrir Square and the Arab Spring would be another example, as 1989 and the fall of walls, curtains, and systems predicated on constraint and keeping apart, or more recently, women taking to the streets, insisting men no longer define their lives, livelihoods, and looks across Iran. The collective moment of Enough! A complicating mix, on one side of indifference, on the other of refusal, resistance, and the reach for being together in the world, with all its messiness to be worked out collectively.

Insistence on the necessity of breath for all animate life and so the universal right to breathe signals the eco-systemic knots tying together wars exemplified by bombs raining down on places of inhabitation, viral pandemics exemplified by being breathed on unmasked by the non-vaccinated, and environmental disaster and refugeedom. These connecting knots concretize the conditions relationally, tying environmental, viral, racial, technological, political, and economic conditions interactively together. Addressing the conditions of possibility for any one of these challenges to planetary life—to the baseline conditions of life itself—requires taking on the underlying ecosystem, making them collectively possible.

Neoliberalization is committed to the privatizing of social infrastructure, its availability only for those who can personally pay for the services it offers. Abandoned or undeveloped baseline living conditions—infrastructures of debilitation or lack of infrastructure at all—are suffered by racially configured populations in informal settlements, indigenous reservations, disinvested neighborhoods, and abandoned towns. An ecology of caretaking demands attending to the quality, equality, and impacts of enabling social design, resources, and infrastructures of living. Hospitals and learning institutions are the most obvious resources to which all should have access, but they are far from the only ones. A caretaking ecology takes as its collective inspiration working together toward putting in place the infrastructural conditions and social practices necessary for all to live dignified lives in the challenged world(s) we cohabit.

Neoliberalism intensified investment in infrastructures of social control: militarisms; digital surveillance, and now tracking; policing and prisons; even restrictive modes of schooling. Contrast with these repressive apparatuses infrastructures of social support and enabling conditions for people to make livable and dignified social arrangements for themselves, investments in which have been partial at best and eroded altogether at worst.

The transformations necessary to address the scope of the challenges faced today are socio-structural and axiological, those transforming states of being for remaking lives and the possibility of life worth living. The turn today is increasingly away from radical individuation and possession to lives and worlds of relation (both epistemologically and socio-ontologically), co-composition, repair, and reconstruction. The fixes are not simply technical: an immunitarian vaccine for the pandemic projected to enable business as before, benefiting at best only the better off; techno-environmental fixes that add as many ecological challenges as the projected objects of the fixes themselves.

Repairing our world(s) is at once a re-pairing, a putting back together in renewed ways, driven by revivified thinking about how to be and do together in and for the collective world. The reparative in this sense concerns addressing new questions of value and ways of being. Rather than individuated and discretely established—the rational subject behind the veil of ignorance—they call for being fashioned anew or reconstructed out of living together connectedly in the world, in this world, facing up to all the messy complexities this involves.

This putting back together anew involves imagining and attending to balancing in reconsidered and reshaped ways the conditions among and between people, states, and social and environmental ecologies constituting what Édouard Glissant referenced as "tout-monde," the world in its entirety. Only once we collectively rise to the deep challenges this worldly reconstitution at large poses for us in all its complexly constitutive connection and relation will the prospect of dissipating dread assume a real and enduring prospect.

2 A phenomenology of anticipation

Experience, culture, social distribution, and collectivity

Christopher Stephan and Devin Flaherty

1. Introduction

Anyone who studies disasters knows how crucial the future becomes in their wake: what will happen in the days and weeks immediately following a disaster, how and when a community will ever feel normal again, and how to prepare for and mitigate the risk of "next time" arise as variously urgent preoccupations in post-disaster contexts. Similarly, the felt possibility of a looming disaster—for instance, flooding of new areas due to climate change—shapes a variety of practices, orientations, and modes of reasoning made meaningful primarily in terms of what is seen as an impending future. Anticipation thus arises as focal point for understanding social processes in disaster contexts. Yet there has been little focused inquiry on the topic or consensus on what anticipation consists of as a distinctive object of study.

Within the social sciences, anticipation has largely been examined as various groupings of techno-political practices of prediction and modes of governance, often framed through concepts of "uncertainty," "risk," "speculation," or "preparedness" (e.g., Adams et al., 2009; Adey & Anderson, 2012; Anderson, 2010; Caduff, 2008; Choi, 2015; Hong & Szpunar, 2019). Anticipation also surfaces in recent work that considers particular representations of possible futures as a symbolic and affective resource for communities (Appadurai, 2013; Piot, 2010). Aptly for this volume, there has also emerged some discussion of anticipation in the context of "eco-anxiety" and other emotional registers in light of anthropogenic climate change (see: Clissold et al., 2022; Panu, 2020; Tyszczuk, 2021). Throughout, "anticipation" is used in a variety of ways, afforded by the term's polysemy: it can refer to particular feelings, forms of knowledge, imaginative previewing, modes of attention, or actions taken in advance (see: Stephan & Flaherty, 2019). Existing work, then, comes from a variety of theoretical and empirical perspectives and is oriented to diffuse conceptions of anticipation. Though much of the literature cited here speaks, often implicitly, to anticipation as lived experience, there is a dearth of systematic theory articulating different forms of anticipatory experience and its relatedness to broader social and cultural phenomena. In this chapter, we develop a synthesis of theoretical resources for that purpose.

In theorizing anticipation as lived experience, we take a phenomenological approach.[1] Phenomenology is a method, first devised in the philosophy of Edmund

DOI: 10.4324/9781003537311-3

Husserl, for systematically analyzing and accounting for the structures of consciousness that furnish our various forms of relation with the world and others. Phenomenological analysis begins by "bracketing" (provisionally putting out of play or suspending judgments about) the taken-for-granted quality of everyday experience in order to turn attention back on these experiences and their objects[2] and inquire into how they are "constituted" in consciousness, interrogating their mode of always partial and perspectival givenness to experiencing subjects.[3] For phenomenology, consciousness is thus indelibly relational (see, e.g., Zigon & Throop, 2021); as Husserl (adapting a concept introduced by his teacher Franz Brentano) asserted, all consciousness is consciousness *of* something. Furthermore, this is not a self-enclosed consciousness, but rather one that is inherently open to—and ontogenetically constituted in relation to—a plurality of others. That is, all experience bears the trace of intersubjectivity. It is by virtue of intersubjectivity that phenomenology addresses itself to a continually constituted and renewed cultural and social world, which is given as common within the experiences of particularly situated subjects. From this, phenomenology comes to address the constitution of traditions, social institutions, and social groups—all of which exceed any individual subject but are nonetheless given in everyday cultural intersubjective encounters and historical experience.

From a foundation of phenomenological insight and concepts, we theorize anticipation as all experiences of feeling into, previewing, or predicting future possibilities.[4] While this may seem a broad definition, this breadth belies what is in fact an organized structure of future-oriented experiences afforded by phenomenological analysis. As we will show, phenomenology enables mutually implicating levels of analysis: from the internal structures of consciousness out to the socialization of an always cultural subject, to the situatedness of that subject in relation to others, to the generative constitution of social acts and orders of reality of a fundamentally intersubjective nature. In this chapter, we chart a narrow course through these levels, building from the origination of anticipation in the temporal structure of consciousness to cultural patterns of attention and developing these themes to characterize anticipatory experiences as both distributed and shared in the social world.

In the first section, "On lived time in a world of others," we introduce the "flexible footprint" of anticipatory experience. Anticipation, we suggest, doesn't bear a single phenomenality but varies in experiential modality (as affective, imaginal, etc.), in its salience and volitionality, and in the clarity and elaboration of its object. With these distinctions in hand, we turn to sketching some of the primary ways in which variable anticipatory experiences are shaped by social and cultural contexts and practices. Here, we emphasize both the importance of the acquisition of habitual modes of anticipation and the sociocultural canalization of attention as particularly important shapers of anticipatory experience.

Having situated individual experiences within social and cultural worlds, the second section ("Questions of anticipatory distribution and sharedness") examines the social organization of anticipation. In any community, responsibilities to anticipate are differentially distributed. We discuss social roles and the embodied and materially scaffolded expertise that these entail as a central motor of this distribution. Taking up disaster response and preparedness as a case in point, we consider both the forms of interdependence that arise from this distribution of relative expertise and the discordances that can surface as differentially positioned individuals reckon with one another's anticipatory horizons. From this, we advance to the question of collective anticipation. While in the social sciences common forms of anticipation are often attributed to particular collections of people (e.g., Adams et al., 2009), there has been a lack of attention to the distinct social phenomenon of *anticipating together*. We draw on recent developments in the phenomenology of collective intentionality and experiential sharing to propose a sketch of the conditions that must be met for an anticipatory experience to be phenomenally "ours." We thus suggest an initial outline of the phenomenology of shared anticipation. This model provides distinctions and projects empirical correlates for researchers looking to study efforts toward collective anticipation.

2.   On lived time in a world of others

2.1   From internal time consciousness to anticipation

From a phenomenological perspective, anticipation is instigated and afforded by the temporal structure of all experience. Rather than characterizing anticipation as existing only as a particular cognitive act (e.g., in which one reflectively projects a future event), phenomenological theory observes that there is some basic element of anticipation built into all experience. What is called "anticipation" can thus be seen, in this view, as an aspect or dimension of experience which may be more or less salient and more or less willfully attended to at a given moment, and which may present its object with varying degrees of clarity or elaborateness: anticipation manifests in a wide variety of forms and has a "flexible footprint" in experience.

It is the always temporalized structure of consciousness that enables a recognition and parsing of the variable experiential manifestations of anticipation. To examine this temporalized structure, it is useful to begin with Edmund Husserl's phenomenological description of "internal time consciousness" (e.g., Husserl, 1964; see also Gallagher, 2013; Zahavi, 2003). On Husserl's account, all experience is integrally temporally structured; for the experiencing subject, lived time is not a series of staggered and unconnected leaps between punctiform moments but a continuous stream with one thing giving way to another. Take, for instance, what Husserl referred to as "temporal objects" such as a melody. We can experience a series of tones as a melody because they present themselves to us as unified in a temporal flow that spans the recent past and stretches toward the unfolding future. Husserl explicated this temporal structure with a threefold scheme: retention— primal impression—protention. While these phases are analytically distinguished, they are not separate moments. "Primal impression" denotes the immediately unfolding phase of the object of consciousness—for instance, the tonal qualities of the presently sounding note. Further, as this note plays, we are aware of its duration, involving the sense of a present note as *still* sounding and of previous notes as having just lapsed. Thus, Husserl introduced the notion of "retention" to describe the conservation of lapsed phases of experience in the experiential now. Finally, we are also conscious of experiences and their objects (like a melody) unfolding and developing into the future. This indicates our "protentional" capacity: the present is structurally open toward more-to-come. Protentions, unlike retentions, are not *content*-ful; when I am listening to a new melody, I do not have in mind some determinate note as coming. Instead, my attention to the melody involves a more or less indeterminate *listening for*. Hence, while protention does not have some determinate content, it is orientated within the field of my present experiences. The fact that I can feel surprised when the next note is "wrong" (e.g., off-key) demonstrates this indeterminate orientedness of protention.

Husserl's trifold scheme illustrates that what is experienced as the present has temporal breadth owing to its complex structure. All experiences of feeling into, previewing, or predicting future possibilities—what we conceive of as anticipation—emerge from this temporal nature of consciousness. Specifically, protention is the condition of possibility, which serves as the ground for all forms of anticipatory experience. The temporal structure of experience describes the unity of all forms of consciousness and is therefore embedded in all anticipatory experiences. There is, however, a key difference between the bedrock protentional dimension of internal time consciousness—in which, for instance, one indeterminately listens toward an unknown next note—and the contentful expectations one holds about the experiences that accompany something like returning home after a day's work. While articulating the precise relationships between protention and the myriad forms of anticipatory experience is a complex task that is outside the scope of this chapter, it is useful to make a brief illustration. The temporal streaming of experience makes possible acts of reflection upon one's own past and one's sense of diachronic unity, characterized by the felt sense of being someone who persists from a past into the unfolding future (Zahavi, 2014, p. 67). It also makes possible the formation of meaningful connections between different events, such as recognizing causal processes and forming typified understandings of situations and people; the remembered past having unfolded with the structure of a sequence makes possible the habitual expectation of how a course of events may run in the future. For instance, during one's daily commute back home at the end of work, one might anticipate the relief of relaxing on the couch, the meal that will satiate one's present hunger, or the comfort of again being home together with loved ones. Our capacity to recollect previous instances of, and anticipate the future recurrence of, this flow of events is built upon the ground of the temporal structure of consciousness.

While we have argued that anticipation is an entailment of consciousness having an inherently temporal structure, it is obvious from the examples that there is more to anticipatory experience than bare protention. What an understanding of the complex temporal structure of consciousness makes us sensitive to, however, is the fundamentally forward-leaning dimension of all forms of experience; our discussion above suggests that, rather than speaking to a putative species of experiences that are anticipatory, it is more appropriate to say that there is an anticipatory aspect to experience *per se*.[5] We write about "anticipatory experience" in order to maintain focus on the range of phenomenality characterizing anticipation. With this in mind, we can begin to consider the manifold variations of anticipation and to inquire into how forms of experience differentially gear into future possibilities. With this in mind, we identify certain experiential variables in anticipation. We parse anticipatory exerpeinces according to their attentional salience, volitionality, the clarity and elaboration of their object, and their experiential modality.

Attentional salience: All experience is shaped through the shifting foregrounding and backgrounding of experiential objects in attention. In thinking about anticipation, the point is that any aspect of anticipatory experience can be more or less salient, from being the primary focus of one's attention at one end of the spectrum, to being at the margins of awareness at the other (Stephan & Flaherty, 2019, p. 4). In short, *that* one is anticipating can be a relatively muted or focal feature of experience. Likewise, *what* one is anticipating can be at the fringes of attention or the theme of one's current interest. The phenomenality of anticipation can fluctuate as attention shifts within and between these. Furthermore, attentional salience is implicated in and affected by all the further variables we describe below.

Volitionality: By volitionality we mean the extent to which an anticipatory experience of something is willfully initiated and orchestrated. In a strict sense, all anticipatory experiences have a passive foundation insofar as all originate from the substructure of internal time consciousness. The variable here, then, is the extent to which these anticipatory experiences *are given as* willfully contrived or unbidden. Volitionally amenable anticipatory experiences are typically salient (e.g., sitting down to think through how to have a difficult conversation with your child later that evening). Indeed, salience can help produce volitionality. Note, however, that it is quite ordinary to have some anticipation surge into direct awareness unbidden (e.g., while happily chatting with a friend, you are suddenly assailed by anxiety about the job interview you have the next morning). While in some cases it is possible to subsequently willfully direct or suppress anticipatory thoughts and feelings, one may also feel a lack of volitional control over a salient anticipatory experience.

Clarity and elaboration: Anticipatory experience inhabits "a spectrum of precision ranging from vague and impressionistic to articulable and precise" (Stephan & Flaherty, 2019, p. 5). For analytical purposes, two abstractable aspects of this continuum can be distinguished. The first is the *clarity* of the object of anticipation. One can anticipate a precise and specifiable object, as in excitement for an upcoming trip to the Grand Canyon, or worry about an upcoming exam. However, one can also feel something like a vague sense of unease or optimism without these feelings taking a specific and easily articulable object. Such moods (see Lee, 1998; Ratcliffe, 2013; Throop, 2014, 2020) and "existential feelings" (Ratcliffe, 2020) may address one's sense of possibility itself rather than a specific future event or experience. Predicated upon clarity, but analytically distinguishable from it, is *elaboration*. Whereas clarity is about the specifiability of the object of anticipation's directedness, the degree of elaboration is the extent to which various activities and occurrences entailed in the object (e.g., steps in a project) are co-attended to within a given anticipatory experience. Elaboration pertains to the diachronic extendedness, including causal and narrative sequences, through which what is anticipated appears.

Modality: Anticipatory experiences are fundamentally multimodal (Stephan & Flaherty, 2019, p. 4). While one may be inclined to think of anticipation as most prototypically entailing some kind of imagination or discursive thought, anticipation takes place across a variety of modalities of experience, including perception, bodily feelings and emotions, and imagination. For example, in Klein's (2017/1998) work on "expert intuition," skilled persons report occasionally acting with tremendous efficacy based only upon strong gut feelings about unfolding events without being able to say how they knew what to do. We can juxtapose this with Casey's (1976) notion of "imagining how," wherein persons may carry out highly detailed previewing of how actions or possible events might go. It is, moreover, possible to recognize an interplay between these experiential modalities such that vivid imaginings or discursive thoughts are founded upon more tacit forms of feeling and perceptual awareness (Stephan, 2019). For example, feelings of stage fright may antecede imagining failure and subsequent shame. We should not, however, think of this interplay as a unidirectional progression: once a thought or imagining is no longer attended to, one can still embody future-oriented feelings such as apprehension or excitement. These different experiential forms of anticipation should not be thought of as discrete or as more or less anticipatory than one another, but as different modes of appearance of anticipatory processes.

The variables we highlight here are not exhaustive. Researchers might also attend to, for instance, the differing degrees of certainty and sense of familiarity or habituality given to particular anticipatory experiences. The central point is that anticipatory experiences have manifold but systematically characterizable phenomenal forms. What this suggests, on the one hand, is that anticipation plays a greater but sometimes more subtle part in everyday life than might be presumed; on the other hand, the flexible footprint of anticipatory experiences indicates that research and theory on anticipation should take this variable phenomenality into account.

2.2 Lived time in cultural lifeworlds

Thus far, we have examined anticipation with respect to its ever-present yet highly differentiated phenomenality. This is far from the whole story. No one anticipates in an acultural way or from and toward a world that (however personal the matter) is not already brimming with other people, artifacts, traditions, and institutions. Rather, culture is present in the very constitution of experience (Csordas, 1990, 1993; Jackson, 1983, 1998; Throop, 2010). In terms of anticipation, this means that individuals' anticipatory experiences unfold in relation to practices and sensibilities that are developed within the particular groups, communities, and institutions into which they are socialized over the life course. Throughout this subsection, we will begin to outline a few of the ways that anticipatory experiences are shaped through the social world.

Anticipatory experiences are future-oriented; yet, in order to begin an analysis of the cultural lifeworld, the term "future" requires some disambiguation. As phenomenological sociologists have shown, the social world is in part constituted through complex layerings of analytically abstractable phenomenal senses of time, spanning four "levels" that run from one's own inner sense of duration to phenomena like daily work schedules and monsoon seasons (see Berger & Luckman, 1991; Schutz, 1951, 1967). Distinguishing these different temporal levels is useful for studying anticipation because the temporal horizon of anticipatory experiences can be anchored in any one of these. Moreover, cultural meanings and practices can differentially elaborate and foreground various levels. The first level is each subject's internal experience of duration; events can feel rapid, thoughts can come to us slowly, etc., and we can sense this and talk about it with no need or intention to refer to external measures of time. Second, in moving and speaking with others, our sense of tempo becomes tethered to and transformed by others. In interaction, for instance, our own expressive actions gear into, await, or forecast those of our co-participants (as we share one another's "vivid present" [Schutz, 1951]). At this level, our sense of temporality is inter-kinetically and interpersonally constituted. Over the life course, we become socialized into situation- and partner-specific rhythms, enabling us to anticipate, interpret and evaluate the flow of intersubjective activity. Third, we live in a world of culturally constituted ways of marking time— rendering it "objective" and ideationally detached from any particular action in social life. We can anchor our plans and actions in clocks and calendars, using these to coordinate with others and delimit expectations for the pacing of our own lives. At the fourth level, processes in the natural world have temporal duration, some of which produce perceptible rhythms within the environment (e.g., the earth spinning on its axis). Discerning the right moment to prepare for a seasonal migration, embark on a fishing expedition, or seek shelter for the night requires embodied cultural knowledge that is discernible from and not necessarily connected to objective units of time measurement. While the difference between these levels is most apparent in abstraction, we would note that individuals may experience one or more of these temporal levels as salient in different anticipatory experiences. Notice that the examples above are suffused with cultural entailments. They not only index practices whose variable existence and meaning are culturally specific; they implicate socialized patterns in attending to the meaningful temporal frames for these practices.

All sociocultural milieus—with their combinations of particular practices, institutional structures, materialities, cultural values, *et cetera*—differentially afford and shape anticipatory experiences, including their patterning, degree of thematization, and form of temporalization across everyday life. Cultural lifeworlds provide an "assumptive background against which anticipatory experience takes shape" (Stephan & Flaherty, 2019, p. 4). For one, cultures constitute "behavioral environments" (Hallowell, 1955) that foundationally shape how the world is given to subjects. What kind of things and beings exist and how to orient in time and space are examples of such basic frameworks. Another component of this cultural diversity is the bevy of "cultural models" available for classifying, explaining, and acting according to socialized patterns (D'Andrade & Strauss, 1992; Holland & Quinn, 1987; Strauss & Quinn, 1998). Cultural models are endemic to anticipatory experiences, providing schema for interpreting events, projecting their relevant possibilities, and informing expectations of others (see Schutz, 2011; Schutz & Luckmann, 1973; Rogers, 1982). Cultural models provide scaffolding for clarity and elaboration within anticipation; the ability to suss out future possibilities is massively supported by not only the socialized capacity to constitute an emerging situation as one of a particular type but also by cultural knowledge of the typical course of such scenarios. What is more, all such models take into account and situationally gear into local material worlds. Societies differ widely in the material artifacts and infrastructures that populate individuals' behavioral environments. The affordances (Dijk & Rietveld, 2021; Gallagher & Aguda, 2019) presented by tools, public infrastructures, and a variety of other material items provide differential possibilities for anticipating an event like "tomorrow's long journey." While the material world is enfolded into anticipatory experience in a variety of ways, artifacts for representing time play a special role as they allow for locating anticipated events within a shared frame of reference, as well as mnemonic devices for prompting anticipatory processes.

Cultural phenomenologists have emphasized the central importance of attention in all of these processes, pointing to "the organization and regulation of attention as a key dimension of our cultural existence" (Throop & Duranti, 2015, p. 1056). For instance, anthropologists (e.g., Aulino, 2019; Csordas, 1993; Geurts, 2002; Luhrmann, 2020; Throop, 2010; Throop & Duranti, 2015) have extensively documented how patterns of attention are culturally "canalized," rendering particular aspects of items, beings, events and modes of experience more or less salient. One implication is that salience, as an experiential variable of anticipation, can be precipitated by cultural emphases (Stephan & Flaherty, 2019, p. 4). That is, it's both that those "cultural objects" that are emphasized within a particular community may be things people are likely to anticipate, but also that the anticipatory activity may itself be more likely to become experientially focal. Not only do particular "cultural objects" (e.g., upcoming rituals, seasonal changes, life stage transitions) become variably culturally constituted as those deserving attention, but cultural practices (perhaps most visibly in institutional contexts) will entail implicit and sometimes explicit norms, which can include what forms of anticipatory experience are valid or desirable. Indeed, skill in a particular cultural domain may entail highly cultivated capacities to "do anticipation" in a situationally appropriate way (see discussion of expertise to follow). Conversely, there are also cultural idioms for emphasizing the importance of, and scaffolding individuals in taking on, practices of intentionally not anticipating in particular contexts (see Flaherty, 2019). Note, however, that cultural patterns of attention are largely habitual; while it is important to take into account the relationship between something being culturally salient and its being experientially salient, it is nonetheless important not to conflate the two.

In most cases, we suggest, anticipation is relatively tacit in instances where cultural practices do not cultivate more explicit formulations. Central to this point is the insight that the majority of experience—including anticipation—is lived out "pre-objectively"[6] (Merleau-Ponty, 2013; see also Dreyfus, 2014), within an immediate, intuitive and absorbed mode of attending to, making use of, and knowing, rather than through mentally stepping back, scrutinizing or pondering. In many ways, the social world functions to sustain individuals' absorption within a taken-for-granted series of events, patterns of action, and expectations of others (see Rogers, 1982). Much anticipation takes place at the fringes of awareness: when social life goes according to expectations, there is no need to further investigate or clearly and elaborately anticipate what might come next. The cultural lifeworld is therefore not only relevant to those moments of anticipation that are marked by high degrees of attentional salience, volitionality, clarity, and elaboration, but also to those that are significantly more habitual and implicit in nature. Further, it is important to attend to the shifting nature of anticipatory experience through time: some future possibility (e.g., a project one must carry out) might appear in a clear, salient object-like way at one moment but be handled in a pre-objective mode of experience at another (e.g., as one is absorbed in a task directed toward this end).

It is also crucial to note, however, that habitual patterns of activities and rela-tions can come to be punctuated by "breakdowns" (see Heidegger, 2010; see also Zigon, 2007) large and small. Heidegger (e.g. 2010) observed that it is in rela-tively rare moments, such as when a tool one reaches for is missing or broken, or when something intrudes on the successful execution of our intended course of action, that our typically tacit and pragmatic mode of engagement in the world breaks down. Schutz's phenomenological sociology suggests a similar pattern with regard to the socially constructed realities we inhabit (Berger & Luckman, 1991, pp. 37–38; Schutz, 2011, pp. 125–128); habitual knowledge, for instance, is always subject to "until further notice" acceptance. When things present themselves as "problematic" or "unfamiliar," one shifts into a mode of investigating social real-ity further that can include making new plans for how to proceed or anticipating a different outcome. What these instances show is that our habitual and pre-objective being in the world is simultaneously an inherent feature of human life and one that is dependent on structures within the world—sociocultural and natural. And, as radically demonstrated in cases of disaster, these structures are subject to disrup-tion and destruction. However, no matter how much breakdowns might instigate a shift in our modes of attention and action, they will nonetheless always take the form of a delimited suspension of our habitual, previously acquired ways of being. The point here is that as sociocultural actors, we never start from scratch in the midst of breakdown: individuals understand problems, imagine solutions and integrate new ways of working from the standpoint of their already habitualized, taken-for-granted way of inhabiting the world.

A final comment is in order. Throughout this subsection, we have kept to broad strokes, writing of cultural meanings and practices as if they were definite, orderly, and fixed. This way of presenting culture is useful for offering a heuristic sketch of areas of inquiry and factors to be taken into account. It is, nonetheless, essential to bear in mind that diversity, disjuncture and distribution exist at all points. In fact, an important methodological premise of our discussions in the sections to follow is that variations in anticipatory experiences within and between social groups must be factored into any theoretical perspective on anticipation.

3. Questions of anticipatory distribution and sharedness

Considering variations within and across social groups is a mainstay of any social scientific approach. Key to thinking through inter- and intra-group processes, however, is pursuing questions of collective social phenomena without collapsing groups into internal homogeneity. Considering anticipation in this light raises two primary questions. First, how are anticipatory experiences distributed within a community, and what social efficacy does that distribution have? This question foregrounds the sociocultural bases and effects of asymmetries within any social group or between interacting members of different groups. Second, what are the characteristics of collective anticipation, and what intersubjective conditions might need to be in place for people to anticipate together? This question recognizes that within any subjectively meaningful group, members will be differently oriented to the possibilities at hand and must come to some awareness of and correspondence with the anticipatory experiences of others. Throughout the remainder of this chapter, we apply our phenomenologically informed perspective to begin answering these questions with an eye toward their specific relevance and application to disaster research. Because these two conceptually and empirically distinct areas of inquiry have largely been elided in existing scholarship, our aim throughout this section is to provide theoretical scaffolding for researchers interested in pursuing one or both of these topics.

3.1 The differential distribution of anticipatory experiences within a community

As we have shown, socialization into a particular community will shape the phenomenality and objects of anticipatory experiences. Nonetheless, anthropologists and sociologists have shown the immense variability that exists among individuals participating in "the same" cultural milieu. On the one hand, people differ on points of view, matters of fact, and temperament (Cohen, 1994; Hollan, 2012; Sapir, 1938; Stromberg, 1986; Wallace, 1970/1961). On the other hand, all individuals inhabit particular "regions" of the social world, taking up a constellation of social roles and acquiring knowledge and habitual forms of action that differentially situate them in regard to interest, expertise, responsibilities, and relationships (Berger & Luckman, 1991). It is this latter source of variation that we are primarily concerned with in this section.

Every individual embodies a changing nexus of social roles as they move through time and through the life course. Roles like "grandfather," "woman," and "teacher" will hold both sociocultural meaning and personal significance; embodying a role informs both who others take one to be and who one sees oneself as being. These differences are concomitant with habits of attention and motive; in terms of anticipation, roles are constituted in part through shared expectations for what should be anticipated and how, as well as by the habitual activities (including regular engagements with particular socio-material environments) through which any role is embodied. As noted by Graeber (2011), for example, labor roles differentially distribute expectations and responsibilities for anticipation.[7] Looking at a community through the lens of anticipation, then, shows us that the great variability of overlapping social roles will be constituted through and manifest in part through differentially distributed dispositions and responsibilities to anticipate.

One of the most important elements of the diversity of social roles is the differential distribution of relative expertise across social domains. By "expertise" we mean to foreground the role of learned, embodied practices that manifest through high levels of competence within any social domain, rather than merely those that are privileged within a given social milieu. This is the form of expertise evidenced, for instance, in Goodwin's (1994) concept of "professional vision"—the socially organized work through which members of a group (such as a profession) accomplish the effective forms of perceiving and understanding that mark competence within that group's domain. Vitally, as Goodwin notes, the exercise of such skill is distributed across discursive, perceptual, cognitive, and material strata. Indeed, we would argue, the development of new capacities for, habits of, and recurrent objects of anticipation are also constitutive of the development of expertise. Goodwin's point holds for all sorts of quotidian knowledge domains, but it is easily recognized in the case of specialized technical artifacts that are relatively unique to a domain of expert practice. In such cases, the very constitution of the object of knowledge depends upon one's ability to competently engage with a given technology. Following Don Ihde's (1990) phenomenology of technology, we can loosely group this constitution into two types: embodiment relations, through which one's capacities for movement or perception are directly enhanced or altered by a technological artifact (e.g., a microscope's effect on vision), and hermeneutic relations consisting in skillful engagements with representations that function in place of direct perception (e.g., flood maps). Verbeek (2011) extends Idhe's insights to observe that technologies can be "moralizing," presenting new morally relevant possibilities (e.g., in the case of obstetric ultrasound). As such, access to these technologies (or lack of access) changes moral stakes. Just as differential material worlds shape possibilities for anticipation within any cultural context, these specialized, relatively sequestered technologies serve to establish differential objects, forms, and habits of anticipation for those working in different domains of relative expertise.

The asymmetries between relative experts and nonexperts in a given domain set up two central points of interest regarding anticipation within and across communities: interdependence and discordance. Interdependence is built into the taken-for-granted nature of social reality. Acting on limited knowledge of the technologies and services we depend on and the institutions we participate in, each person relies upon more or less anonymous others whose knowledge and skills extend and supplement their own (Berger & Luckman, 1991; Schutz, 1967). A complementary point is that anywhere differentiation in roles and expertise is observable, we should find cases where persons are to some degree responsible to anticipate on behalf of others.

Thinking with a case study is useful here. In the aftermath of disaster (be that days, months, or years after the event), disaster experts of various kinds descend upon communities. The usefulness of these disaster experts consists, in part, in their having been habituated into particular forms of anticipation; these will include forms of attention, methods of planning, and technologies for predicting in post-disaster contexts that will not be shared by community members. The very purpose of these kinds of experts is to take on the responsibility of anticipating for the community at large, putting programs and initiatives into motion that will, from their perspective, most optimally support the community in recovering and (in many contexts) preparing for or mitigating the risk of the next possible disaster. This kind of "expert anticipation" is in many ways afforded not only by esoteric knowledge and embodied skills but also by a variety of technologies and other material artifacts not accessible to members of the impacted community. For instance, in the years of recovery after Hurricane Maria hit St. Croix, US Virgin Islands, the main conference room at the island's Disaster Response Center featured a large color-coded map that represented the island's geography through its differential risk for flooding.[8] Similarly, familiarity with algorithms for predicting the likelihood and severity of potential future disasters in a given location, or various forms of statistics, graphs, and charts that quantitatively render the effects of disaster on a community are relatively sequestered parts of the everyday worlds of disaster experts that significantly shape what and how they anticipate on behalf of the community they are working in.

While distributed relative expertise is a condition of possibility for interdependence, discrepancies in these background assumptions and techniques also produce discordant anticipations. Persons with expertise in common may disagree among themselves, but they rarely have to deal with the problem of communicating the relevance or legitimacy of their anticipatory objects to one another from scratch. This ceases to be the case when seeking to motivate or convince domain-relative novices. It would be tempting to treat this as an "education" problem— and, indeed, this is a dominant paradigm through which such issues are often viewed (e.g., Codreanu et al., 2014; Kitagawa, 2021; Preston, 2012). Yet, we mean to point to a more fundamental issue: from the phenomenological standpoint, what is obvious and relevant is embedded in "the world within reach" of people's day-to-day projects and encounters (Schutz, 1945). Discordances between habitual horizons of anticipation arise because persons operating in different domains can be significantly out of sync in terms of their everyday means of constituting reality. Co-constituting and co-orienting to meaningfulness across standpoints can rarely, if ever, be achieved through simply making new information available. Discrepant orientations pose a further problem whenever accomplishing efficacious actions or projects across domains of expertise requires forms of cooperative action with relative nonexperts.

To return to the case study: in post-disaster contexts, there is a subset of experts who are responsible for trying to make sure the affected community is prepared for the next disaster. This often involves engaging community members in particular forms of anticipation that align with the expectations and predictions produced from the standpoint of a disaster expert. For instance, in regions like the Caribbean where severe hurricanes are recurrent, disaster experts in community-engaged roles are responsible, in post-hurricane contexts, for motivating community members to take action or adjust their behavior in order to be best prepared for the next hurricane. However, an eye toward the phenomenology of anticipation shows many reasons why this poses a huge social challenge. For one, it requires recruiting community members to shift into forms of anticipation that are not in alignment with the habitual modes of anticipating that arise from and are afforded by their everyday worlds. Second, it can be predicated on a shift from habitual modes of understanding and expectation regarding the division of anticipatory responsibility along lines of expertise. For instance, in the post-Maria context on St. Croix, many community members felt that it was the responsibility of local government entities (including disaster experts who had contracted with them) to take care of doing everything necessary to prepare for the next severe hurricane: they were, after all, the experts. On their part, however, disaster experts working with the local government were laser-focused on "educating" the community so that *they could better prepare themselves* for when the next severe hurricane struck. From their point of view, this was the central missing piece to achieving satisfactory island-wide preparedness for the next storm.

Problematic asymmetries between community members and disaster experts in contexts of disaster recovery and preparation have been documented and analyzed across global contexts (e.g., Barrios, 2010, 2016, 2017; Choi, 2015). For instance, Roberto Barrios (2016, 2017) has shown that the success or failure of disaster recovery projects hinges on whether disaster experts adequately attune and respond to community members' own priorities for the recovery process.[9] Attending to asymmetries in anticipation through the framework of expertise, however, can lend new insight into these often fraught engagements. In particular, enduring asymmetries in habitual objects and forms of anticipatory experience between community members and disaster experts can manifest empirically through unsuccessful disaster education or preparation programs in which recovery workers fail to recruit community members into particular modes of future orientation.

What a brief summary of these cases points to is the deeply embedded nature of anticipation; anticipatory experiences arise within the context of each individual's skillful inhabiting of their everyday world. Considered at a community level, this skillful inhabiting can be productively approached as the differential distribution of relative expertise. Both interdependence and discord between different habitual orientations and styles can become especially noticeable wherever people are intervening in the lives of others. The situated and habitual means through which future possibilities are felt, projected, or predicted in anticipatory experience are the source of both the interdependent nature of people's anticipatory horizons and the discordances that can become prominent and urgent issues of accommodation or conflict.

3.2 Anticipating together

Considering the distribution of anticipatory experiences forms but one side of an account of the social nature of anticipatory experience. It is also necessary to consider the nature of collective anticipation. The empirical stakes of this are made exceptionally clear in the cases of disaster response and preparation: the asymmetrical distribution of relative expertise can manifest in substantial inter- or intra-group challenges for achieving aligned orientations toward the future. Despite its particular problems, what this example points toward is by no means an unusual situation; rather, anticipating together is a common undercurrent within social life. When working on a team project, making plans for a trip with a significant other, or sharing concerns over the fragile health of an elderly relative, people are (at least at times) doing more than informing one another of their individual anticipatory feelings and projections. They are also shaping one another's anticipatory experiences and coming to feel that they are facing some future possibility together. We would suggest, then, that anticipation can be undertaken collectively and that this is something we can *experience as such*. It is significant that while collective anticipation seems implicit within at least some of the forms of collective action and experiential sharing highlighted in the phenomenology of "collective intentionality" (e.g., Caminada, 2018; Chelstrom, 2013; Szanto, 2016; Tollefsen, 2014) and "shared emotions" (e.g., León et al., 2019; Salice, 2016), it has not, as of yet, been theorized within either of these literatures. We can, however, leverage some of the conceptual tools derived from theories of collective intentionality and experiential sharing to provide an initial sketch of the intersubjective conditions that are conducive to collective anticipatory processes.

As a first step, it is important to clarify what we are talking about when we speak of "collective" anticipation. Over the last forty years, philosophers, psychologists, and social scientists have dedicated concerted attention to the problem of "collective intentionality" (e.g., Bratman, 2014; Gilbert, 2014; Tollefsen, 2015; Tuomela, 2016). Weighing the merits of different theories has required scholars to carefully delimit what is meant by the term "collective." Even within the phenomenological literatures, there is noteworthy variability in how scholars articulate and differentiate these notions (see Schmid, 2023; Szanto, 2024). Without rehashing these positions, we think it is sufficient to offer a few takeaways: First, classical phenomenologists including Husserl, Scheler, Stein, Gurwitsch, and Schutz observe that the collective is what is irreducibly intersubjective but recognizable at the level of the individual. A central theme of their arguments is that there are forms of first-person plural experience that are *given* as "ours"—they are phenomenally a "we experience" (Szanto & Moran, 2016; Walsh, 2020; Zahavi, 2014).[10] In a sense that will be expanded upon shortly, we would suggest that this "collective" form of experience entails undergoing something alongside and in relation to others' experiences of it. Second, the first-person plural form of experience does not amount to a single collective consciousness. There is no "us" without a differentiable "you" and "I." Third, taking the phenomenological view, the meaningful sense of "collective" does not entail some kind of "phenomenal fusion" wherein there is putatively one, unified experience undergone by two or more persons (see León et al., 2019 and Zahavi, 2018 for critiques of the "phenomenal fusion" view). Hence, in theorizing collective-level anticipation, it is also important to preserve both self-other differentiation and asymmetries between persons. Finally, what is "collective" cannot necessarily be defined from an externalist view as that extent to which an action, attitude, etc. is "the same" across a category of persons.

A significant benefit of this final point is that we can meaningfully differentiate the kind of claims made about collective lived experiences from generalizations about social categories—two distinct types of claims that can otherwise easily be conflated.

Inspired by (though, admittedly, simplifying) Szanto's (2016) synthetic account of a Husserlian model for collective intentionality, we would propose that the basic case of collective anticipatory experience is characterized by (1) mutual awareness, (2) reciprocal influence, and (3) mutual incorporation. We will illustrate how these three conditions are met by the following example: Amery is a new participant in an improv comedy workshop, regularly attended by his friend Laura. They have been made scene partners for a sketch in front of a live audience and are waiting together backstage. As their turn on stage approaches, Amery begins to feel stage fright and glances at Laura. Laura is looking forward to the performance, but seeing Amery's nervous look, she realizes he might freeze during the sketch if he cannot loosen up. She makes a silly face and gives him a playful punch in the arm. Amery laughs, and his attention shifts toward the goal of having fun with his friend.

The first condition identifies that to share in or achieve collective experience entails *mutual awareness*. Minimally and sufficiently, collective experiences involve a low-level awareness of one or more other persons as having their own subjective standpoints. In our example, Amery and Laura are attentive to one another. This awareness need not be focal at all moments, but it may become so. As such, when Amery glances at Laura, she is in a position to observe that Amery is nervous. Notably, the mutual awareness condition already entails empathy. Phenomenologically, empathy is the quasi-perceptual appearance of another person as a minded, experiencing being—another center of orientation within the world (Szanto & Moran, 2016; Throop, 2023; Zahavi, 2001). It is critical to empathy's fundamental role in intersubjectivity that its essential manifestation does not entail a kind of inference to the best explanation, cognitive perspective-taking, or affective resonance. While in some cases we may engage in more imaginative or inferential ways of understanding others, the passive immediacy with which we get the gist of another's meaning in the most elementary forms of empathy is vital to our capacity to condition one another's perspectives and responses (see Stephan, 2023). From this, follow the next two conditions.

The second condition specifies further that in order to anticipate together there must be some *reciprocity of influence* between the individuals involved. Reciprocal influence is characterized by mutually motivating one another's experiences. Motivation, in the sense employed here, is not a psychological state but a connectedness of experiences; for one experience to motivate another is for the latter to emerge from the former (Stein, 2000/1922, ch. 3 §1). In mutual motivation, each interactant's anticipatory experience is spurred by that of the other(s). As such, collective anticipation is never a one-sided effect. Even the most minimal interactions involve reciprocal influence in the form of mutual motivation. Returning to our example: Amery's nervous glance instigates Laura's own silly response, and Amery reacts in turn.[11] Note that reciprocal influence highlights the significance of intersubjective temporality to collective anticipation. For illustration, we restrict our considerations to real-time interactions, but the crucial dynamic is interpersonal synchronization which does not necessarily have to unfold within immediate bodily copresence.[12]

Finally, the basic case of collective anticipation involves *mutually incorporating* the *directedness* of one another's experiences. While this condition involves individuals being directed toward a common concern (though the participants need not be in the same position with respect to a developing situation/possibility), it is not satisfied merely by each being directed toward the self-same object of attention. Rather, by "mutually incorporating," we mean that the individuals in question must each enfold one another's orientations into their own. Thus, in order to anticipate together, Amery and Laura must mutually orient to some future possibility in light of one another's orientations to this future possibility—in this case, their upcoming sketch. Amery's shift from anxiety to playfulness responsively incorporates Laura's attitude, just as Laura's goofy response aims at putting Amery into a more appropriate emotional orientation for the coming performance. At this point, they are collectively anticipating—each contributing to the other's anticipation and co-constituting its object by virtue of their shared involvement in each other's anticipatory experiences.

Within collective anticipation are complex interactions between individuals' anticipatory experiences. As we noted above (Section 2), anticipation involves a variety of experiential registers, comprising a range from the most implicit and passive forms of embodied awareness, such as moods, to the articulable and volitionally amenable, such as imagination or ratiocination. These modalities of anticipatory experience can manifest in interaction (with or without becoming topical or explicitly articulated). It is here that asymmetries between participants become a productive source of an emergent collective anticipation irreducible to the experiences of each individual involved (this becomes more evident in the case of larger social collectives). When people are reciprocally engaged, as in coactivity and conversation, the actions of each take account of the other. In interaction, each participant affects the other's attention to aspects or entailments of the situation at hand. This involves an interchange of two kinds, which is nonetheless realized within a single ongoing process. First, participants may draw one another's attention to aspects of a situation that either modify each other's attention to and understanding of a jointly attended object or begin to constitute a new object of attention. Second, as Schutz (1967, §34) observed of all face-to-face situations, it is possible for forms of anticipation that are more implicitly undergone by one person to be recognized by another in a more determinate fashion. In doing so, the moods, feelings, emotions, or imagined possibilities of one participant can inform the responses of another—a process that makes possible a kind of feedback loop that can bootstrap reflectively available forms of anticipation within interaction (see Stephan, 2020, pp. 150–153). Notice here that, precisely because the emergence and course of collective anticipation is predicated as much on productive asymmetries between individuals as on their coalescence, the account preserves the particularity of each subject's experience.[13] It is not necessary, nor is it possible, that Laura's perspective on Amery's nervousness be identical to Amery's own experience.

Our objective here has been to sketch out the implications for anticipation of a phenomenological argument regarding the basic case of collective experiencing. Consequently, we have left aside some pertinent but complex considerations. On the one hand, by offering an example of just two people anticipating together, some of the modifications that arise in triadic interactions (and larger collectives) have been bracketed for the time being. It is important to make one note, however: when subjects anticipate together in larger social collectives, they do not devote thematic attention to each and every other subject at each and every moment. Amery and Laura are in a position to continuously track one another; a group of ten people in a meeting, for instance, cannot. Consequently, much happens that no one individual can keep account of. The three conditions we describe, therefore, are not concurrently symmetrically fulfilled by each participant at all moments. The value of the model we endorse here is that it grounds sufficient criteria for claims to collective anticipation and provides a set of empirical correlates for the study of anticipating together. On the other hand, we have not delved into social developments that might arise from collective anticipation. And yet, beyond the basic case, there are further varieties of experiential sharedness with relevance to collective anticipation (see León & Zahavi, 2016). For instance, anticipating together can develop into arriving at explicit agreements and plans (see Szanto, 2016 for a discussion of this in the context of collective intentions). However, it is important to bear in mind that this is not an inevitable development. Anticipating together is not necessarily a volitional undertaking, such as is the case when participants in a group project set about making plans; it is possible to find oneself caught up in collective anticipation without decision or conscious effort. It may be that anticipating together is an important antecedent for (if not a guarantee of) developing common perspectives on what is at stake, potentiating agreement or shared goals for the future. In the case of collective anticipation, we would suggest that there is also a sense of ownership at stake (the sense that *we* have anticipated something). It is evident, then, that the basic case can ground inquiry into applied questions of collectivity. Among these are issues of the cooperative means—for instance, in disaster response and preparedness—through which individuals mutually attune toward how possible futures matter now.

4.   Conclusion: lessons for researchers

In concluding, we return to major points in order to draw out their implications for future qualitative research on anticipation. Anticipation is a basic feature of experience, bootstrapped from the temporal flow of consciousness itself. Accordingly, anticipatory experiences can entail a manifold of bodily feelings, emotions, intuitions, imaginative projections, and ratiocinations. This "flexible footprint" of anticipatory experiences opens up a range of questions regarding their phenomenality in any given instance, as well as the relationship between forms of anticipatory experience and sociocultural context. We have identified attentional salience, volitionality, clarity and elaboration, and experiential modality as key variables researchers of anticipation should attend to when delimiting their research objectives, gathering qualitative data, and developing theory. We would note that these phenomenological variables make anticipatory experiences differentially articulable by individuals and differentially available to an outside observer (researcher) across moments in time, calling for a variety of coordinated methods of data collection sensitive to these variable showings. Moreover, since anticipatory experience shifts through time, we suggest that analyses of anticipation must attend to this temporality, eschewing static generalizations. For many research projects, gearing into this temporal dynamism can be best achieved by taking a diachronic perspective.

The objects and qualities of anticipatory experience vary within and between communities. It is, of course, important to take into account different customs and kinds of events, considering these alongside diverse beliefs, forms of knowledge and attitudes. Yet a cultural phenomenological perspective aims to go further by examining the constitution of cultural objects, practices, and events in their very modes of appearances to cultural actors. Anticipation evinces cultural schema and patterns of attention, but these are analytic abstractions from what must be understood first and foremost as a lived situation; efforts to understand anticipation as a lived experience should be located within the horizons of people's everyday engagements within the social world. Researchers interested in some particular anticipatory object (e.g., flooding from anthropogenic climate change) must take into account how the bevy of anticipatory orientations individuals enact are embedded within and take shape against a background of their pre-objective and reflective activity in the cultural lifeworld.

In coming to grips with how future possibilities are handled within a particular cultural community, it is important to consider what members of a community recognize and respond to as the anticipatory dimension of one another's experience. Complementing this point, we would note that it will often be appropriate to pair this inquiry with one that considers prevailing social arrangements for who anticipates what. One available route highlighted here is to examine the differential responsibilities to anticipate customarily ascribed to and taken up by members of a social group. Expertise is a key concept for thinking about the differential distribution of anticipation. While here we took the example of professional expertise in disaster response and planning, we would emphasize that expertise should be considered something everyone has in some form. Keeping in mind the material scaffolding of anticipatory experiences, it could be productive for disaster researchers to attend not only to the cultural habits and role responsibilities enacted by various community members but also to the varying degrees of access persons may have to tools and techniques for evoking particular future possibilities. Further, social dynamics arising around bridging expertise, including contrasting (and not always complementary) perspectives, is a productive space for researchers to attend to.

Collective-level anticipation has special relevance for disaster research, but it is also a theoretically and methodologically delicate analytic object. When theorizing collective orientations toward the future, there is always a risk of making generalized claims about groups from an external perspective without making it clear how this can be empirically traced or offering a theory of how such collective orientations may be achieved. We suggest that the phenomenological model presented here avoids both of these problems. In anticipating together, each person's anticipatory experience, while never being a microcosm of the collective-level process, would not have taken the course it did without reciprocally incorporating the anticipatory experiences of others. Beyond contributing to theoretical distinctions, this model indicates empirical correlates that enable researchers to directly study collective processes of anticipation; in so doing, the model offers an approach to examining anticipation within social groups. Moreover, considering collective anticipation as consisting of individuals mutually conditioning one another's anticipation provides a further methodological gain insofar as it permits us to distinguish claims made about genuinely collective anticipatory processes from generalizations ascribed to a social category. While the latter can be useful, confounding the two could easily lead to muddled theory. Qualitative research in this area could contribute to differentiating collective anticipatory processes, particularly by taking into account their cultural variations and material scaffolding.

Acknowledgements

Research and writing for this text conducted by Christopher Stephan was supported by funding from the Carlsberg Foundation (Grant ID: CF-18–1107). The ethnographic fieldwork drawn on in this text was funded through a Wenner-Gren Foundation Post-PhD Research Grant awarded to Devin Flaherty. The authors thank both of these sources for their support.

Notes

1 We cannot offer an extensive discussion of phenomenology as a philosophical tradition or its development within the social sciences here. However, for an easy introduction, see Zahavi (2019). For a discussion of phenomenological anthropology, see Desjarlais and Throop (2011) and Zigon and Throop (2021). For a discussion of the influence of phenomenology in sociology, see Overgaard and Zahavi (2009).
2 In phenomenology, an "object" is anything toward which consciousness is directed, be it an entity or event in the world, or something that manifests in thought (e.g., in imagination). A subject's own thoughts and feelings can become "objects" in this sense when the subject's attention is turned back upon them in an act of reflection. The "object," then, is the *something* toward which our thoughts, feelings, and perceptions are directed. Yet there are subtleties to observe here. As our chapter will make clear, for instance, the objects toward which anticipations are directed do not always appear in a finely delimited, determinate manner.
3 From a phenomenological standpoint, the ultimate point of reference being the object's appearance to consciousness places a certain primacy on the experiencing subject. In taking this position, phenomenology does not, however, provide an endorsement of methodological individualism (Salice & Schmid, 2016, pp. 4–5), nor does it speak only to first-person perspectives (see Zigon & Throop, 2021). The point is that superindividual social phenomena must be understood in their experiential givenness, not that all objects are reducible to the level of individual minds (singularly or in the aggregate).
4 The risk of offering a definition is always that it will come to be treated as a standalone argument or analytic tool. We would caution against this here. This definition is merely a product of the analytic procedure and the conceptual rationale we develop here and

should be interpreted as a waypoint in the analysis rather than a conclusive finding or end point.

5 As our discussion of variables in anticipation below illustrates, this is not to deny that there are some experiences in which the anticipatory process is more focal and integral to the subjective meaning of what we are up to. Rather, we consider that attributions to this effect should arise from within an analysis that accounts for the variable phenomenality of anticipatory experience rather than a predetermining of what "counts" as an instance of anticipation.

6 Merleau-Ponty introduced this term to evoke the embodied, involved immediacy in which subjects live in the world. While his nomenclature is slightly different from the Husserlian terminology we have mainly drawn on here, the term "pre-objective" does not contradict the basic idea that consciousness is always directed toward *something* (the "object" of consciousness).

7 It is important to note that Graeber's (2011) observation is, more precisely, that these differential responsibilities to anticipate often mirror and perpetuate forms of social and economic inequality. While we don't develop the point here, we would note that Graeber's work illustrates how attending to these asymmetries is one way that the study of anticipation lends itself to critical insights.

8 It is interesting to note that not only was this kind of map not available to most community members in their everyday lives, but that you in fact needed various forms of security clearance in order to set foot in this conference room.

9 Barrios's work (e.g., 2016, 2017) compellingly shows the repeated failure of disaster experts across contexts to adequately bridge these asymmetries. In particular, Barrios (2016) points out that it is disaster recovery experts' failure or willingness to recognize their own expertise as mutable and being open to acknowledging the expertise of disaster survivors as to the needs and aspirations of their community that can determine the relative success of disaster recovery and reconstruction projects.

10 Furthermore, it should be noted that there are degrees of intensity and integratedness to "we experiences"; as such, readers should bear in mind that everything we describe in the abstract admits degrees of realization in any given case. In application, we think it is advisable to be skeptical: where the phenomenal characteristics of collective anticipatory experience are seemingly not present, one should consider alternative possibilities (conceptual or practical).

11 Note that we are keeping to minimalistic examples in order to keep attention on the basic conditions of possibility for collective anticipation. In most real-world instances, conversational interactions will take these dynamics beyond mere mutual noticing; we often articulate our feelings, imagined possibilities, or explicitly formulated predictions. Yet it is important to note that even this on its own is not yet sufficient to share an anticipatory experience. For that, we need the third condition to be met: that one's own anticipatory experience *involves* that of the other/s.

12 We do not rule out that there may be forms of socially extended anticipation that take place asynchronously, but do observe that these will not have the same phenomenality. They may involve, for instance, admixtures of what Schutz (1967) called "the world of predecessors" and "the world of successors." Often materially mediated, we might think of intergenerational efforts to incite recollection and, in so doing, jog anticipatory processes. The tsunami stones found scattered around the Japanese coastline, or the "hunger stones" found in rivers throughout Europe may be particularly rich examples for disaster researchers.

13 We would suggest that it is important to maintain a distinction between shared anticipation and analogous anticipation: collectively anticipating emergently shifts what is anticipated for the parties involved such that shared anticipatory experience is irreducible to the individual anticipatory experiences of those involved—they are neither the same for each nor what either could experience alone.

References

Adams, V., Murphy, C., & Clarke, A. E. (2009). Anticipation: Technoscience, life, affect, temporality. *Subjectivity*, *28*, 246–265.

Adey, P., & Anderson, B. (2012). Anticipating emergencies: Technologies of preparedness and the matter of security. *Security Dialogues*, *43*(2), 99–117.

Anderson, B. (2010). Preemption, precaution, preparedness: Anticipatory action and future geographies. *Progress in Human Geography*, *34*(6), 377–398.

Appadurai, A. (2013). *The future as cultural fact: Essays on the global condition*. Verso.

Aulino, F. (2019). *Rituals of care: Karmic politics in an aging Thailand*. Cornell University Press.

Barrios, R. (2010). If you did not grow up here, you can't appreciate living here: Neoliberalism, space-time and affect in post-Katrina recovery planning. *Human Organization*, *70*(2), 118–127.

Barrios, R. (2016). Expert knowledge and the ethnography of disaster reconstruction. In G. V. Button & M. Schuller (Eds.), *Contextualizing disaster* (pp. 134–152). Berghahn.

Barrios, R. (2017). *Governing affect: Neoliberalism and disaster reconstruction*. University of Nebraska Press.

Berger, P. L., & Luckman, T. (1991). *The social construction of reality: A treatise in the sociology of knowledge*. Doubleday.

Bratman, M. E. (2014). *Shared agency: A planning theory of acting together*. Oxford University Press.

Caduff, C. (2008). Anticipations of biosecurity. In A. Lakoff & S. J. Collier (Eds.), *Biosecurity interventions: Global health and security in question* (pp. 257–278). Columbia University Press.

Caminada, E. (2018). Husserl on the common mind. In F. Kjosavik, C. Beyer, & C. Fricke (Eds.), *Husserl's phenomenology of intersubjectivity: Historical interpretations and contemporary applications* (pp. 263–279). Routledge.

Casey, E. S. (1976). *Imagining: A phenomenological study*. Indiana University Press.

Chelstrom, E. (2013). *Social phenomenology: Husserl, intersubjectivity, and collective intentionality*. Lexington Books.

Choi, V. Y. (2015). Anticipatory states: Tsunami, war, and insecurity in Sri Lanka. *Cultural Anthropology*, *30*(2), 286–309.

Clissold, R., McNamara, K. E., & Westoby, R. (2022). Emotions of the anthropocene across Oceania. *International Journal of Environmental Research and Public Health*, *19*(11), 6757.

Codreanu, T., Celenza, A., & Jacobs, I. (2014). Does disaster education of teenagers translate into better survival knowledge, knowledge of skills, and adaptive behavioral change? A systematic literature review. *Prehospital and Disaster Medicine*, *29*(6), 629–642.

Cohen, A. (1994). *Self consciousness: An alternative anthropology of identity*. Taylor & Francis.

Csordas, T. J. (1990). Embodiment as a paradigm for anthropology. *Ethos*, *18*(1), 5–47.

Csordas, T. J. (1993). Somatic modes of attention. *Cultural Anthropology*, *8*(1), 135–156.

D'Andrade, R. G., & Strauss, C. (Eds.). (1992). *Human motives and cultural models*. Cambridge University Press.

Desjarlais, R., & Throop, C. J. (2011). Phenomenological approaches in anthropology. *Annual Review of Anthropology*, *40*, 87–102.

Dijk, L. van, and Rietveld, E. (2021). Situated anticipation. *Synthese*, *198*(1), 349–371.

Dreyfus, H. L. (2014). *Skillful coping: Essays on the phenomenology of everyday perception and action*. Oxford University Press.

Flaherty, D. (2019). 'Takin it one day at a time': (Not) anticipating as moral project. *Cambridge Journal of Anthropology*, *37*(1), 61–76.

Gallagher, S. (2013). Husserl and the phenomenology of temporality. In H. Dyke & A. Bardon (Eds.), *A companion to the philosophy of time*. John Wiley & Sons.

Gallagher, S., & Aguda, B. (2019). Anchoring know-how: Action, affordance, and anticipation. *Journal of Consciousness Studies*, *27*(3–4), 11–37.

Geurts, K. L. (2002). On rocks, walks, and talks in West Africa: Cultural categories and an anthropology of the senses. *Ethos*, *30*(3), 178–198.

Gilbert, M. (2014). *Joint commitment: How we make the social world*. Oxford University Press.

Goodwin, C. (1994). Professional vision. *American Anthropologist*, *96*(3), 606–633.

Graeber, D. (2011). *Revolutions in reverse: Essays on politics, art, violence, and imagination*. Autonomedia.

Hallowell, A. I. (1955). *Culture and experience*. University of Pennsylvania Press.

Heidegger, M. (2010). *Being and time* (J. Stambaugh, Trans.). State University of New York Press.

Hollan, D. (2012). On the varieties and particularities of cultural experience. *Ethos*, *40*(1), 37–53.

Holland, D., & Quinn, N. (Eds.). (1987). *Cultural models in language and thought*. Cambridge University Press.

Hong, S., & Szpunar, P. M. (2019). The futures of anticipatory reason: Contingency and speculation in the sting operation. *Security Dialogue*, *50*(5), 314–330.

Husserl, E. (1964). *The phenomenology of internal time-consciousness* (M. Heidegger, Ed.; J. S. Churchill, Trans.). Indiana University Press.

Ihde, D. (1990). *Technology and the lifeworld: From garden to earth*. Indiana University Press.

Jackson, M. (1983). Knowledge of the body. *Man*, *18*(2), 327–345.

Jackson, M. (1998). *Minima ethnographica: Intersubjectivity and the anthropological project*. University of Chicago Press.

Kitagawa, K. (2021). Conceptualising 'disaster education'. *Education Science*, *11*(5), 233.

Klein, G. (2017). *Sources of power: How people make decisions*. MIT Press.

Lee, N.-I. (1998). Edmund Husserl's phenomenology of mood. In N. Depraz & D. Zahavi (Eds.), *Alterity and facticity* (pp. 103–120). Kluwer Academic Publishers.

León, F., Szanto, T., & Zahavi, D. (2019). Emotional sharing and the extended mind. *Synthese*, *196*(12), 4847–4867.

León, F., & Zahavi, D. (2016). Phenomenology of experiential sharing: The contribution of Schutz and Walter. In A. Salice, & H. B. Schmid (Eds.), *The phenomenological approach to social reality: History, concepts, problems* (pp. 219–234). Springer.

Luhrmann, T. M. (2020). *How god becomes real: Kindling the presence of invisible others* [The Lewis Henry Morgan Lectures]. Princeton University Press.

Merleau-Ponty, M. (2013). *Phenomenology of perception* (D. Landes, Trans.). Routledge.

Overgaard, S., & Zahavi, D. (2009). Phenomenological sociology. In M. H. Jacobsen (Ed.), *Encountering the everyday: An introduction to the sociologies of the unnoticed* (pp. 93–115). Palgrave-Macmillan.

Panu, P. (2020). Anxiety and the ecological crisis: An analysis of eco-anxiety and climate anxiety. *Sustainability*, *12*(19), 7836.

Piot, C. (2010). *Nostalgia for the future: West Africa after the Cold War*. University of Chicago Press.

Preston, J. (2012). *Disaster education*. SensePublishers.

Ratcliffe, M. (2013). Why mood matters. In M. Wrathall (Ed.), *The Cambridge companion to Heidegger's being and time* (pp. 157–176). Cambridge University Press.

Ratcliffe, M. (2020). Existential feelings. In T. Szanto & H. Landweer (Eds.), *Routledge handbook of phenomenology of emotions* (pp. 250–261). Routledge.

Rogers, M. F. (1982). The topic of power. *Human Studies*, *5*(1), 183–194.

Salice, A. (2016). Shared emotions—a Schelerian approach. *Thaumàzein*, *3*, 83–102.

Salice, A., & Schmid, H. B. (2016). Social reality—the phenomenological approach. In A. Salice, & H. B. Schmid (Eds.), *The phenomenological approach to social reality: History, concepts, problems* (pp. 1–14). Springer.

Sapir, E. (1938). Why culture needs the psychiatrist. *Psychiatry, 1*(1), 7–12.

Schmid, H. B. (2023). *We, together: The social ontology of us*. Oxford University Press.

Schutz, A. (1945). On multiple realities. *Philosophy and Phenomenological Research, 5*(4), 533–576.

Schutz, A. (1951). Making music together: A study in social relationship. *Social Research, 18*(1), 76–97.

Schutz, A. (1967). *Phenomenology of the social world*. Northwestern University Press.

Schutz, A. (2011). Reflections on the problem of relevance. In L. Embree (Ed.), *Collected papers V: Phenomenology and the social sciences* (pp. 93–199). Springer.

Schutz, A., & Luckmann, T. (1973). *Structures of the life-world, vol. 1*. Northwestern University Press.

Stein, E. (2000). *Philosophy of psychology and the humanities* (M. C. Baseheart, & M. Sawicki, Trans.). ICS Publications.

Stephan, C. (2019). A generative theory of anticipation: Mood, intuition, and imagination in architectural practice. *Cambridge Journal of Anthropology, 37*(1), 108–122.

Stephan, C. (2020). 'Focus on the users': Empathy, anticipation, and perspective-taking in healthcare architecture [Doctoral dissertation]. UCLA Department of Anthropology.

Stephan, C. (2023). The passive dimension of empathy and its relevance for design. *Design Studies, 86*, 101179.

Stephan, C., & Flaherty, D. (2019). Experiencing anticipation: Anthropological perspectives. *Cambridge Journal of Anthropology, 37*(1), 1–16.

Strauss, C., & Quinn, N. (Eds.). (1998). *A cognitive theory of cultural meaning*. Cambridge University Press.

Stromberg, P. G. (1986). *Symbols of community: The cultural systems of a Swedish church*. University of Arizona Press.

Szanto, T. (2016). Husserl on collective intentionality. In A. Salice & H. B. Schmid (Eds.), *The phenomenological approach to social reality: History, concepts, problems* (pp. 145–172). Springer.

Szanto, T. (2024). Collective intentionality as a concept in phenomenology. In N. de Warren & T. Toadvine (Eds.), *Encyclopedia of phenomenology*. Springer.

Szanto, T., & Moran, D. (2016). Introduction: Empathy and collective intentionality—the social philosophy of Edith Stein. *Human Studies, 38*(4), 445–461.

Throop, C. J. (2010). *Suffering and sentiment: Exploring the vicissitudes of experience and pain in Yap*. University of California Press.

Throop, C. J. (2014). Moral moods. *Ethos, 42*(1), 65–83.

Throop, C. J. (2020). Meteorological moods and atmospheric attunements. In V. Browne, D. Rosenow, & J. Danely (Eds.), *Vulnerability and the politics of care: Transdisciplinary dialogues* (pp. 60–70). Oxford University Press.

Throop, C. J. (2023). Empathy and its limits. In F. Mezzenzana & D. Peluso (Eds.), *Conversations on empathy* (pp. 27–33). Routledge.

Throop, C. J., & Duranti, A. (2015). Attention, ritual glitches, and attentional pull: The president and the queen. *Phenomenology and the Cognitive Sciences, 14*, 1–28.

Tollefsen, D. (2014). A dynamic theory of shared intention and the phenomenology of joint action. In S. R. Chant, F. Hindriks, & G. Preyer (Eds.), *From individual to collective intentionality* (pp. 12–33). Oxford University Press.

Tollefsen, D. (2015). *Groups as agents*. Polity.

Tuomela, R. (2016). *Social ontology: Collective intentionality and group agents*. Oxford University Press.

Tyszczuk, R. (2021). Collective scenarios: Speculative improvisations for the Anthropocene. *Futures, 134*, 102854.

Verbeek, P.-P. (2011). *Moralizing technology: Understanding and designing the morality of things*. University of Chicago Press.

Wallace, A. F. C. (1970). *Culture and personality*. Random House.

Walsh, P. J. (2020). Intercorporeity and the first-person plural in Merleau-Ponty. *Continental Philosophy Review*, *53*(1), 21–47.

Zahavi, D. (2001). Beyond empathy: Phenomenological approaches to intersubjectivity. *Journal of Consciousness Studies*, *8*(5–7), 151–167.

Zahavi, D. (2003). *Husserl's phenomenology*. Stanford University Press.

Zahavi, D. (2014). *Self and other: Exploring subjectivity, empathy, and shame*. Oxford University Press.

Zahavi, D. (2018). Collective intentionality and plural pre-reflective self-awareness. *Journal of Social Philosophy*, *49*(1), 61–75.

Zahavi, D. (2019). *Phenomenology: The basics*. Routledge.

Zigon, J. (2007). Moral breakdown and the ethical demand: A theoretical framework for an anthropology of moralities. *Anthropological Theory*, *7*(2), 131–150.

Zigon, J., & Throop, J. (2021). Phenomenology. In F. Stein (Ed.), *The Cambridge Encyclopedia of Anthropology*. https://www.anthroencyclopedia.com/entry/phenomenology

3 We are the times

Temporal agency of utopian, dystopian, and (post)apocalyptic futures

Monika Gabriela Bartoszewicz

1. Introduction

The uncertainty of the future begins to reveal things we had no inkling of. Such was the case 10 years ago when the world was momentarily gripped by a fever over the announcement of the end of the world, which was to be meticulously predicted by the Mayan calendar for Saturday, 22 December 2012. Life in the prospect of the definite end, even among sceptics and agnostics, not to mention pop culture, for a while began to focus on the question of the possibility of reaching a destination, some kind of fulfilment or completion. Let us leave aside for a moment the consideration that the Mayan calendar indicated not so much the end of the world but merely—according to Mayan reckoning—the end of a single calendar cycle, a recurring event. What is more, the ancient Yucatán people's understanding of this moment was also quite different from its reception in the clearly more catastrophically inclined 21st century. For the Maya were waiting not for an end but for a new beginning. This indeed resonates strongly also in the ears associated with our cultural circle, rooted in the Christian idea of the world. In the case of Western civilisation, the roots lie deep in precisely these aspects of eschatology. However, Christianity, with its vision of the end, has made a severe breach in the model that prevailed in earlier cultures based on cyclicity and repetition. The Christian eschatological idea broke the recurring loop, and history ceased to turn constantly in the myth of the eternal beginning; it straightened its line, which inevitably began to run in an unknown direction.

This linear concept bridged the gap between the utopia of Eden and the horror of an apocalyptic end, in whose shadow everything remained—the culmination, bringing history to its finale. The vision of the Parousia became the point of arrival, the longed-for fulfilment of history, which was proceeding according to a soteriological plan. Initially, in the first generations after Christ, it was embodied in the expectation of the imminent Apocalypse; then it was integrated into a longer perspective, which at the same time never invalidates it. The utopian new beginning after the apocalyptic climax illustrates the tension between the incompatibility of the present disastrous condition of the world and a particular desire for carefree happiness, which humans carry within. If we turn to Eric Voegelin's (1987) concept and consider that bringing the eschaton down to earth is a function

DOI: 10.4324/9781003537311-4

of the politicality of the modern age, then the revolutionary fervour of invalidating the existing order at the expense of trying to build the new, so present throughout recent centuries, is all the more unsurprising. However, even in an age marked by dystopian totalitarianism and nihilism, futures are still stretched on a continuum between a vision and a nightmare (Moriarty & Honnery, 2018).

Each civilisation brings with it not only changes in how people treat time (Koneczny, 1991, p. 26) but also changes in the understanding of this strange thing called time that we normally use without thinking about it. This realisation brought about the temporal turn in social sciences, which conceptualised temporality as time perception based on subjective measurements (Samimian-Darash, 2022, p. 92), mostly following the Aristotelian division into the technique, knowledge, and ethics of time (Bear, 2016, p. 489). To borrow the elegant description from D'Angelo and Pijpers (2018, p. 215), to talk about temporality is to talk about

> durations, rhythms and cycles—with different velocities, intensities and extensions—that different social actors try to know, tame or manipulate by (de)synchronizing them in line with contingent and often conflicting strategic interests. To use the word 'temporality' in the plural does not only mean exploring, recognizing and describing these different levels and types of temporalities, but also understanding how they are socially and culturally constructed and manipulated by teratogenous social actors in specific political and economic contexts.

The realm of temporality is punctuated by dyads: we talk of static versus flux time, objective and subjective time perception, linear and sequential contrasted with non-linear circular time, and last but not least, past versus future-oriented temporalities. However, the temporal orientation is more than merely a technical distinction. According to Antonello and Carey (2017, p. 185), among the divergent constructions of time across many societies and throughout history, past, present, and futures are widely conceived divisions that allow humans to orient themselves, but more importantly, they are the tool used for articulating people's *agency* (emphasis mine). Agency, in its broadest sense, denotes the human capacity to (re) act (Ahearn, 1999). Nonetheless, Emirbayer and Mische emphasize that agentic processes can only be understood if they are intrinsically linked to the changing temporal orientations of situated actors (1998, p. 967).

Therefore, an inquiry into the temporal dimensions and orientations, which are both projected onto the future and simultaneously entail strategic engagement with the past (D'Angelo & Pijpers, 2018, p. 219), allows for analysing the timescapes of utopian, dystopian, and apocalyptic realities in the context that ties them together with the notion of agency, that is, human response to them. As Bear insists (2016, p. 489), this heuristic perspective of timescape allows for tracing how human practices of time intersect and affect the sphere of sociopolitical. In this sense, the chapter looks not only into the temporality of these polar opposite extremes but glimpses into their historicity, understood as making sense of the past while anticipating the future under constraints of ontological forms of reality (Hirsch &

Stewart, 2005). Variability in temporal orientations is therefore used as a means for studying how we orient ourselves to futures (Bryan & Knight, 2019) and as a lens to study sociocultural temporalities that are also inherently political.

Social actors do establish and maintain specific temporal regimes (Jordheim, 2014) as the order of time governs all the everyday endeavours of men (Canetti, 1996, p. 457). However, the temporal agency does not merely imply an exploration of how time is conceived in differing situations; there is also the question of its agogics. The notion of "flow," or "flux" of time, and certain preoccupations with change and fluidity are, according to Hodges (2008, p. 416), a symptom of our contemporary "runaway" civilisation, brought by liquid modernity (Bauman, 2013). The pacing of time is in lockstep with the orientation: we know time flows, but what kind of flow can be observed, if at all? This second axis complements temporal orientation and allows us to look at futures both developing in time and shaped by its tempo in their divergent modalities.

In what follows, I do not intend to homogenise the temporal differences or to fixate on their linearities, but to flesh out and explore their implications. To this end, I will first explore the agency of deep futures by looking into their respective temporal orientations and the agogic of their time. Second, I will use this framework to examine how such temporal agencies reverberate in their sociopolitical dimensions. Simply put, if time matters to how people act and react, what kind of human action can be expected in a utopian, dystopian, or apocalyptic setting?

2.   The agency of deep futures

The conceptual frame for our inquiry requires then to have a clear understanding of what the possible deep futures imply and how they are related to their temporal realities of agency, conceived both in terms of orientation and in terms of agogics.

In the sequencing frame, utopia and dystopia are not bound together by the apocalypse but rather by myopia, which serves as an enabling condition, as shown in Figure 3.1. Dystopias are customarily defined as futuristic, fictional universes in which the illusion of a perfect society is maintained through some kind of control, be it moral, technological, bureaucratic, corporate, or totalitarian. Typical dystopia is an exaggerated worst-case scenario formulating a criticism about a current trend, societal norm or political system; usually set in an imagined future (Bartoszewicz et al., 2022). However, as Jill Lepore (2017) aptly observed, dystopias follow utopias the way thunder follows lightning.

Utopia is the vision of a perfect world that erases the original sin of all sociopolitical deficiencies rooted in the past. Unlike in a dystopian future, utopian perfection is not faked and does not have to be enforced. However, dystopias are, in their essence, nothing else but dysfunctional utopias. They typically appear when a myopic policy is implemented to make a utopia come true. Dystopias, thus, never exist in a void; they are always connected with some utopian vision. Even semantics follows this sequencing logic: Utopia, while named by Thomas More in 1516, effectively goes back to Plato's Republic, that is, 380 BC. Conversely, the first recorded use of the word dystopia is relatively young, as we can find it in the

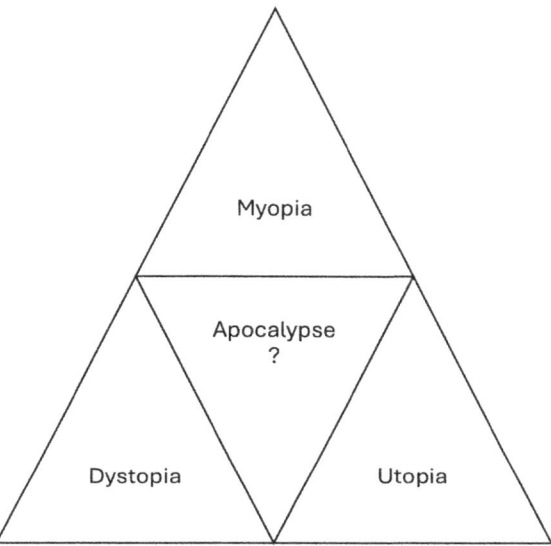

Figure 3.1 Inter-relatedness of utopia, dystopia, and the apocalypse (figure by author).

1868 speech made in the House of Commons by the Victorian philosopher John Stuart Mill.

Similarly, while utopia gives shape to human hopes cast into the future, dystopia is connected to the way society fears. This is relevant when we consider that in recent years, safety has been sacralised to the point that it has become a foundational value for our societies (Furedi, 2018). Furedi argues that security, the meaning of safety, has expanded to the point that it guides virtually every dimension of life. Effectively, as a dominant (principal) value of society, it has acquired a sacred status, and its moral authority is frequently used to justify the introduction of a variety of measures for regulating life. Dystopia reflects such an uncompromising and regressive vision of politics (Van Rythoven, 2018), and since dystopian visions reveal a profound pessimism, they, therefore, lead to the politics of fear (Shames & Atchison, 2019). As Ratzinger (2011, p. 347) put it, "we fear a future whose paths we do not know and the ceaseless dwindling of our own share in that future."

The apocalypse, on the other hand, when removed from the religious register, means either the end of the world or the end of the world as we know it. This seemingly trivial distinction has far-reaching ramifications. The end of the world implies the end of times, whereas the end of the world as we know it suggests the possibility of post-apocalyptic temporalities. Either we are running out of time, or we use the moment of apocalyptic catharsis as a springboard that will catapult us into a new era. In the second scenario, it is not that the world will end, but rather our world will exist no more as "the accepted texture of reality is about to undergo a staggering transformation, in which the long-established institutions and ways of life will be destroyed" (Barkun, 1983, p. 258). Unsurprisingly, in his reflections on the apocalypse, René Girard observed that the history of people driven by the principle of destruction manifests itself in the apocalypse, but the apocalyptic spirit has nothing to do with nihilism because the rush to the worst can only be understood in the context of a profound hope (Girard, 2018, pp. 196–197). Thus, in an apocalyptic future, the hopes and the fears are indelibly linked. Apocalypse may lead to a utopia of paradise regained, but it can give birth to terrible dystopias with equal ease.

In his seminal work on speed and politics, Paul Virilio (2008) demonstrates how velocity is the engine of destruction. Apocalypse is the climax of speeding temporality. In clear opposition to the apocalyptic sense of urgency, both utopian and dystopian agogics are that of times slowing down in perfectly mirrored antithesis of one another. Where utopia is inherently future-oriented and renders the past irrelevant or undesirable, dystopia suspends the future in the perpetual present. The past is corrected in the former; in the latter, it must be erased because the monstrous dystopian now is an inheritance of history. In the former, errors of history are corrected, while in the latter, the only option is to erase the past that gave rise to that dystopia. Table 3.1 elucidates the agogic and orientation nexus.

2.1 Utopia

Utopias are nothing else than visions of a boring happily ever after that never ends, suspended in the constant present. Utopias are built on the belief that by removing the rubble of the past, a path to creating a new society will be cleared. In such utopian renewal, time reinvents itself in perfection. Accordingly, utopia is governed by something that Mircea Eliade (1974, p. 87) would instantly recognize as the eternal present tense. In other words, it is constituted by an eternal present that is infinitely recoverable and, in some respects, can be likened to eternity. At the same time, suspended in the ever-present, utopia is future-oriented: the past has been conquered and, therefore, is irrelevant. It is the future that is supposed to regenerate *sensum temporis*, that is, to restore it to its original purity and fullness. Since the past has been rectified and the future is all that matters, the only concern in the utopian temporality is that tomorrow should look exactly like today since today is perfect.

Considered from this vantage point, utopianism is not just an "imaginative" or an "intellectual exercise" regarding sociopolitical systems, but according to

Table. 3.1 The matrix of temporal agogic juxtaposed with dominant orientation

	Past-oriented	*Future-oriented*
Decelerating temporality | Time irrelevant (frozen)	Dystopia	Utopia
Accelerating temporality | Time running out	Apocalypse-never; (post-)apocalypse	Apocalypse-now

Thomas Steven Molnar (1921–2010), Hungarian philosopher, historian, and political theorist, it "forms an autonomous category of thought" (Molnar, 1967, p. 3). In his book, Molnar (1967, p. 225) delves deeply into the revolutionary utopian mind set against "things as they are." Molnar (1967, p. 6) claims that utopians believe in an unspoiled beginning and attainable perfection. Inherent to this optimism towards societal perfection (vibrant despite pessimism towards human nature) (Molnar, 1967, p. 61) is the concept of an unspoiled beginning. Molnar (1967, p. 16) explains that "The concept of 'unspoiled beginning' is not exhausted by insistence on the cyclical theory of time; it posits also an imaginary first state of affairs . . . which serves for the model of restoration of the end of the cycle." In this sense, potentiality is the utopian counterpart to bureaucratic dystopian futures of risk and threat. Grounded in the future-oriented, decelerating temporality, "(t)he utopian, in this speculation, ignores human nature, the rhythm of change, the fact that change involves not only a gain but loss as well, the reality of time and the essential freedom of the soul" (Molnar, 1967, p. 227). The utopian stasis is perhaps best captured by The Transhumanist Manifesto (*Humanity Plus*), which sees "aging is a disease" and immortality as a prerequisite to "expand human capabilities."

In secular, contemporary utopia, the divine kingdom ("the 1000-year rule of Christ," cf. Revelation, 20, pp. 2–3) is substituted with an ideal society in which all is possible; there are minimum amounts of pain and toil in labour. A radical departure from our current state of affairs and a one-way transition into permanent bliss. Rutger Bregman's bestseller *Utopia for Realists* starts with an explicitly temporal opening: "In the past, everything was worse." It discusses a positive, brighter future, a "future faced with unprecedented enthusiasm" and "awash in leisure." Bregman clarifies that he does not want to predict the future but to unlock it and direct the minds of his readers into it. In the past, Bregman observes dryly, "nearly everyone, everywhere was still poor, hungry, dirty, afraid, stupid, sick, and ugly" (2017, p. 15), but subsequently goes even more provocative by stating that it is "the dystopia we are living in today" (2017, p. 28) only to urge to "transcend this confining zeitgeist," which precisely what he aspires to do in his book where he discusses digitization of life, universal basic income "end of poverty," 15-hour workweek, and no national borders.

Given the dominant themes in his book, it is unsurprising that in 2019 Bregman was invited to a panel debate at the World Economic Forum (WEF), an organisation that also serves as a hub for modern utopian thinking. In this regard, two books penned by its founder, Klaus Schwab, are particularly interesting. In Fourth Industrial Revolution (2017), Schwab expects the new era to be ushered by breakthroughs in emerging technologies and hence shape the "future-oriented communities" (2017, p. 118). Subsequently, in *Great Reset* (first, a book co-authored with Thierry Malleret in 2020 and then a proposal of post-pandemic recovery developed by the WEF, where *The Fourth Industrial Revolution* is included as a solution to create a new, post-pandemic world), Schwab offers an overview of the future landscape and envisions a digital revolution that is characterised by a fusion of technologies and blurring the lines between physical, digital, and biological spheres, which, through unlimited access to knowledge, will raise global income level and improve the quality of life. Schwab's utopia needs a reset because, in his view, Covid-19 has "torn up the existing script" of governance; it nearly amounts to an apocalypse as it is a defining moment that changes many things forever. Therefore, Schwab sketches a path forward "to a better world: more inclusive, more equitable and more respectful of Mother Nature" (2020, p. 4–5). His vision of the future gives shape to something he calls a "new normal," a temporality "radically different from the one we will be progressively leaving behind" (2020, p. 16). Schwab also perfectly captures the unidirectional orientation of utopian temporality. He poses a hypothetical question of when humanity will go back to the broken past and answers it promptly and categorically: "The short response is: never. Nothing will ever return to the 'broken' sense of normalcy" (2020, p. 15). Utopia is a point of no return. Other contemporary utopian projects like the United Nations Agenda 2030 for Sustainable Development, which preaches a world free of hunger, disease, fear, and violence, but with universal healthcare and social protection "where physical, mental, and social well-being is assured" or project Ecotopia 2121, a compendium of 100 stories how different cities from around the world can transform into Green Utopias by the year 2121, also exude this perfection homed in a timeless future.

2.2 Dystopia

In her reflections on time, Laura Bear (2016, p. 489) shares Bregman's pessimism as she writes: "We live in a period in which futures have lost their utopian qualities." Our dystopias consist of Derrida (1990) normal monstrosities whereby the current source of horror is cast into the future as an extrapolation of current trends that form hypothetical chains of events (Hjerpe & Linnér, 2009). Dystopia reflects an unyielding and regressive vision (Van Rythoven, 2018), depicting horrifying societies and highlighting the dangers lurking in the future. Although dystopia takes the undesired qualities of contemporary society as a point of departure, it functions as more than merely a scenario that provides a coherent and plausible story about the future (Hjerpe & Linnér, 2009, p. 241). However, a distinction should be introduced here: Dystopian looming becomes something more than merely a normative narration capable of tapping into societal anxieties and exploring societal fears. It becomes the future invading the present. Dystopia incarnated, on the other hand, stops looking into the future as there is no future, and time becomes irrelevant.

Hodges (2008, p. 404) was the one to capture the best the unchanging nature of dystopia outside of the realm of human agency, rendering it "fundamentally untensed" akin to the Bergsonian *durée* in which particular moments merge together in such a way that the past, present, and future merge into one another. Nonetheless, dystopia is undeniably past-oriented, which does not mean that it believes that the love of the past can be a remedy for the evils of the present and future worlds. On the contrary, because the current dystopian condition has its roots in what had been, it means that either the past must be entirely eradicated so that it does not repeat ever again or the present it led to is so overwhelming it leaves no space for any futures.

This condition is aligned well with dystopian temporality: When staying safe and surviving appears to have become the pivotal issue around which everything else turns, no goals can be projected into the future. Dystopia also requires a set of wider structural settings that enable a situation where humanity becomes obsessed with a particular form of security to such an extent that we have lost sight of the rest. Fear is mediated and regulated not only via the immediacy of the threat but primarily via its connection to the past that gave birth to current troubles in the first place. To illustrate this dynamic, let us choose an alternative path to reminiscing the dystopian qualities of the Covid-19 lockdown regime and instead look into contemporary dystopian literature. In this, we will follow the footsteps of Marshall McLuhan (1964), who famously said, "I think of art, at its most significant, as a DEW line, a Distant Early Warning system that can always be relied on to tell the old culture what is beginning to happen to it." Seen from this vantage point, written dystopias can act as an early alarm signal, enabling us to gain insights into the future to prepare us to cope with them. Interestingly, the 2010s saw a rapid rise in dystopian literature focused explicitly on the Young Adult audience.

Contemporary dystopias are historically informed but go beyond the *Brave New World* of 1984 dichotomy. We know that the *Animal Farm* does not have to be a labour camp; it can be an amusement park. Nevertheless, they also go beyond the tensions between anarchy and totalitarianism so visible in *A Clockwork Orange* by Anthony Burgess (1962) or *V for Vendetta* by Alan Moore and David Lloyd (1982–1985) or *Lord of the Flies* by William Golding (1954). They moved on to specific fears/insecurities, such as environment, fertility, technology, or politics (e.g., migration).

Jean Raspail was the precursor of the latter in how he depicted the destruction of western civilisation by mass migration. In *The Camp of the Saints* (1973), one million people from India leave their country on huge boats while the world follows their journey and final destination. Finally, boats arrive on the French Riviera, and migrants peacefully invade the European continent while everything is covered live by the media. *The Wall* by John Lanchester (2019) picks up on this imagery as it depicts a future in which the seas rise and Britain walls itself off to keep people out. The country's youth are selected to defend the Wall against both the rising sea and dangerous Others. In the book, the past is flooded, but simultaneously, the Others are the flood that needs to be warded off at all costs.

However, very often, dystopias illustrate the sheer impossibility of attaining the future. The *Future Home of the Living God* by Louise Erdrich (2017) explores evolution in reverse, with each generation becoming more primitive than the previous one. The story follows a pregnant woman who is searching for her own roots and starts writing a diary to give to her unborn child. The mother-to-be is a Native, and the baby that is to receive the heritage is symbolically due on December 25.

Among the reproductive dystopias, two prime examples are Margaret Atwood's *The Handmaid's Tale* (1985) and Oxford-born P.D. James' *Children of Men* (1992). The latter was set in the city of Oxford in 2021 (alas, a dated one already) in a world where no children are born anymore. What a hauntingly poignant way to capture dystopian temporality. When the main character sits in one of the college chapels listening to a recording of a children's choir, he knows that humanity has reached the end of its road. In a different vein, *The Handmaid's Tale* is a story told by a woman whose life had been destroyed and remade by a religious revolution that, on the dying embers of the United States, created a monstrous nomocracy where a warped theology shapes all dimensions of life and enforces observance of certain norms by all means available, including violence. It is a world doomed from the beginning, built on a lie and kept up carefully strengthened by hypocrisy enforced by violence, where the past is perpetually demonised and kept alive to be used as a legitimising vehicle for the regime. Atwood writes about the slippery slope of birth rates sliding past the zero line of replacement due to air too full of chemicals, radiation, and water full of toxins. *Who Runs the World?* by Virginia Bergin (2017) takes us to a world where the past vanishes with one of the sexes. It takes place 60 years after a global pandemic that nearly wipes out all men; a teenage girl named River finds a young boy named Mason to find that her version of the past was a lie.

Technocracies, oligarchies, and capitocracies are the usual dystopian culprits. *Blade of Tyshalle*, a dystopian world where corporations used the pandemic to eliminate states and introduce a caste-based system of total control, was written by Matthew Stover 20 years before Covid−19. *The Traitor Baru Cormorant* by Seth Dickinson (2015) introduces an empire, The Masquerade, which brings prosperity, sophisticated engineering, advanced science, and modern medicine to the conquered lands. Through civilisational advancement, it imposes its rules and ideas of social order. The only price one must pay is their own past and accumulated wisdom of indigenous heritage. The *Divergent* by Veronica Roth (2011), *Red Rising* by Pierce Brown (2014) and *The Hunger Games* by Suzanne Collins (2008) are by far the most popular triad in this group. Each of those captures dystopian temporality in a different way. In *Red Rising*, the oppressed Reds are kept in an underworld hell in a suspended state of looped reality. They think they are terraforming a planet that has long been terraformed and is habitable; their present is the past long gone for everyone else. *The Hunger Games* exorcise the past through ritual violence. Games are a reminder but simultaneously also a fetish that keeps the past at bay. As long as they recur, the sociopolitical system is stable. After all, Canetti (1996, p. 457) already noticed that the one essential thing for any dystopian power is that it must never end.

However, when it comes to worlds without a past and without a future, *The Giver* by Lois Lowry (1993) is the undisputed winner. It is set in a seemingly utopian society characterised by Sameness: In Sameness, there is no war or pain or colour. In this community run by the Elders, every person is assigned a role. The main character, Jonas, is selected to inherit the position of Receiver of Memory, the person who stores all the past memories of the time before Sameness. The Elders understand that there may be times when one must draw upon the wisdom gained from history to aid the decision-making, but they believe the past to be a dangerous toy that, if re-enacted, could threaten the very survival of the community. It is fitting to juxtapose *The Giver* with *Station Eleven* by Emily St. John Mandel (2014).

It portrays the after-effects of a flu pandemic that wipes out most of the civilisation through the eyes of a band of survivors, a nomadic troupe called The Symphony, who, 20 years later, still perform *King Lear* throughout the countryside. The central theme of this dystopian novel is: Survival is not enough. Careful reading lets us understand that it is not enough to warrant a future.

The danger of knowledge buried in the past is also well explored in dystopian literature. *Fahrenheit 451* by Ray Bradbury (1953) presents a dystopian society in which books, as a source of knowledge and wisdom, are banned. In *Anathem*, Neal Stephenson (2008) takes one step further. He created a world where intellectuals enter *concents* (monastic communities) to protect their activities from the collapse of society. The *avout* (intellectuals separated from *Sæcular* society) are banned from possessing or operating the most advanced technology and are normally allowed to communicate with people outside the walls of the *concent* only once every year, decade, century, or millennium, depending on the particular vows they have taken. Only the arrival of an impendent apocalypse changes that. Each chapter should normally be in a separate file. The chapter title should be typed in with the first letter of important words capitalized.

2.3 Apocalypse—now

Apocalypse is the before/after moment; a clear demarcation point between two temporalities. It is inherently future-oriented in how it awaits the inevitable and the un-whenable; a catastrophe that must come but whose exact timing is not known. Hence, the defining trait of the apocalypse is its temporality of urgency (Samimian-Darash, 2022, p. 90) brought by social, political, and economic turbulences, which organise their threat projections (Clark, 2000) so that the future can be discerned only through the lens of looming disaster.

The "end of the world" is, of course, not an exclusively Christian idea. There are several analogous pre-Christian concepts also in civilisations that had no contact with the idea of the end of the world. We can talk here about religious as well as philosophical concepts (the Stoic cycle of *ekpyrosis* and *apokatastasis*). Most of them framed the end of the world in cyclical terms. Contemporary apocalyptic narrative differs from its predecessors in that it is totally pessimistic. This might be partially rooted in the obsession related to the eschatological recognition of human fears concerning the end of the individual, the community, and the whole of humankind. Partially in the resignation that just like Chronos, the primordial divinity that devours his own children, time becomes the master of men. As it devours us, we have to hasten. In the climax of future-oriented, ever-accelerating temporality, there is no time left. The apocalypse happens now, or—to put it more provocatively—the time to seek it is now "before we have acquired the perfect insouciance of those who prefer perdition" (Weaver, 2013, p. 10). The hectic apocalyptic temporality manifests itself in what Christopher Rowland (2014, p. 407) calls apocalyptic radicalism, an interpretation of apocalyptic texts that leads to a political critique or an actual confrontation with the political authorities in the name of that higher authority or alternative perspective.

This proactive, apocalyptic agency, the active waiting, has its perfect reflection in the rise and collapse of the Islamic State of Iraq and Syria.[1] Just like in Christianity, a sense of apocalyptic urgency drove the early period of Islam. Since Muhammad was viewed as the last prophet, Muslims expected the imminent end of the world (Wessinger, 2014). Sookhdeo (2015, p. 47) describes what Sunnis believe to be the "Signs of the Hour," including the lesser signs like moral decay, crime, natural disasters, and wars and the greater signs that constitute a veritable map of the future. Unsurprisingly, eschatological beliefs still resonate with many contemporary Muslims, who are awaiting a messianic saviour figure. Specifically, radicals assume the role of God's weapon of wrath manifested in the jihad against unbelieving, immoral enemies. The vision of an incoming, imminent apocalypse predisposes them to appropriate violence. Terrorism, in this understanding, is akin to God's cleansing fire preparing the way for the promised deliverer. Such an approach allows us to see this phenomenon as an apocalyptic calamity.

In the radical milieu, the Islamic State (IS) is unique in how the organisation not only perceived its activities as a part of the end-of-times scenario but sought an active role in provoking and hastening the final cataclysmic struggles. We know the Islamic State of Iraq and the Levant (ISIL) existed as one among many Islamist groups operating in the Middle East, long before it captured the attention of global media and world politicians. In the summer of 2014, the Islamic State in Iraq and Syria (ISIS) seized vast swaths of territory, creating a terrorist proto-state (Bartoszewicz, 2020). Wood's (2015) thorough analysis of the group suggests that ISIS "rejects peace as a matter of principle; that it hungers for genocide; that its religious views make it constitutionally incapable of certain types of change, even if that change might ensure its survival; and that it considers itself a harbinger of apocalypse—and headline player in—the imminent end of the world." In other words, religion is an essence, an axis of the *modus vivendi* as well as *modus operandi*, and the strategic goals of the group to this extent that one could claim IS to be a unique case of using politics for furthering religious agenda rather than the other way round (Bartoszewicz, 2016). This emphasis on eschatology was a powerful recruitment motivator (Karataş, 2021) as the group called the faithful to participate in the final battles of history (Mauro, 2014), but also a convenient propaganda tool. Fromson and Simon (2015) argued that what made ISIS's caliphate particularly appealing was that it made apocalyptic prophecy a lived reality rather than a hypothetical goal, as it was for Al-Qaeda.

In his book, McCants (2015) captured the apocalyptic moment of ISIS, which lasted roughly from the proclamation of the caliphate in June 2014 to May 2015, when the group's territorial expansion ceased. ISIL's public framing of itself as a harbinger of the final hour enabled the group to become the masters of their own apocalyptic narrative. Consequently, Fromson and Simon (2015) argue that the idea of the apocalypse has been no less potent in animating their doctrines and recruitment and that even battlefield strategy grounded it in apocalyptic theology. For instance, Abu Ayyub al-Masri, one of the post-Zarqawi leaders in Iraq, instructed his men to build pulpits for the Mahdi as the Islamic saviour would be arriving soon in his view (Byman, 2016, p. 138).

The group has focused on the small Syrian town of Dabiq (captured already in August 2014) because it features in Islamic prophecies as the site of a great end-time battle between Muslims and their enemies, ushering in the final victory of Islam. Suffice it to mention that Dabiq was chosen as the title of the official magazine of the IS, but also it featured in the group's "promotional" materials, such as the beheading of the American hostage Peter Kassig in December 2014 (BBC, 2016). "We are waiting for you in Dabiq," ISIS touted the West (McCants, 2016) as the jihadis wanted to provoke the final apocalyptic war of end times, which Muslims are divinely promised to win. This eschatological impatience was also the primary reason why ISIS was discouraged neither by the United States and allied military intervention nor by its own high death tolls. On the contrary, these were actually encouraging, as the jihadis believed themselves to be on the threshold of the promised final victory. And yet, the apocalypse never materialised.

2.4   Apocalypse—never (but always)

If the apocalypse never comes, that is one dilemma. Another is when the future arrives only to grip humanity by the throat and does not want to let go. Never becomes an always when what was supposed to be once in a lifetime becomes a permanent fixture. In such a case, we are faced with a never-ending apocalypse, or what Shellenberger (2018, p. 240) called a "replacement Apocalypse," denoting a continuous series of crises whereby one begins immediately upon another. Omnipresent securitisation and the explosion of risks so presciently diagnosed by Furedi (2007) have facilitated the projection of threat scenarios and the invention of ever-new threats and dangers. Bear (2016, p. 493) writes that these apocalyptic scenarios generate affects of fear and urgency and reveal the emergence of preparedness as a form of anticipatory temporal knowledge to the extent that anticipation has become a dominant new virtue with a particular temporal orientation. Such living in anticipation has been developed into an analytical notion by Reidar Staupe (2021, p. 89), who explains it as a state when expected future calamities shape and even overshadow life in the presence, and by doing so, they become real even in the absence of their actual occurrence.

The standard apocalyptic temporal perspective is that there is precious little of time left; in the never-coming but never-ending apocalypse, Hemingwayan gradually—then suddenly, defines the *zeitgeist*. Nevertheless, the continually receding horizon of the future means that where utopia posits the present vis-à-vis the always, apocalypse faces us with the never. The apocalypse-never reworks the Christian mindset known as a man in the state of *homo viator* or his *status viatoris*. The state of the "not-yet." Here, a permanent crisis is rooted in the shrinking future, which emerges from the inevitable via catastrophic scenarios of ever-accelerating doom. The collapse will not be a single event but a slide into what the world systems analyst Giovanni Arrighi (1999) calls "systemic chaos."

The changing narrative of environmental disasters serves as a perfect exemplar of this temporal dynamic. From the early 1970s that touted global cooling, to the 1980s with the dominant theme of acid rain and the 1990s that focused on the ozone layer and pollution, to global warming in the 2000s only to arrive in the 2010s at the *perpetuum mobile* of climate change. Climate change epitomises the apocalypse-never temporality because of its sheer open-endedness. The threat is not one effect but many different consequences. Most conveniently, any unusual phenomena can be co-opted as yet more evidence of climate change—because the climate really is constantly changing. Unlike acid rain, global warming or cooling, climate change is impervious to the anathema of failed prophecies. Due to the nature of the threat, we cannot expect to verify it. All the foretold apocalypses that can be traced on the extinction clock website, starting from the very first prediction made by Paul Ehrlich, who in 1970 prophesied that "America will be subject to water rationing by 1974 and food rationing by 1980" via a whole host of modern doomsayers to the most recent prediction that 80% of Emperor penguins will be extinct by 2100 without Paris Agreement (Lee et al., 2022) threaten the legitimacy of the apocalypse. With the advent of climate change, contradictions can be absorbed in the apocalyptic narrative as inevitable since the climate is so complex; it is not a mono-causality but a spaghetti of many different malfunctions. Furthermore, the concept of climate change covers everything that could possibly be wrong about the natural environment. Too hot? Too cold? Too rainy? Not rainy enough? These are all the horsemen. Therefore, the incoming apocalypse has to be accepted not primarily on empirical grounds but first and foremost on the basis of temporal claims. The contest is no longer between the arguments you are hearing and the reality you are seeing but between you and the future.

The latest Intergovernmental Panel on Climate Change report prompted precisely this apocalyptic response in the media and beyond (Crowley, 2023). However, if humanity is on the threshold of our last chance to act before climate-change damage becomes irreversible, then preparedness and anticipation will not suffice. A terminally violent event, like a catastrophic global disaster, is also met with what Wessinger (2014, p. 426) diagnosed as avertive apocalypticism, which comes to the fore with all the radicalism of solutions directed against the present on which the whole future existence relies upon. The belief that humanity is facing possible extinction in the next century or sooner lies at the heart of the Extinction Rebellion and its spin-off, Just Stop Oil. Both organisations show that the apocalyptic nature of contemporary environmentalism is no mere rhetorical flourish. Its temporality structures the thought and deeds of activists. The protesting has gradually taken a more drastic turn, spraying paint on symbolic or just well-known targets. This is often accompanied by the activist glueing themselves to the target, making it difficult to remove them or creating other obstructions. The climate apocalypse groups justify their actions with a lack of alternatives, excusing their threats and methods with their important message of incoming doom. The activists feel obligated to escalate their actions because climate change is imminent and poses a much more significant threat to humanity and future generations. Their perception of the future shrinks to a very narrow field to the extent that the only way to have a future is to eschew it altogether, the thinking that manifests itself best through the Stop Having Kids (2022) movement: "We think it's best and most considerate for humans to not come into existence, which for them will be facing serious and severe problems (that could have been avoided) and exacerbating problems that threaten all life and ecosystems on Earth."

The temporality of apocalypse-never happening but always present is most conducive to a panicked frenzy. However, an individual processes constant doomsday claims that do not materialize either through the continuous never or through the ever-present always. The apocalypse never coming but always present may equally inspire boredom with its legacy of failed predictions that inspire jaded scepticism. In the "boring apocalypse" (Liu et al., 2018) scenario, the catastrophic mindset can continue to work over openly illegitimate postulates or phenomena detached from the immediate experiences to conjure something that, borrowing from Gendron (1977, p. 68), we can call a "half-baked" or "mixed" or "intermediate" apocalypse. Those forecasts of the inevitable social disaster brought about by omnipresent climate change align within Cattarinussi's "whimper theory," which envisions not a single calamity (a bang) but gradual slow-motion destruction. Both of these reactions contribute to a broader societal pessimism that undercuts any prospects for positive social change. In this sense, apocalyptic temporality might not encourage creativity, but the decay of time is a good compost that fertilizes the soil for the expected tomorrow.

3. We are the times

Even deep futures must still be regarded from the vantage point of a human lifespan despite the accelerating pace of change in our contemporary temporality, which has the effect of compressing the present moment and distancing the past, as suggested by the ever-insightful Ratzinger (2011, p. 350):

> Human life changes ever more rapidly: it is used up sooner, so that the difference between past and present becomes steadily greater, the present moments become ever shorter, and the past recedes faster and faster and ends up at an increasing distance from the present. This, however, means that man is thrust into the past at an increasingly earlier point and belongs to it longer. It also means that increasingly divergent times must coexists within single time and that increasingly sharp tensions must be endured within one and the same time, which in fact consists of stratification of contradictory times.

An inquiry into the variability in the timescapes of utopian, dystopian, and apocalyptic futures conducted along the two axes that together shape human agency revealed several tensions highlighted in this quote above. The human agency, that is, the ability to act in the time given to us, is shaped by the temporal realities, both in terms of orientation and agogics. As this chapter demonstrated, rather than accelerating urgency, utopian and dystopian agogics exhibit times slowing down. Utopias assume that by eliminating the rubble of the past, a new society can be built. In this utopian renewal, time is reinvented in a perfect state. Simultaneously, utopias are future-oriented, and the past is irrelevant since it has been conquered. Dystopias cease to consider the future because of their preoccupation with past disasters and crises. This happens because dystopia necessitates a set of broader structural arrangements that establish a scenario in which humanity becomes obsessed with a specific type of security to the extent that everything else is overlooked.

Dystopias frequently demonstrate that attaining the future is impossible, with their protagonists caught in a suspended state of looped reality of the never-changing present. Finally, the apocalypse anticipates the inevitable and the un-whenable catastrophe, making it inherently future-oriented. The contemporary apocalyptic narrative is entirely pessimistic and manifests itself in a future-oriented, ever-accelerating temporality. The apocalypse occurs now, or, more provocatively, the time to seek it is now because the apocalyptic agency is both proactive and impatient. However, there are two dilemmas: the apocalypse may never arrive, or the future arrives and refuses to let go. The constantly receding horizon of the future means that the temporality of the apocalypse-never arriving but always present is most conducive to a panicked frenzy. Nevertheless, an individual who continually processes doomsday claims that do not come to pass may become bored with the legacy of failed predictions. It does not entail a complete disappearance of belief in the end of the world but rather a far-reaching devaluation of grand cosmic eschatological narratives in favour of individual eschatologies that rationalise the apocalypse by equating the end of the world with the end of individual existence. This infuses apocalyptic agency with cynicism, scepticism, and a broader societal pessimism that undercuts any prospects for positive social change.

Nevertheless, it was St. Augustine of Hippo who famously said, "We ourselves are the times!" against his malcontent contemporaries, who were complaining about how bad the times were. This sentiment is seconded by Ratzinger, who concludes that human beings, with their changing ways, make up the times. To again use Ratzinger's phrase (2011), man can raise his head above the waters of time and thus master it. The attempt to control the pasts or the futures is grounded in the temporalised action in the present. However, to fully understand deep futures' agency, we also need to answer the immediately arising question, who controls the time? Time, as Hodges (2008, p. 406) reminds us, is also a dimension for the exercise of power that can be neutral, benign in utopian settings or malign, as we have seen in dystopian examples of history politics expressed in the power of what to remember or attempts to constantly rewrite history. In utopian, dystopian and apocalyptic settings, certain groups or individuals may have the power to determine and enforce a dominant temporal regime. Breaking such monopoly might be the shortcut to what Alvin Toffler (1986, p. 404) called *praktopia*, a world neither the best nor the worst possible. Praktopia differs from utopias in that it is not static, frozen in unreal perfection, and at the same time, it is devoid of atavism that would shape it to resemble some imaginary ideal from the past, thus turning it into a dystopia. Simultaneously, praktopia offers a way out of an apocalypse, as it is looking beyond its own demise, beyond the coming crisis, beyond the ongoing end of the world.

Acknowledgements

I would like to express my most profound gratitude to Dr Jan C. Bentz (Blackfriars Priory, Oxford), whose work on utopianism as political Gnosticism, and specifically, Molnar's critique of the utopian mindset enriched this chapter immensely.

Note

1 I am using ISIS (Islamic State of Iraq and Syria; Islamic State of Iraq and al-Sham) and ISIL (Islamic State of Iraq and Levant) intermittently. There are also names that draw directly from the Arabic language: *Al Daw-lah* (State) or *Da'esh/Da'ish*, being an acronym for Arabic words: *ad-Dawlah al-Islāmiyahfī 'l-Irāq wa-sh-Shām*, that is, the same ones that make up the English name of ISIS.

References

Ahearn, L. M. (1999). Agency. *Journal of Linguistic Anthropology*, *9*(1/2), 12–15.

Antonello, A., & Carey, M. (2017). Ice cores and the temporalities of the global environment. *Environmental Humanities*, *9*(2), 181–203.

Arrighi, G. (1999). *Chaos and governance in the modern world system*. University of Minnesota Press.

Atwood, M. (1985). *The Handmaid's Tale*. Houghton Mifflin.

Augustine of Hippo. (1888). *Sermon 30 on the New Testament* (R. G. MacMullen, Trans.). In P. Schaff (Ed.), *Nicene and Post-Nicene fathers, first series* (Vol. 6). Christian Literature Publishing Co. Revised by K. Knight. http://www.newadvent.org/fathers/160330.htm

Barkun, M. (1983). Divided apocalypse: Thinking about the end in contemporary America. *Soundings: An Interdisciplinary Journal*, *6*(3), 257–280.

Bartoszewicz, M. G. (2016). Fortress Europe: Terrorist threat in the context of ISIS. *Studia Polityczne*, (44), 205–224.

Bartoszewicz, M. G. (2020). Siła czy przesilenie? Działalność i znaczenie Państwa Islamskiego. *Przegląd Bezpieczeństwa Wewnętrznego*, *12*(22), 39–65.

Bartoszewicz, M. G., Eibl, O., & El Ghamari, M. (2022). Securitising the future: Dystopian migration discourses in Poland and the Czech Republic. *Futures*, 102972.

Bauman, Z. (2013). *Liquid modernity*. John Wiley & Sons.

Bear, L. (2016). Time as technique. *Annual Review of Anthropology*, *45*, 487–502.

Bergin, V. (2017). *Who runs the world?* Macmillan Children's Books.

Bradbury, R. (1953). *Fahrenheit 451*. Ballantine Books.

Bregman, R. (2017). *Utopia for realists: And how we can get there*. Bloomsbury Publishing.

Brown, P. (2014). *Red rising*. Del Rey.

Bryant, R., & Knight, D. M. (2019). *The anthropology of the future*. Cambridge University Press.

Burgess, A. (1962). *A clockwork orange*. W. W. Norton & Company.

Byman, D. (2016). Understanding the Islamic state—a review essay. *International Security*, *40*(4), 127–165.

Canetti, E. (1996). *Masa i władza*. Czytelnik.

Cattarinussi, B. (1977). The dimensions of utopia. *The Philosophy Forum*, *15*(1–2), 1–13.

Clark, G. A. (2000). Darwinian dystopia: The shape of things to come. *Futures*, *32*(8), 729–738.

Collins, S. (2008). *The Hunger Games*. Scholastic Press.

Crowley, M. (2023, March 26). The cult of the climate apocalypse. *Spiked*. https://www.spiked-online.com/2023/03/26/the-cult-of-the-climate-apocalypse/

D'Angelo, L., & Pijpers, R. J. (2018). Mining temporalities: An overview. *The Extractive Industries and Society*, *5*(2), 215–222.

Derrida, J. (1990). Some statements and truisms about neologisms, newisms, postisms, parasitisms, and other small seismisms. In D. Carroll (Ed.), *The states of "Theory": History, art, and critical discourse* (pp. 63–94). Columbia University Press.

Dickinson, S. (2015). *The Traitor Baru Cormorant*. Tor Books.

Eliade, M. (1974). *Sacrum. Mit. Historia*. Państwowy Instytut Wydawniczy.

Emirbayer, M., & Mische, A. (1998). What is agency? *American Journal of Sociology, 103*(4), 962–1023.

Erdrich, L. (2017). *Future home of the living god*. HarperCollins.

Fromson, J., & Simon, S. (2015). ISIS: The dubious paradise of apocalypse now. *Survival, 57*(3), 7–56.

Furedi, F. (2007). *Culture of fear revisited*. Continuum.

Furedi, F. (2018). *How fear works: Culture of fear in the 21st century*. Bloomsbury.

Gendron, B. (1977). The brave new world reconsidered. *The Philosophy Forum, 15*(1–2), 49–68.

Girard, R. (2018). *Apokalipsa tu i teraz*. Wydawnictwo WAM.

Golding, W. (1954). *Lord of the flies*. Faber and Faber.

Hirsch, E., & Stewart, C. (2005). Introduction: Ethnographies of historicity. *History and Anthropology, 16*(3), 261–274.

Hjerpe, M., & Linnér, B. O. (2009). Utopian and dystopian thought in climate change science and policy. *Futures, 41*(4), 234–245.

Hodges, M. (2008). Rethinking time's arrow: Bergson, Deleuze and the anthropology of time. *Anthropological Theory, 8*(4), 399–429.

James, P. D. (1992). *The children of men*. Knopf.

Jordheim, H. (2014). Introduction: Multiple times and the work of synchronization. *History and Theory, 53*(4), 498–518.

Karataş, İ. (2021). The role of apocalyptic prophecies in ISIS terrorism. *Journal of College of Sharia & Islamic Studies, 39*(1), 193–212.

Koneczny, F. (1991). *O ład w historii*. Michalineum.

Lanchester, J. (2019). *The wall*. W. W. Norton & Company.

Lee, J. R., Terauds, A., Carwardine, J., Shaw, J. D., Fuller, R. A., Possingham, H. P., & Chadès, I. (2022). Threat management priorities for conserving Antarctic biodiversity. *PLoS Biology, 20*(12), e3001921.

Lepore, J. (2017, June 5). A golden age for dystopian fiction. *New Yorker*. https://www.new-yorker.com/magazine/2017/06/05/a-golden-age-for-dystopian-fiction

Liu, H. Y., Lauta, K. C., & Maas, M. M. (2018). Governing boring apocalypses: A new typology of existential vulnerabilities and exposures for existential risk research. *Futures, 102*, 6–19.

Lowry, L. (1993). *The giver*. Houghton Mifflin.

Mandel, E. (2014). *Station eleven*. Vintage.

Mauro, R. (2014, November 18). The Islamic State seeks the battle of apocalypse. *The Clarion Project*. http://www.clarionproject.org/analysis/dabiq-islamic-state-wants-battle-end-days

McCants, W. F. (2015). *The ISIS apocalypse: The history, strategy, and doomsday vision of the Islamic state*. Macmillan.

McCants, W. F. (2016, October 17). Apocalypse delayed. *Brookings*. https://www.brookings.edu/blog/markaz/2016/10/17/apocalypse-delayed/

McLuhan, M. (1964). *Understanding media: The extensions of man*. McGraw Hill.

Molnar, T. (1967). *Utopia. The perennial heresy*. Shed and Ward.

Monitoring, BBC. (2016). Dabiq: Why is syrian town so important for IS? *BBC News*. https://www.bbc.com/news/world-middle-east-30083303

Moore, A., & Lloyd, D. (1982–1989). *V for Vendetta*. DC Comics.

Moriarty, P., & Honnery, D. (2018). Three futures: Nightmare, diversion, vision. *World Futures, 74*(2), 51–67.

Raspail, J. (1973). *The camp of the saints*. Editions Robert Laffont.

Ratzinger, J. (2011). *Dogma and preaching*. Ignatius Press.

Roth, V. (2011). *Divergent*. Katherine Tegen Books.

Rowland, C. (2014). Apocalypticism and radicalism. In J. J. Collins (Ed.), *The Oxford handbook of apocalyptic literature* (pp. 407–421). Oxford University Press.

Samimian-Darash, L. (2022). Scenarios in a time of urgency: Shifting temporality and technology. *Social Anthropology/Anthropologie Sociale, 30*(4), 90–109.

Schwab, K. (2017). *The fourth industrial revolution.* Crown Business.

Schwab, K., & Malleret, T. (2020). *The great reset.* World Economic Forum.

Shames, S. L., & Atchison, A. L. (2019). *Survive and resist: The definitive guide to dystopian politics.* Columbia University Press.

Shellenberger, M. (2018). *Apocalypse never.* HarperCollins.

Sookhdeo, P. (2015). *Unmasking islamic state.* Isaac Publishing.

Staupe-Delgado, R. (2021). *Disasters and life in anticipation of slow calamity: Perspectives from the Colombian Andes.* Routledge.

Stephenson, N. (2008). *Anathem.* William Morrow.

Stop Having Kids. (2022). *We ought to consider future problems.* https://www.stophaving-kids.org/

Stover, M. R. (2001). *Blade of tyshalle.* Del Rey.

Toffler A. (1986). *Trzecia fala.* Państwowy Instytut Wydawniczy.

Van Rythoven, E. (2018). Fear in the crowd or fear of the crowd? The dystopian politics of fear in international relations. *Critical Studies on Security, 6*(1), 33–49.

Virilio, P. (2008). *Prędkość i polityka.* Sic!

Voegelin, E. (1987). *The new science of politics: An introduction.* University of Chicago Press.

Weaver, R. M. (2013). *Ideas have consequences: Expanded edition.* University of Chicago Press.

Wessinger, C. (2014). Apocalypse and violence. In J. J. Collins (Ed.), *The Oxford handbook of apocalyptic literature* (pp. 422–440). Oxford University Press.

Wood, G. (2015). What ISIS really wants. *The Atlantic.* http://www.theatlantic.com/magazine/archive/2015/03/what-isis-really-wants/384980/

4 Disasters as time, time as disasters

Tomás J. Usón and Cécile Stephanie Stehrenberger

1. Introduction

"Dirt is matter out of place," famously affirmed Mary Douglas in her book *Risk and Blame*. This pivotal phrase—originally proposed by William James (2004/1902, p. 107)—came to offer one of the most straightforward explanations of how people make sense of danger and calamity. In a time when scholars were convinced that environmental hazards were objective events that could be measured, assessed, and, as such, avoided, Douglas proposed an alternative view in which hazards and their risks were not external phenomena but an intrinsic component of societies that set clear boundaries with actors and situations that put their internal functioning at risk. By understanding social pollution beyond disposal escaping from society's control and functioning, Douglas suggested that the definition of pure and impure elements and bodies responded more to a way of setting the boundaries between an inside and outside that can—and must—be controlled. Danger, in this sense, relies more on a chaotic arrangement that threatening bodies and events may present for a certain social group rather than on a strictly essentialized condition of what a hazard entails.

Although sometimes criticized for applying a rather static and generalized model to understand risk components for different societal groups (and presenting a conservative approach to environmental movements; see Lupton, 2013), Douglas' understanding of danger, threats, and risks has strong relevance even today. First, it helps emphasize that threats, rather than being fixed and essential situations, are deeply connected with the very understandings that societies make of them. This societal perspective also challenges the all-too-common individualistic view of risks, where the individual is the ultimate actor in charge of facing and coping with generalized risks and threats. Second, it shows us that even chaotic and disruptive moments can have a logical construction and arrangement, after all. No matter how disorienting and messy the outcomes of threats and hazards might be, they can always, at the end of the day, be classified in a certain way of understanding the chaos and destruction they portray.

This last point seems to be a fundamental issue when dealing with the analysis of disasters, especially from a temporal perspective, as this chapter aims to do. In the past decades, several approaches have sought to redefine the temporal

DOI: 10.4324/9781003537311-5

assumptions behind the classic understandings of disasters as disruptions, arguing that the explosive moments with which disasters are normally associated are not always the norm. Under the notion of slow disasters (Williamson & Courtney, 2018; Anderson et al., 2020; Stehrenberger, 2020), critical approaches in this regard have pursued a research agenda where the different rhythms and paces of disastrous processes can be taken into consideration. Inspired by the notion of slow violence (Nixon, 2011), slow disasters emerge as a political contestation to an unfair homogenization of the diverse ways in which the unbearable consequences of disasters can take form and expression. However, they still operate under a very strong assumption: that disasters, rather than being producers of a certain form of time and temporality, are processes—whether fast or slow—that take place in time and are contained within it. Yet, if we take Mary Douglas' assumption seriously when she affirms that hazards are boundaries societies create to recognize and classify elements that put their internal functioning at risk, it is worth asking what type of temporal arrangements disasters produce at a societal level.

As Michael Guggenheim (2014) prolifically suggests, disasters as politics remind us that extreme events and their disruptive effects within society can be powerful sources of political response and reaction. Politics as disasters, moreover, aim to tell us that, rather than situations beyond social control, disasters are situations produced by political decisions in the first place. In similar terms, what we aim to argue here is that while disasters can be placed within temporal moments and periods, they are also sociopolitical arrangements that produce certain forms of time: times of disruption, systemic failure, and ultimately suffering, but also times of emergency management, recovery, and preparedness.

In this chapter, we aim to delve deeper into these issues by exploring the entangled connections between disasters and time. Specifically, we seek to review the main temporal assumptions that have shaped the studies of disasters and risks over the past decades, emphasizing both the hazard- and vulnerability-based paradigms and their understandings of disasters as situations taking place in time. In a second section, we offer some alternative approaches to the notion of disasters beyond their eventual and processual nature, particularly positions related to science and technology studies (STS) and assemblage thinking. By addressing the notion of chronopolitics, we propose in a third section to reconsider the main temporal assumptions behind disaster studies and consider catastrophes as complex arrangements, further conceptualized as assemblages, that allow us to articulate the notion of time in the first place.

2. Defining disasters: from events to processes

Problematizations around the notion of disaster are as old as humanity itself. Explanations behind calamities have always been a leading and central issue in different societies. Whether acts of gods, misfortune due to misbehavior, or simply the result of external, uncontrollable forces, catastrophic situations have been a source of all kinds of speculations—a sign of an "ill star," from the Latin, leading to unexpected calamities.

Despite the long-standing tradition around explanations behind disasters—the "forensic theory of danger," as Mary Douglas (1994) defines the social necessity of understanding the source of calamities—ways of assessing threats and their consequences have varied considerably throughout history. Similar to Douglas, scholars like Niklas Luhmann (2005) would suggest that the main difference in risk and danger estimations can be found in the classical distinction between the so-called premodern and modern societies. Whereas the former would be driven by a notion of fate in which calamities were the consequences of a destiny practically impossible to change, the latter would revolve around the idea of individual decision-making and its consequences in terms of loss and gain. Yet, the main distinction between Douglas and Luhmann seems to be the origins of that change. For Douglas, transformations in the explanatory systems to make sense of danger might be related to a change in the role that individuals as owners of rights started to fulfill in modern societies—something that would give them the capacity to decide over their lives. For Luhmann, moreover, switching from fate to decision would have less to do with the new roles that individuals as owners of rights started to fulfill in modern societies and more to do with new notions of time that would emerge with the Industrial Revolution.

According to the author, time in its traditional form was conceived as a totality that could only be differentiated from eternity. The fate of humans was immersed within time but depended on the will of eternal entities, with God as the ultimate observer and ruler of human destiny. But with modernity,[1] the notion of eternity, and thus an absolute, omnipresent God, would be replaced by a differentiation taking place within time: past and future. Although not exclusively modern, for Luhmann, these two stages would take control over time semantics in industrial societies and provide new capacities for managing reality and, thus, the destiny of people at their own hands:

> The advantage point from which the totality of time could be simultaneously observed had previously been eternity, and the observer had been called God. Now it was each present that reflected on the totality of time in dividing up between the past and the future of this particular present, and the observer was the human being.
>
> (Luhmann, 2005, p. 40)

Risk, under this vision, would be the form that modernity would develop to deal with the uncertainties that a life with a dead God leaves aside. Structured under the notions of past and future, modern societies would base their hazard estimations in terms of risks emerging from decision-making in the present, the ultimate moment where the difference between past and future flourishes. Disaster, under this view, would be the direct result of decisions, referring to the incapacity—or reluctance—to deal with possible hazards accordingly. It is thus no wonder that risk would come to be placed as a central element of modern life—"an essential need of the soul," as Simone Weil (2005, p. 134) defines it—the ultimate capacity of humans to control, or even colonize, the future in pursuit of influencing present affairs and actions (Beck, 1998).

Despite the efforts to overcome so-called premodern explanations regarding disasters as unbearable and unavoidable forces, early scholars working on this issue maintained an approach that conceived disasters as *external* events—as external as God—around which society needed to adjust its behaviors. The early work of authors like Samuel Henry Prince (1920), Lowell Carr (1932), and Gilbert White (1945) focused on strategies to counteract physical singularities produced by geophysical and technological events, emphasizing the necessity of adjusting human behavior accordingly and managing the affected population. In the 1960s, moreover, authors like Charles Fritz (1961) expanded the focus to individual and organizational behavior in the pre- and post-stages of the disturbance. However, disasters would continue to be considered "an event, concentrated in time and space, in which a society or a relatively self-sufficient subdivision of a society undergoes severe danger and incurs such losses" (Fritz, 1961, p. 655). Amid this externally triggered disruption is the challenge that society needed to deal with, while scarce historical and sociocultural patterns were considered to put the disruption into context in the first place (Hoffman & Oliver-Smith, 1999, p. 1).[2] Risks, under this vision, would be considered objective issues with an independent existence from our capacity to observe and assess them (Tierney, 2014).

Conceiving disasters as concrete events taking place in space and time, these early groups of scholars were particularly interested in defining the diffuse contours and limits of those disruptions. In their studies, authors like Fritz and Charles Wallace (1961) analyzed not only the immediate implications of and reactions to extreme events but also the long-term consequences that disruptive moments might arouse among individuals and society. By exploring the transformations happening in the aftermath, they soon started reflecting on the costs but also the opportunities for progress that catastrophes and crises could elicit. Disasters would be turned into prolific moments for social resurrection and "amplified rebound" (Fritz, 1961, p. 692), an opportunity to turn misfortune and tragedy into learning and growth—common assumptions shaping the current therapy culture and self-help consumerism of our times, as Timothy Recuber (2016) suggests. Just as with the notion of risk, temporal reflections on disasters presented a strong future orientation where decisions in the aftermath would be concerned with returning to a lost normality—the myth of an ordinary life that needed to be recovered (Hewitt, 1983b: 22)—with the highest reward as possible.

These early event-based, naturalistic, or "hazardist" approaches to disasters, shaped by progress-based assumptions, had a significant influence on the development of reactive action plans. Driven by a military ethos of control and "peace restoration," efforts for risk reduction followed a centralized managerial logic, portraying exposed populations as defenseless victims in need of protection (Davis, 2007; Masco, 2014), with a strong emphasis on infrastructure and zoning efforts to address hazards (Hewitt, 1983b). The role of centralized institutions, under these terms, took center stage in the discussion for many years, promoting an emergency-based response with a milder focus on the social and political conditions leading to crises. The notions of risk acceptability and risk perception were applied to understand the reluctance of people to incorporate allegedly objective risk assessments into their own perceptions and judgments. Communication became a highly relevant topic for risk management, encouraging decision-makers and technicians to replace top-down communication mechanisms with constructive debates among all the actors involved. The dominant belief at this point was that the knowledge used to dictate public policies needed to be not only true but also clear (Wynne, 2002). However, analysts still replicated reductionist perspectives by considering people as irrational or ignorant and seeking to convince them to accept certain risks in the name of progress and development—especially those related to technological interventions like nuclear plants or industrial facilities (Strydom, 2002).

Hazardist approaches to disasters began to be contested by new theoretical and empirical approaches integrated into the field during the seventies and, notably, the eighties and nineties. The work of new scholars offered alternative approaches to the notion of social disruption, emphasizing both symbolic experiences of meaning production and the relevance of societal processes to understand the causes of disasters. Inspired by the early work of authors like Phil O'Keefe, Ken Westgate, and Ben Wisner (1976), who called for a reconsideration of the "naturalness" of natural disasters, and the work of Kenneth Hewitt (1983a) on the notion of vulnerability as a fundamental dimension to understand human compromise amid extreme events, new perspectives in disaster studies criticized the pro-Western, pro-capitalist, and technologically driven biases that the view of disasters as single events arouse. Approaches in this regard aimed to emphasize the inherently political nature of disasters (Brown & Goldin, 1973), offering new perspectives to inquire into the sociopolitical conditions leading to the concatenation of social disruptions. Disasters, under these terms, began to be conceptualized as processes: long-standing phases of pressure accumulation related to social inequalities, fragile environments, and a lack of proper risk management systems that could ultimately be released through an extreme event like an earthquake or a landslide (Blaikie et al., 1994).

The impact of more critical, processed-based approaches would be manifold. First, the objective assumptions of risk assessment proposed by a positivist, event-based research agenda would be soon contested by constructivist perspectives placing special emphasis on the values and social conditions leading to prioritizing certain forms of risk assessments over others. The early work of authors like Mary Douglas (1966; 1994), exploring cultural and symbolic aspects defining the notions of risk and danger within societies, would be followed up by authors like Ulrich Beck (1992) and Anthony Giddens (1991) and their theory of risk society, where risk comes to be conceived as an intrinsic form of sociopolitical organization in today's world. The problem of scarcity and distribution of wealth, under this scenario, is overlapped by "the problems and conflicts that arise from the production, definition, and distribution of techno-scientifically produced risks" (Beck, 1992, p. 19). Under this view, the same notion of expertise, together with the expert-lay knowledge dichotomy, would be equally problematized. The local population would cease to be considered a passive group that needs to be protected and educated and would instead be turned into an active, engaged part for the articulation of values, explanations, and strategies to deal with risks and extreme events (Callon, 1999; Brian Wynne, 2004; Collins & Evans, 2009; Callon et al., 2011).

Furthermore, critical perspectives on disasters would recognize temporal arrangements of disasters that escape from the instantaneous disruption of events like earthquakes, floods, or tornadoes. Scholars in this regard would follow Rob Nixon's (2011, p. 2) argument around the notion of slow violence, that is, "violence that occurs gradually and out of sight, a violence of delayed destruction that is dispersed across time and space, an attritional violence that is typically not viewed as violence at all." Studies of this kind would explore alternative configurations where disruptions are not based on immediateness but on the incremental accumulation of social and environmental inequalities across generations (Williamson & Courtney, 2018; Anderson et al., 2020; Stehrenberger, 2020). The slow onset of disasters, under this view, would start to be considered not an exception to the rule but the intrinsic characteristic of processes ultimately leading to explosive disruptions within society. It is the slow accumulation of inequalities that would ultimately create the perfect scenario for explosive situations of destruction, loss, and trauma.

This problematization of temporal rhythms would come together with another central assumption among critical approaches to the field: the exceptional condition of disasters and crises. Rather than being anomalies within a prevailing normality, disasters, emergencies, crises, and catastrophes would be portrayed as states of exception that sustain and perpetuate an allegedly normal notion—the norm of a capitalist system exacerbated by the neoliberal agenda (Agamben, 2005). The enactment of crisis and catastrophic stages, moreover, would be used to call for interventions that, in many cases, operate as shock doctrines for deep social interventions, aiming to exacerbate ongoing processes of privatization and deregulation (Klein, 2008).[3] These perspectives aim to question the very understanding of what is conceived as normal by exploring the specific set of values, norms, political conditions, and social configurations that allow structural inequalities to become the rule. Rather than placing them in context, crises would be conceived as the context itself, a persistent and chronic condition—"the result of slow processes of deterioration, erosion and negative change—of multiple traumas and friction" (Vigh, 2008, p. 9).

3.   Assembling disasters

The peerless contributions that hazard- and process-based approaches have made to the study of disaster have also been their main limitations. The hazard paradigm has strongly influenced the development of plans and programs to deal with extreme events at an institutional level, while more critical perspectives have challenged commonly accepted positivist assumptions regarding disaster rhythms, social justice, and knowledge production. Yet, both paradigms have also promoted what Michael Guggenheim (2014) defines as the naturalization and culturalization of disasters, views that have tended to excessively simplify the complexity that such massive disruptions entail. The main reason behind this issue seems to be the unresolved tension about the "real nature" of disasters: one that requires us to conceive them as real social issues while at the same time neglecting their non-social condition by defining them as ("natural") events taking place outside the societal order; an anomia that needs to be avoided rather than fully embraced as an inherent component of society.

The all-too-technocratic positions that hazard-based approaches promote have led to the idea of disasters as situations that, with the proper preparation and response capacity, can be avoided and prevented. The outsider condition of catastrophes as events taking place beyond the norm and, thus, external to the proper function of society, has led to an uncritical view that necessarily hides the inherently social and political condition of disasters. The naturalization of disasters, in this regard, operates as a strategy that aims to externalize the occurrence of extreme, disruptive events. There are social factors contributing to the calamities a disaster entails. But the source is always outside, after all.

Some critically driven approaches to disasters, moreover, have tended to a form of culturalization that operates in a paradoxically inverse, yet similar, way. By embracing the fully social conditions of disasters, some critical voices have implicitly denied the material component of catastrophes. The neglect of the "real" condition of disasters, related to their processual nature that has little to do with the occurrence of external events and more to do with the internal operation of the social, commonly leads to the idea that disasters, rather than objectively defined events, are interpretations of reality without a place in the real world. Defined as analytical conceits, disasters are conceived as "interpretive fictions" (Hagen & Elliott, 2021; Horowitz & Remes, 2021) aim to hide social inequalities and structural violence through the occurrence of extreme events. Some critical positions, in this sense, have turned disasters into a construction, a vacuum existing only in institutional explanations unwilling to deal with environmental injustice. As politics, paraphrasing Guggenheim, disasters are nothing but distinctions: forms of classification following a political orientation (Bond, 2013; Fortun et al., 2016). This full internalization of the idea of disasters, moreover, leads to an inevitable conundrum: if disasters do not exist in reality, how can we explain the capacity they have to arrange the world—as a concept but also as an experience?

With these arguments, we do not want to assert that critical scholars aim to relativize the material consequences that extreme events and poor political implementations have on the population. As Horowitz and Remes (2021, p. 4) suggest, "the consequences of 'disaster' as a belief are made real in the distribution of sympathy, material resources, and state power." Yet, giving up the notion of disaster and its real, ontological existence runs the risk of losing sight of how disasters are practically articulated—not only by an institutionality unwilling to tackle structural factors leading to societal collapse but also by the same population and communities exposed to those situations. The existence of disasters must be placed both beyond the external position of extreme events outside society and beyond the internal configuration of politics. They portray an incommensurability that escapes any human capacity to fully embrace them—something that attracts us, in a threatening way, to the point of trying to name it. As Maurice Blanchot (1995, p. 5) brilliantly affirms, "the disaster is unknown; it is the unknown name for that in thought itself which dissuades us from thinking of it, leaving us, but its proximity, alone." Disasters are a diffuse excess; an effort to name something that escapes our understanding. This incommensurability is defined by Manuel Tironi (2014, p. 117) as an excessive type of controversy: "situations in which a matter controversial is always outstripping, vitally plethoric and abundant, involving life's liveliness itself." The excessiveness disasters arouse relates to the Kantian sublime, the pleasure the mind experiences when the imagination reaches its limits due to pain (Ray, 2005). This "negative" pleasure is the only way the impotent mind has to set certain boundaries under a situation that is entirely out of hands. And it is precisely this excessiveness that is missed when we treat disasters as a simple conceit.

Taking into consideration these conceptual limitations, alternative approaches to the study of disasters have aimed to overcome the dichotomous naturalist and culturalist—also hazard-based and process-based—positions by suggesting that it is not possible to conceive disasters only as events or processes. Related to the field of STS, scholars have come to define disasters and their management as a meshwork, complex entanglements connecting actors, materialities, and practices that turn them into dynamic realities difficult to fully localize in a particular time and space (Rodríguez-Giralt et al., 2014). Highly inspired by assemblage theory and the principles of flat ontology and more-than-human associations (Donovan, 2017; McGowran & Donovan, 2021), scholars have aimed to expand the set of elements considered when dealing with disasters—commonly enclosed under the classical risk formula as the occurrence of an event crossed by the levels of exposure and vulnerability of a certain social group. Assemblage thinking, as Amy Donovan (2017) suggests in this regard, can help to open up disaster risk reduction research by expanding the components involved in the process. "Disasters are more than natural, but they are also more-than-human," affirms the author (Donovan, 2017, p. 5), inspired by Sarah Whatmore's (2006) more-than-human geography. As assemblages, Donovan (2017, p. 8) continues, disasters "are characterized by complex ideas, physical processes, physical-human interactions (e.g., via affect and imagination), human cultures and technologies that experience a varying power distribution in time." Dealing with this vast set of components and entities shaped and shaping these distributions of power, Donovan suggests, implies including different types of ontologies and epistemic regimes that move beyond classical scientific and local knowledges. In this sense, Peter McGowran and Amy Donovan (2021) affirm, disasters are signified not by what is conceived as scientifically validated or not, but through the relations among the elements composing the vast network of actors, associations, triggers, and concepts entangled in the diffuse boundaries of the disaster. This perspective necessarily requires moving beyond anthropocentric approaches prioritizing human actors and expanding the analysis to the socio-material components involved, as well as the relations between them.

Defined as assemblages, disasters unveil not only the present spatiotemporal circumstances that give rise to a particular disturbance but also the discourses and statements that provide meaning to that chaos, while projecting it into potential future scenarios of political oversight and handling. This differentiation between the socio-material and interpretative elements shaping disasters, echoing Deleuze and Guattari's (1987) distinction between the mechanical and enunciative state of assemblages, aligns with the approach that scholars in STS have termed a material-semiotic perspective for delving into reality (Barad, 2007; Law, 2008; Haraway, 2018). Disasters, as both concrete realities and conceptual devices, following Donna Haraway (2018), operate as sets of relations that have to do with meanings and materials. Like cyborgs, disasters entail both a social reality and fictional constructs—arrangements that are messy and multiple, always in-the-making (Adam & Groves, 2007; McGowran & Donovan, 2021). The multiplicity that disasters represent is given not only due to the multiple explanations around extreme events but mostly because a disaster "indirectly depicts, enacts, and manifests a range of realities" (Law, 2004, p. 94). This multiplicity is what makes disasters an elusive reality, a pure excess that escapes our capacity to fully enclose their occurrence into one single coherent explanation.

In recent years, several scholars have called upon assemblage thinking to explore how disasters—as massive, ever-changing ecological arrangements—operate in the intersection of multiple and potentially conflicting societal projects. John Law (2004) applies a material-semiotic perspective to analyze the multiple explanations emanating from the 1999 Ladbroke Grove train collision in the vicinity of London, an accident that left more than thirty fatalities and hundreds injured. By defining the collision as an allegory, the art of "hold[ing] two or more things together that do not necessarily cohere" (Law, 2004, p. 90), Law describes the accident as a scene that creates a range of realities that escape any coherent effort to explain "what really happened." Without a single explanation that could clarify the origin of the accident, authorities and public opinion had to deal with a noncoherent multiplicity incapable of offering a so-needed singularity that can be used to establish who should be held responsible for the accident. "Singularities are not only sought, but they are normatively enacted. A good reality is one that is centrally coordinated," affirms Law (2004, p. 100). Yet, this singularity cannot be reached without restricting multiplicity to express itself. It is when multiplicity is restricted that political projects try to reduce the complex scenarios that extreme events leave for society. However, those discursive restrictions can never eliminate the multiple realities that disasters as assemblages configure, leading to an always incomplete operation of preparedness, response, and recovery stages.

Inspired by authors like John Law and others close to the field of Actor-Network Theory, a series of scholars have embarked on the task of overcoming the two classical movements to conceptualize disasters previously presented: the naturalization and culturalization of the problem. In a pivotal issue of the journal *Sociological Review* from 2014 titled "Disasters and Politics: Materials, Experiments, Preparedness," Manuel Tironi, Israel Rodríguez-Giralt, and Michael Guggenheim, together with other authors, reflect on the challenges and possibilities of embracing disasters as complex entanglements where actors, materials, practice, and relations come into play. In the volume, Ignacio Farías (2014b) explores the dramatic consequences left by the 2010 earthquake and tsunami over the coastal areas of central

Chile to ask what happens when planetary forces are neglected as truly political agents.

As an event initially discarded by the Chilean emergency system, the 2010 tsunami caught authorities and citizens by surprise upon its arrival on the country's coast, raising the question of how such an event, which should have been properly predicted, was able to bypass the procedures and standards of monitoring agencies. Building on Nancy Fraser's notion of recognition, Farías concludes that acknowledging the ontological existence of nonhuman forces—and their political impact—needs to go hand in hand with cosmopolitical recognition that takes into account the unpredictable nature of forces like tsunamis. Rather than events that can be unequivocally predicted, the author suggests that political frameworks need to open up to the incapacity to fully control planetary entities—treating them as political actors with their own agency. This cosmopolitical recognition emphasizes the active role that planetary forces play in the constitution of our common worlds and expands the political arena by allowing nonhuman entities to take part in it.

Farías further explores these issues alongside Manuel Tironi when examining processes of recovery and reconstruction in Constitución, a coastal city severely impacted by the 2010 tsunami in Chile (Tironi & Farías, 2015). In this context, the concept of the assemblage, particularly in its urban consideration (Amin & Thrift, 2002; Farías & Bender, 2009; Farías, 2011; McFarlane, 2011), plays a crucial role in understanding the critical role that planetary forces have in the reconfiguration of cities as inhabited atmospheres. The authors draw on Peter Sloterdijk's notion of immunization, a highly contested concept for being applied elsewhere as a normative justification to define which actors and bodies should be considered as agents in tune with Europe's needs and goals and which ones should be excluded. Immunization, in that case, operates as an inclusive exclusivity (Wambacq and van Tuinen, 2017), a membrane that creates a safe interior while shielding and expulsing any pathogen body. However, instead of applying immunization from a normative perspective, the authors use it as an analytical device to explore precisely which bodies, materials, entities, and practices are enabled to inhabit the urban world and at what cost—a boundary work that resonates with Mary Douglas' notions of danger and purity.

By examining the construction of an urban park designed to operate as a natural shield against future tsunamis, the authors explore how the city's new master plan, which functions as a cosmical diagram—or cosmogram (Tresch, 2007; Farías, 2014a)—envisions cohabitation with earthly powers. The inability to diplomatically manage forces like tsunamis leads to the necessity of creating inclusively exclusive membranes that prevent these forces from fully participating in the urban atmosphere. However, instead of completely restricting the presence of these earthly powers, the cosmogramatic operations create new urban configurations where forces like tsunamis, rather than being excluded entities, become crucial components. It represents a movement of opening up rather than closure (Wambacq and van Tuinen, 2017), a recognition of the tsunami as a force that must be considered, albeit in negative ways, within the new cosmopolitical configuration of the city.

Elizabeth Angell (2014) similarly employs the notion of assemblage when examining earthquakes in Istanbul to understand how they create new connections between the city's materiality and its inhabitants. These connections, the author suggests, give rise to novel forms of causality shaped by survivors' intimate experiences and urban politics related to recovery and mitigation plans. "The concept of urban assemblage," Angell (2014, p. 676) remarks, "offers a way to consider disaster as a phenomenon that is not just destructive, but productive—a force that participates in the constant reassembling of the city." As disruptions of the actual version of urban projects, disasters are a fundamental part of the urban composition, "an actualisation of one of many possible futures of an assemblage of expressive and material components" (McGowran & Donovan, 2021, p. 8). They are not pure chaos, but a chaos that can be named and partially, only partially, made sense of.

4.   Temporizing assemblages: disasters and chronopolitics

Considering disasters as assemblages, leaves, however, a central question unresolved: how to deal with time around disasters and the temporalities making sense of these events in-the-making in the first place. Mostly, what role do disasters play in the understanding of time as an ontological dimension and a historical event, "as a transcendental fact (being in time is always the condition of being)" and "as a condition always embedded in contingent situations of a precise moment" (Torres, 2021: xv)?

Behind this question lies a similar conundrum as the one that Ulrich Beck (1992) and Anthony Giddens (1991) faced when reflecting on late-modern societies: the paradox of risk not as an object located out there waiting to be located but instead as a result, a consequence of modernity, and the same voices claiming to work toward risk reduction. In other words, tools to estimate risk are not applied in a specific risky context; they create the context and the surrounding risk. In a similar vein, disaster is the result of the same voices calling upon its control and management. It is a monster out of control, a creature whose magnitude escapes any possibility of contention and limitation. And one of the main—yet not only—ways of aiming to control that excessiveness, we argue, is through the creation of concrete forms of time that seek to enunciate the unmanageable massiveness disasters entail.

We could say that defining a disaster as a moment of time production is nothing novel, as any form of event—or process—can be considered based on this premise. Any event, in other words, produces a break from normality that requires us to reflect on the actual order of things and intervene in the rules of a concrete situation, as Alain Badiou (2007) affirms. In a similar way, any process implies a passage of time—a time that, according to Gilles Deleuze (1995) when dealing with the notion of becoming, leads to a permanent movement of territorialization and de-territorialization. Yet, the rupture that disasters entail responds to a form of "hyper-eventuality," paraphrasing Tim Morton (2013): a kind of disruption of such intensity that cannot be simply explained through the unfolding of the issues leading to the occurrence of a certain event but through a massive multiplicity that cannot be fully contained. Here is where the double condition of assemblages—as machinic and enunciative arrangements—becomes a complementary tension:

whereas disasters are moments, "times" of unbearable chaos, they are also a formulation, a "conceit" that seeks to contain that chaos. And one of the most common ways of containing that chaos is, precisely, bestowing it with time. Disasters, in other words, are temporizing assemblages that base their functionality on both the disruption and reconfiguration of temporal schemas.

Producing forms of time—times and rhythms of response and recovery but also anticipation, preparedness, and prevention—is an exercise that reveals how disasters, as Mike Michael suggests, are "a punctuation in the flow of normality" (Michael, 2014, p. 237). "The temporal foldable diversity of a disaster is not located within (. . .) parameters that lie outside of its eventuation. Rather, what is to count as (the measure of) temporality can be regarded as emergent from within the event of a disaster," the author continues (Michael, 2014, p. 240). Those rhythms and times are precisely what are revealed when exploring disasters from a temporal approach. This revelation also helps to explain why disasters can be conceived both as processes and events in the first place. In tune with Niklas Luhmann's argument affirming that danger and risk are two forms of responding to the—sometimes overwhelming—incommensurability of time and eternity, both in their processual or eventual condition, disasters operate as elements that aim to make sense of the very same disruption they evoke. They are not only taking place at a specific spatiotemporal scale; they are those issues that allow us to make sense of those scales in the first place.

The creation of temporal arrangements around and throughout disasters can be traced back to the very first studies about them. By exploring the cargo ship collision that triggered the Halifax explosion more than a century ago, Samuel H. Prince (1920) already identified three main temporal stages of catastrophes: a preliminary stage where the conditions for the occurrence of the event accumulate, the manifestation stage where the event itself takes place, and the reorganization and readjustment stage. This temporal formula would be maintained and perpetuated over the decades, with some variations adding more complexity to the disaster cycle but keeping the same logic, after all. It is a temporal construction that has been fundamental not only for studies in this regard but also for the operation of risk reduction efforts across the decades. As Ben Anderson (2010) rightfully affirms, anticipatory actions amid disasters are nothing more than the creation of a present normality that needs to be protected against the vicissitudes of the future. Anticipation, in its Western, positivist understanding, entails the creation of an "as if" future configured around a time of precaution, preemption, and preparedness. It is precisely these types of temporal arrangements that disasters produce that show us the temporal capacity of these arrangements—a form of political intervention that we further conceptualize as chronopolitics.

Originally coined by George W. Wallis (1970, p. 102) as a way of emphasizing "the relationship between the political behavior of individuals and groups and their time-perspectives," we understand chronopolitics as the strategies to create synchronicity and diachronicity amid moments of a-synchronized pluralism. Synchronicity, as disasters require us to restore the present temporal orders; and diachronicity, because they also mandate us to deal with them from a historical, say long-term, perspective. Politics of time, in this sense, are focused not only on the question of how to maintain social normalcy. They are also strongly focused on the question of change: how to understand transformation and how to deal with it. This turns especially crucial when confronting moments of unmanageable multiplicity, as the previous examples have shown—moments in which the temporal tensions that disasters produce are sought to be managed through singular explanations of the facts—and the promotion of straightforward politics of recovery, mitigation, and preparedness.

To exemplify these ideas, we want to briefly introduce a case that both of us have extensively studied in the past: the 1970 earthquake that struck the region of Ancash in Peru (Usón & Stehrenberger, 2021). With more than seventy thousand fatal victims and millions of victims, the earthquake is remembered in Peru as the deadliest catastrophe in the country's history and certainly one of the most dramatic seismic-based events worldwide. Yet the relevance of this event at a national level relies not only on the magnitude of its destruction. The 1970 earthquake was also the perfect scenario in which the revolutionary government of Juan Velasco Alvarado, a leftist military regime that aimed to promote a national project based on social justice, land reforms, and state modernization, aimed to promote a series of policies to rebuild the region of Ancash from the ground. "The earthquake of the 31st of May 1970 confirmed the unequal and unjust socioeconomic and political order existing in the Affected Zone, a situation that as revolutionary Peruvians we have the obligation to change through the tasks of Reconstruction and Rehabilitation," stated CRYRZA (1972, in Bode, 2001, p. 178) at the time, the agency in charge of leading the reconstruction process. Rather than complete mayhem, the situation was seen by authorities as an opportunity for progress, a historical moment to bury the old colonial order for good and bring the Andean population into the modern era.

The relevance of this event was not only national. Framed within the Cold War's disaster diplomacy (Birn & Muntaner, 2020), the earthquake turned into the perfect "battleground," where both geopolitical blocs of the time came to show their political power and economic superiority by sending any form of aid support imaginable, from clothing and blankets to heavy machinery and prefabricated hospitals, including also vast amounts of healthcare volunteers and professionals. One of the first internationally broadcast disasters, thanks to the presence of journalists from all over the world, the earthquake became one of the first expressions in the history of international aid amid a "natural" disaster, embracing a sense of global solidarity that, at the same time, came together with all sorts of temporal configurations. The "poor, vulnerable" local victims, commonly portrayed as uneducated groups of people living in "the past," were the subjects of all sorts of labels that, interestingly, would be later replicated in other countries during other equally dramatic events. The work of psychiatrists and mental health professionals in the affected region would push forward the diagnosis of post-traumatic stress disorder (PTSD) among the survivors, a recently coined condition at the time emerging from diagnoses conducted on soldiers after the war. As a field highly influenced by military operations (Davis, 2007; Masco, 2014), disaster management efforts would apply

PTSD as a form of reinforcing the idea of the victim, justifying with it the necessity of implementing all sorts of healthcare interventions that were necessary not only for recovering people's "mental normality" but also to take them out of poverty toward the "modern times."

As with any other historical moment of deep political transformations, the earthquake's aftermath was a highly contested scenario of mixed feelings and attitudes—both from the authorities and the local population. With time, Velasco Alvarado's ambitious recovery plan encountered several challenges in being fully implemented and achieved. Besides material limitations and logistic difficulties, the government faced strong opposition from the local population regarding its plans for urban modernization and social justice. Survivors, who experienced the earthquake as a dramatic moment of deep loss and trauma, saw Velasco Alvarado's plan as "the real disaster" (Oliver-Smith, 1986, p. 106). In addition to what they considered insufficient and unequal aid distribution and generalized state abandonment, survivors viewed the reconstruction as the main loss that the earthquake left. The ambitious governmental plan of urban modernization was, for them, a moment in which their old, idyllic Andean world was destroyed for good. Rather than promoting social justice and inclusion, the reconstruction of the urban zones led to, according to urban survivors, a process of uncontrolled rural migration that ended up reversing the old Andean order. Rural actors, from this perspective, were seen by the urban world as part of the catastrophe, and their incorporation into the new urban settlements was seen as the main reason for a dramatic loss of identity and values. Far from being a moment of progress and development, for urban survivors, the disaster was related to stagnation and backlash, a process that has continued until nowadays.

The case of the 1970 earthquake briefly exposed shows us how disasters, as temporizing assemblages, are applied to create new forms of chronopolitical interventions while reinforcing many of the temporal arrangements already configuring society. The earthquake was portrayed by authorities as a possibility for individual and social growth—a narrative all too common amid moments of tragedy and crisis. The possibilities that "building back better" offered were filled with a developmentalist impulse that promised to overcome the mistakes of the past. The times that the disaster destroyed and buried were surrounded by loss and horror but also related to an opportunity for society to grow. Yet the disaster was also a moment of stagnation and grievance. What the government saw as the possibility of wiping the slate clean, local urban survivors saw as the loss of their own world for good. The political transformations promoted at the time opened the doors to rural actors previously excluded from the urban world—according to urban survivors, the real source of the social catastrophe experienced in the aftermath. By making the rural world responsible for the social hecatomb lived afterward, urban survivors were perpetuating colonial discourses against rural inhabitants, reinforcing stereotypes of racial discrimination. As a temporizing device, the earthquake was evoked as a form of remembering and revendicating a lost, idyllic past while condemning the future possibilities that the process of recovery and reconstruction left in the region.

5. Conclusion

In this chapter, we have explored the complex entanglement between disasters and time. Through an initial historical review of how disaster studies have conceptualized catastrophes, initially as events and later as processes, this work has sought to put forward an alternative to previous positions by considering disasters as an uncontrollable excess that needs to be named and managed. Rather than moments or processes, here we have reflected on how disasters, as temporizing assemblages, are machinic and enunciative devices that allow us to (re)articulate time in situations of plural a-synchronicity. This enunciative condition of disasters, which we also relate to the notion of chronopolitics, is what helps to explain why disasters are strongly defined through temporal categories: moments or processes shaped by linear stages of prevention, preparedness, response, and recovery.

Considering disasters as temporizing assemblages, needless to say, does not aim to leave out other main configurations that disasters, as hyper-controversies (Tironi, 2014), can elicit. The chronopolitical dimension that disasters present does not exclude the geopolitical component, configuring management systems around them. As Ian Klinke (2013) rightfully suggests, chronopolitics should not be understood as an alternative or replacement for geopolitics but as an intrinsic part of it. What we suggest here is that chronopolitics are not only a geopolitical exercise but, above all, a cosmopolitical one: an effort to transform the multiplicity that disasters as excess produce into single explanations, versions, and lines of response—a common world amid the heterogeneity that moments of systemic collapse produce.

Mentioning the geopolitics of disaster also brings us to underline that the question of the chronopolitics of disasters is inextricably linked to that of their spatiality. This interconnectedness could be analyzed on several levels, including that of the history of science and knowledge of disaster thinking. It is, for example, no coincidence that the notion of disaster as a process emerged at a moment and from a context in which the unequal global but also regional geographical distribution of hazards and risks was problematized. Among these contexts were the 1980s (activist)-scholarship on the "imperialist" international trade of toxic waste, but also on the "environmental racism" that was interpreted as a cause for the high concentration of environmental disasters in places predominantly inhabited by people of color in the United States.

Concerns about the spatiality of the multiple temporal rhythms that disasters present have been a decisive issue in the current discussions trying to conceptualize, in novel terms, the planetary scale of the environmental crisis we are experiencing. The Anthropocene (Crutzen & Stoermer, 2000), plantationocene (Haraway, 2015), capitalocene (Malm, 2016; Moore, 2017), and wasteocene (Armiero, 2021) are expressions that have emerged to emphasize, in one way or another, the entangled connections between fast and slow disasters with different forms of spatiality. Whereas the notion of the Anthropocene has tried to fulfill this through a sometimes-criticized universalizing "anthropos" and the notion of deep time that fails to grasp the extremely different ways in which human beings are involved in and impacted by the creation of an era shaped by multiple catastrophes, notions like plantationocene and capitalocene have placed emphasis on the colonial legacy and regional orientation of the crisis by providing a concrete place that the Anthropocene lacks. Wasteocene, moreover, has been oriented to a similar endeavor by seeking to make explicit the porous boundaries between bodies and ecosystems, the social process of "wasting," and the resulting "transcorporeal toxicity" as "the salient feature of the present condition of humans and more-than-humans" in the "age of waste" (Iengo & Armiero, 2023, p. 189). All these concepts exemplify the necessity of enunciating, of putting into words, in novel ways, the entangled connections between disasters, space, and time.

The arguments exposed in this chapter should also not be considered a rejection of previous critical studies that have aimed to reconceptualize disasters and their temporal rhythms. Academic works referring to disasters as processes of slow violence, also framed under the notion of slow disasters, have been a fundamental contribution to reflect on how the explosive condition commonly attributed to catastrophes and crises is rather an exception installed as a rule. Situations of environmental degradation, pollution, and the accumulation of social inequities are all-too-common issues that the idea of disasters as abrupt transformations cannot deal with. The structural inequalities that the notion of slow disaster reveals place it as a fundamental abstraction to further explore the colonial, ecological, and class-based violence to which many groups and communities are constantly exposed. Rather than positioning against such contributions, we think that conceiving disasters as temporizing assemblages helps to further explore those violences by placing disasters not only as moments where social injustice and violence flourish but also as a conceptual device that can be applied to create forms of time that perpetuate social injustice in the first place.

Exploring disasters from a temporal lens, in this sense, aims to expand the study of the dramatic consequences that risk management systems at a central level may have for local communities affected both by extreme events and the governmental responses in the aftermath. Approaches in this line may help to reveal how recovery and preparedness plans are commonly shaped by temporal assumptions in which local populations are placed in particular moments of time: a vulnerable group that, incapable of dealing with the consequences of a disruptive event, needs to be put at safe and educated toward modern, future-like understandings of risks. By making explicit the temporal positions promoted by risk management systems, scholars can reveal the patronizing perspectives commonly operating behind risk management agencies. Yet, it can also be a way of embracing the new stages that disruptions produce without falling into the temptation of "returning to a lost normality."

By making explicit the temporal arrangements built around the idea of a lost normality that needs to be recovered, disaster studies can help conceive new forms of dealing with the consequences of environmental crises without seeking to return to a lost, yearned past. It can also help avoid falling into catastrophic readings that impede us from seeing the fundamental scientific and ethical labor required to halt environmental degradation. By reflecting on the temporal assumptions behind disaster risk management efforts, studies in this regard can help promote new forms of horizon work (Petryna, 2022) and novel ways of creating livable futures amid the uncertainties that environmental crises, as moments of excessive plurality, bring with them.

Notes

1 Besides the emergence of a diverse set of specialized function systems, as classical sociological theory explains the rise of modernity, Luhmann places special relevance to the development of the printing press for this, a technology that "revealed how much knowledge already exists simultaneously, so that new selection and classification requirements arose" (Luhmann, 2005, p. 38).
2 Quarantelli and Dynes (1977) referred to this issue by affirming that some studies at the time had already warned about the limited vision that event-based perspectives around disasters constrained. However, they dismissed these claims by affirming that "the implication of this for research, if it is a valid position, has so far been unrecognized" (Quarantelli & Dynes, 1977, p. 24).
3 Despite the novelty of Naomi Klein's notion of the shock doctrine and its uses for political purposes, this argument is not entirely new. Risk and crisis have been long-standing subjects of Marxian and Marxist theory, considered fundamental elements for transcending the limits of capital accumulation during capitalist expansion. As Jane Roitman (2013, p. 73) suggests, "for neo-Marxist analysis, risk is equated with the tendency toward crisis that is endemic to capitalism, being structural and necessary for historical transformation; crisis is due to an erroneous model of compound growth and harbors the missed revolution."

References

Adam, B., & Groves, C. (2007). *Future matters: Action, knowledge, ethics*. Brill.
Agamben, G. (2005). *State of exception*. University of Chicago Press.
Amin, A., & Thrift, N. (2002). *Cities: Reimagining the urban*. Blackwell Publishers.
Anderson, B. (2010). Preemption, precaution, preparedness: Anticipatory action and future geographies. *Progress in Human Geography*, 34(6), 777–798.
Anderson, B., Grove, K., Rickards, L., & Kearnes, M. (2020). Slow emergencies: Temporality and the racialized biopolitics of emergency governance. *Progress in Human Geography*, 44(4), 621–639.
Angell, E. (2014). Assembling disaster: Earthquakes and urban politics in Istanbul. *City*, 18(6), 667–678.
Armiero, M. (2021). *Wasteocene: Stories from the global dump*. Cambridge University Press.
Badiou, A. (2007). *Being and event*. Bloomsbury Academic.
Barad, K. (2007). *Meeting the universe halfway: Quantum physics and the entanglement of matter and meaning*. Duke University Press.
Beck, U. (1992). *Risk society: Towards a new modernity* (1st ed.). SAGE Publications.
Beck, U. (1998). The politics of risk society. In J. Franklin (Ed.), *The politics of risk society* (pp. 8–22). Polity Press.
Birn, A.-E., & Muntaner, C. (2020). Latin American social medicine across borders: South-South cooperation and the making of health solidarity. In E. E. Vasquez, A. G. Perez-Brumer, & R. Parker (Eds.), *Social inequities and contemporary struggles for collective health in Latin America* (pp. 41–58). Routledge.
Blaikie, P., Cannon, T., Davis, I., & Wisner, B. (1994). *At risk: Natural hazards, people's vulnerability and disasters*. Routledge.

Blanchot, M. (1995). *The writing of the disaster*. University of Nebraska Press.
Bode, B. (2001). *No bells to toll: Destruction and creation in the Andes*. iUniverse.
Bond, D. (2013). Governing disaster: The political life of the environment during the BP oil spill. *Cultural Anthropology*, *28*(4), 694–715.
Brown, M., & Goldin, A. (1973). *Collective behavior: A review and reinterpretation of the literature*. Goodyear Publishing.
Callon, M. (1999). The role of lay people in the production and dissemination of scientific knowledge. *Science, Technology & Society*, *4*(1), 81–94.
Callon, M., Lascoumes, P., & Barthe, Y. (2011). *Acting in an uncertain world: An essay on technical democracy* (G. Burchell, Trans.). The MIT Press.
Carr, L. J. (1932). Disaster and the sequence-pattern concept of social change. *American Journal of Sociology*, *38*(2), 207–218.
Collins, H., & Evans, R. (2009). *Rethinking expertise*. University of Chicago Press.
Crutzen, P. J., & Stoermer, E. F. (2000). The 'Anthropocene'. In L. Robin, S. Sörlin, & P. Warde (Eds.), *The future of nature: Documents of global change* (pp. 479–490). Yale University Press.
Davis, T. C. (2007). *Stages of emergency: Cold War nuclear civil defense*. Duke University Press.
Deleuze, G. (1995). *Difference and repetition* (Rev. ed.). Columbia University Press.
Deleuze, G., & Guattari, F. (1987). *A thousand plateaus: Capitalism and schizophrenia*. University of Minnesota Press.
Donovan, A. (2017). Geopower: Reflections on the critical geography of disasters. *Progress in Human Geography*, *41*(1), 44–67.
Douglas, M. (1966). *Purity and danger: An analysis of concepts of pollution and taboo*. Routledge.
Douglas, M. (1994). *Risk and blame: Essays in cultural theory*. Routledge.
Farías, I. (2011). The politics of urban assemblages. *City*, *15*(3–4), 365–374.
Farías, I. (2014a). Planes maestros como cosmogramas. *Revista Pléyade*, *14*, 119–142.
Farías, I. (2014b). Misrecognizing tsunamis: Ontological politics and cosmopolitical challenges in early warning systems. *The Sociological Review*, *62*(6), 61–87.
Farías, I., & Bender, T. (Eds.). (2009). *Urban assemblages: How actor-network theory changes urban studies*. Routledge.
Fortun, K., Knowles, S. G., Choi, V. Y., Jobin, P., Matumoto, M., de la Torre III, P., Liboiron, M., & Murillo, L. F. R. (2016). Researching disaster from an STS perspective. In U. Felt, R. Fouche, C. A. Miller, & L. Smith-Doerr (Eds.), *The handbook of science and technology studies* (4th ed., pp. 1003–1028). The MIT Press.
Fritz, C. (1961). Disasters. In R. K. Merton & R. A. Nisbet (Eds.), *Contemporary social problems* (pp. 651–694). Harcourt, Brace & World.
Giddens, A. (1991). *The consequences of modernity*. Blackwell Publishers.
Guggenheim, M. (2014). Introduction: Disasters as politics—Politics as disasters. *The Sociological Review*, *62*(1), 1–16.
Hagen, R., & Elliott, R. (2021). Disasters, continuity, and the pathological normal. *Sociologica*, *15*(1), 1–9.
Haraway, D. J. (2015). Anthropocene, capitalocene, plantationocene, chthulucene: Making kin. *Environmental Humanities*, *6*, 159–165.
Haraway, D. J. (2018). *Modest_Witness@Second_Millennium.FemaleMan_Meets_OncoMouse*. Routledge.
Hewitt, K. (Ed.). (1983a). *Interpretations of calamity: From the viewpoint of human ecology*. Routledge.
Hewitt, K. (1983b). The idea of calamity in a technocratic age. In K. Hewitt (Ed.), *Interpretations of calamity: From the viewpoint of human ecology* (pp. 3–32). Routledge.
Hoffman, S. M., & Oliver-Smith, A. (1999). Anthropology and the angry earth: An overview. In A. Oliver-Smith & S. M. Hoffman (Eds.), *The angry earth: Disaster in anthropological perspective* (pp. 1–16). Routledge.

Horowitz, A., & Remes, J. A. C. (2021). Introducing critical disaster studies. In J. A. C. Remes & A. Horowitz (Eds.), *Critical disaster studies* (pp. 1–10). University of Pennsylvania Press.

Iengo, I., & Armiero, M. (2023). Toxic bios: Traversing toxic timescapes through corporeal storytelling. In S. M. Muller & M. O. Nielsen (Eds.), *Toxic timescapes: Examining toxicity across time and space* (pp. 187–211). Ohio University Press.

James, W. (Ed.). (2004). *The varieties of religious experience*. Routledge.

Klein, N. (2008). *The shock doctrine: The rise of disaster capitalism*. Picador.

Klinke, I. (2013). Chronopolitics: A conceptual matrix. *Progress in Human Geography*, *37*(5), 673–690.

Law, J. (2004). *After method: Mess in social science research*. Routledge.

Law, J. (2008). Actor network theory and material semiotics. In B. S. Turner (Ed.), *The new Blackwell companion to social theory* (pp. 141–158). Blackwell.

Luhmann, N. (2005). *Risk: A sociological theory*. Aldine Transaction.

Lupton, D. (2013). *Risk* (2nd ed.). Routledge.

Malm, A. (2016). *Fossil capital: The rise of steam power and the roots of global warming*. Verso Books.

Masco, J. (2014). *The theater of operations: National security affect from the Cold War to the War on Terror*. Duke University Press.

McFarlane, C. (2011). Assemblage and critical urbanism. *City*, *15*(2), 204–224.

McGowran, P., & Donovan, A. (2021). Assemblage theory and disaster risk management. *Progress in Human Geography*, *45*(6), 1601–1624.

Michael, M. (2014). Afterword: On the topologies and temporalities of disaster. *The Sociological Review*, *62*(1_suppl), 236–245.

Moore, J. W. (2017). The capitalocene, part I: On the nature and origins of our ecological crisis. *The Journal of Peasant Studies*, *44*(3), 594–630.

Morton, T. (2013). *Hyperobjects: Philosophy and ecology after the end of the world*. Combined Academic Publishing.

Nixon, R. (2011). *Slow violence and the environmentalism of the poor*. Harvard University Press.

O'Keefe, P., Westgate, K., & Wisner, B. (1976). Taking the naturalness out of natural disasters. *Nature*, *260*(5552), 566–567.

Oliver-Smith, A. (1986). *The martyred city: Death and rebirth in the Andes*. University of New Mexico Press.

Petryna, A. (2022). *Horizon work: At the edges of knowledge in an age of runaway climate change*. Princeton University Press.

Prince, S. H. (1920). *Catastrophe and social change: Based upon a sociological study of the Halifax disaster*. Columbia University.

Quarantelli, E. L., & Dynes, R. R. (1977). Response to social crisis and disaster. *Annual Review of Sociology*, *3*, 23–49.

Ray, G. (2005). Reading the Lisbon earthquake: Adorno, Lyotard, and the contemporary sublime. In G. Ray (Ed.), *Terror and the sublime in art and critical theory: From Auschwitz to Hiroshima to September 11* (pp. 19–23). Palgrave Macmillan.

Recuber, T. (2016). *Consuming catastrophe: Mass culture in America's decade of disaster*. Temple University Press.

Rodríguez-Giralt, I., Tirado, F., & Tironi, M. (2014). Disasters as meshworks: Migratory birds and the enlivening of Doñana's toxic spill. *The Sociological Review*, *62*(1_suppl), 38–60.

Roitman, J. (2013). *Anti-crisis*. Duke University Press.

Stehrenberger, C. S. (2020). Annobón 1988: Slow disaster, colonialism, and the Franco dictatorship. *Art in Translation*, *12*(2), 263–287.

Strydom, P. (2002). *Risk, environment, and society: Ongoing debates, current issues, and future prospects*. Open University Press.

Tierney, K. (2014). *The social roots of risk: Producing disasters, promoting resilience.* Stanford Business Books.

Tironi, M. (2014). Atmospheres of indagation: Disasters and the politics of excessiveness. *The Sociological Review, 62*(6), 114–134.

Tironi, M., & Farías, I. (2015). Building a park, immunising life: Environmental management and radical asymmetry. *Geoforum, 66*(11), 167–175.

Torres, F. (2021). *Temporal regimes: Materiality, politics, technology.* Routledge.

Tresch, J. (2007). Technological world-pictures: Cosmic things and cosmograms. *Isis, 98*(1), 84–99.

Usón, T. J., & Stehrenberger, C. S. (2021). A temporal device: Disasters and the articulation of (de)acceleration in and beyond 1970 Ancash's earthquake. *Res Publica. Revista de Historia de las Ideas Políticas, 24*(3), 467–480.

Vigh, H. (2008). Crisis and chronicity: Anthropological perspectives on continuous conflict and decline. *Ethnos, 73*(1), 5–24.

Wallace, A. F. C. (1961). *Culture and personality.* Random House.

Wallis, G. W. (1970). Chronopolitics: The impact of time perspectives on the dynamics of change. *Social Forces, 49*(1), 102–8.

Wambacq, J., & van Tuinen, S. (2017). Interiority in Sloterdijk and Deleuze. *Palgrave Communications, 3*(1), 1–7.

Weil, S. (2005). *An anthology.* Penguin Classics.

Whatmore, S. (2006). Materialist returns: Practising cultural geography in and for a more-than-human world. *Cultural Geographies, 13*(4), 600–609.

White, G. F. (1945). *Human adjustment to floods: A geographical approach to the flood problem in the United States* [PhD dissertation]. University of Chicago.

Williamson, F., & Courtney, C. (2018). Disasters fast and slow: The temporality of hazards in environmental history. *International Review of Environmental History, 4*(2), 5–11.

Wynne, B. (2002). Risk and environment as legitimatory discourses of technology: Reflexivity inside out? *Current Sociology, 50*(3), 459–477.

Wynne, B. (2004). May the sheep safely graze? A reflexive view of the expert-lay knowledge divide. In S. Lash & B. Szerszynski (Eds.), *Risk, environment, and modernity: Towards a new ecology* (pp. 44–83). SAGE Publications.

5   Surviving (in) time

National history and memory as temporal factors underlying ontological and national security

Piotr Gil

1. Introduction

When it comes to scientific reflection on human life, one of the most crucial starting points (although there are others, not less significant, that can be conceived of) concerns its temporality. Human beings, along with the communities they create and in which they live, always exist within the boundaries of a certain period and the specific historical-cultural conditions resulting from it. Also, they tend to devise and strive to bring into being multifaceted visions of a desirable future. In the case of a community such as a nation-state, those visions involve inter alia improving relations with "significant others" that are circumscribed in geopolitical codes (Flint, 2006, pp. 55–56); augmenting national power (Morgenthau, 1949, pp. 80–108) and thus elevating the state's position in the international "pecking order"; increasing the wealth of the society; and, last but not least, ensuring national security. However, individuals and nations neither emerge in the world *ex nihilo* nor do they craft the visions of their future out of thin air. Whatever they do at present or wish for to happen in the future, those things are inexorably rooted in the past. From the sociological perspective, it can be comprehended by referring to the elegant concept of social fact, coined by Durkheim (2007), who claimed that in society there exist *a priori* certain phenomena, institutions, and patterns of behavior that not only precede the existence of individuals (and, arguably, also communities) but also impose themselves on them and force them to comply, referred to as social facts. It is also true that human beings are not only conditioned by such structures but also capable of molding them at their own will, as held by Berger and Luckman (1966) and Giddens (1984). However, the inescapable truth that people's past continues to remain one step ahead of them and, as such, exerts its irresistible influence upon their lives compels them to account for it in their daily *praxis*.

One field of human life in which the pragmatics of temporality are to be accounted for is (striving for) national security. Arguably, the very notion of (any type of) security cannot be fathomed without referring to time, since being (or at least feeling) secure denotes certainty of further existence. In other words, if one is secure, then he or she is expected to go on in time. But before one can go on, it is first necessary to know where (and *when*) he or she comes from. What this means is that for a vision of a safe and secure future to be implemented, its authors must

DOI: 10.4324/9781003537311-6

first realize in what way and by what means their past conditions are present and mark out the most coveted avenues for future development.

In the case of national security, the temporal factors underlying it are twofold. First, some pertain to the "content" of national history, that is, the answers to the following questions: Where and *when* do we come from? What events that have happened throughout our history have made us be us? To what extent does the common past of us and our "significant others" continue to shape our common present (and possibly future, too)? Should we follow the path that has brought us here, or should we look for a different one (and if we do, what will happen to us?)? Second, it is also the meaning of the national history itself that demands further inquiry due to its intrinsic duality or, to make it more precise, the difference between "history" and *historics*. In the words of Ricoeur (2004, pp. 297–298), "the notion of the makeability of history is so tenacious (. . .) because it aims at aligning our twofold relation to history-making history and the making of histories *(faire l'histoire et faire de l'histoire)*." Put simply, the duality of the commonsensically understood notion of history is that it does not only happen but is also made to happen, which is obviously in line with the vision of a nation as an "imagined community" (Anderson, 2016). This effect is achieved through measures such as (politics of) memory, narratives, or discourses, since memory can be comprehended as the (fragments of) history that have been chosen to be remembered. The consequences of that choice for national security are many, complex, and serious.

Regarding national security, the practices of history-making bear profound and significant consequences, both at the level of the former's philosophical tenets and political pragmatics. Political leaders who are responsible for developing and implementing national security policies have to decide not only what is the content of the history of their nation and state, but also what is history as a social phenomenon and thus what should and can be done to ensure national security. Is history a value that should be cherished and preserved? A source of knowledge that can be tapped into and used as an asset? A tool for acquiring political power? Or a formidable force in social reality that brings security in or brings it down? Each one of the above approaches to history yields different consequences for the politics of memory and therefore also for ontological and national security, which can be conducive or pernicious for it.

This chapter seeks to examine the relationship between national history and memory on the one hand and the security of the nation-state on the other, which is done through the prism of the Ontological Security Theory (OST) that is employed in an interpretative and expanded manner to grasp in greater detail the temporal implications of its core tenets. In the first step, the very concept of survival is subject to discussion to unpack its complexity and explain in what ways a social entity such as the nation-state can survive (or fail to do so) and what role in this regard is played by national history. An attempt is made to unveil the significance of preserving (historically established) identity and narratives to ensure national security, with ontological security treated as its cornerstone and *conditio sine qua non*. National identity, being the pillar of the ontological security of the nation-state, is presented in this context as the bridge between the history and memory of a given nation-state and its security. The OST can illuminate, in a sense, the interweaving of time and values that are constitutive and of paramount importance to the nation-state (being not the only human community to which they are applicable though), such as its identity, historical legacy, survival, and growth. Second, attention is turned over to the politics of memory to unpack the reasons and ways of using instrumentally national history and memory to achieve political ends, which are not always congruent with national security principles. This depends on whether such politics aim to cement the memory of national history to use it to bolster national identity and security in the process, or to manipulate it to prevail in political conflicts. What comes to the forefront here is the malleability of history, which can at the same time play the role of an objective phenomenon and be played out. Finally, conclusions are drawn that address the policy of security formation and its temporal determinants, such as national history, myths, and politics of memory. Those conclusions are modeled on the approach to security represented by, respectively, Cox (1986, p. 207) and Booth (2007, pp. 220–221). Cox's famous contention that "theory is always for someone and for some purpose" can be paraphrased into "national history and memory are always (made) for someone and for some purpose." What is important regarding national security is to make sure that neither national history is made, nor the politics of memory, is used toward the ends that could eventually undermine national security rather than bolster it. Booth's emancipatory approach is also applicable to history, as he stresses that because history is made by people, it can also be unmade to free them from the errors of the past, such as, for example, slavery (Booth, 2007, pp. 127, 220). By applying the imperative of emancipation to the interplay between history and security, it is made sure that making histories (rather than *making history*, as per the distinction by Ricoeur) involves accountability for ramifications of the latter.

2. Survival of the nation-state and its temporal essence

As already mentioned, the essence of security is about enduring. This is primarily understood as physical survival as a result of either the absence of threats or the referent object's capability to repel them. Also, being secure involves the prospect of future growth and improvement of the quality of existence. In the words of Booth (2007, p. 39), "Security implies *survival plus*, and for a species with a highly developed consciousness, this means creating space for human self-invention beyond merely existing." In other words, for the nation-state to be secure means not only to be able to last but also to do so in a way that viably guarantees the improvement of the quality of its existence. However, survival means more than that and is not confined (nor it should be) to the purely physical/material dimension of human existence (either individual or communal). For any referent object of security, the nation-state being no exception, to survive means not only to preserve its corporeal body but also the spiritual and cultural Self. This leads to the struggle for the preservation of identity and fulfillment of ontological security needs, with the latter being discussed at length further in this text.

The desire of political leaders to ensure the physical security and survival of their nation-state is essentially self-evident and begs no explanation. If the nation-state is to exist, any threat that challenges the physical integrity of the former and puts in jeopardy the life of the members of the latter must be then eradicated. The case of Poland and its history furnishes a good illustration of the above. After its last partition in the year 1795, the Polish state effectively vanished from the map of Europe. As for its nation, it was also divided and incorporated into the societies of the invaders that occupied Poland. Thus, in terms of Poland's history, a temporal "gap" occurred and lasted for 123 years before the Polish state and nation were restored in the year 1918. Unlike the course of Poland's history, however, the "Polishness" endured and for decades fuelled the resolve of the next generation generations of Poles to resist the efforts by the occupiers to denationalize them. Reversely, one could also conceive of an inverse process wherein a given nation-state or even a civilization continues to exist on the physical plane and yet at the same time it is decaying from within. Some claim that this is the case with contemporary Europe (Murray, 2017). This indicates that, in comparison to national security, it is much more difficult to grasp the essence of ontological security, especially over time and from the perspective of *longue durée*. As far as the latter is concerned, one could argue that security and survival as its fundamental goal are, in a sense, about passing the "test of time." As hinted at above, that test effectively consists of two parts: (1) to survive *de jure* and (2) to survive *de facto*. Survival *de jure* refers to the tangible, that is, physical aspect of existence. The Roman Empire ceased to exist more than 1.5 thousand years ago, but even after its demise, it has continued to exert influence upon Western civilization through its cultural legacy (Beard, 2015, pp. 535–536). Therefore, the passage from Horace's ode *non omnis moriar, multaque pars mei vitabit Libitinam: usque ego postera crescam laude recens* (Naylor, 1922, p. 184) is applicable to ancient Rome. At the other end of the spectrum lies the United Kingdom (UK), once the largest empire ever to exist in the world's history. For the UK, it only took approximately 150 years to lose the status of the world's largest-ever empire, naval superpower, and even its membership in the European Union (EU). Unlike Poland or Germany, it never ceased to exist, nor was it partitioned, but its position in the international system and therefore also its identity (Ferguson, 2003) have changed and dwindled drastically. In this case, the following question arises: Can one claim that the UK has truly "survived" the downfall of its empire?

Thus, one could assume that neither of the two great empires has fully passed the test of time. What is more, those cases shed light on another curious aspect of security that is associated with time. On the one hand, as mentioned before, security denotes the ability to endure in time by overcoming threats. But on the other hand, with time the appraisal of security is likely to change. From the short-term perspective, for the UK to repel the German attempt to invade the British Isles and to emerge victorious from World War II (WWII) was undoubtedly a glorious achievement. In hindsight, though, the end of WWII ultimately sealed the fate of the UK as one of the global powers and reduced its status to the second-tier regional power. This prompts us to focus to a greater extent on the ontological aspect of the survival and security of the nation-state. What is more, attention must also be paid not only to surviving in time but also the time, that is, the influence exerted by frequently staggering temporal processes.

3.   Duration of self and ontological security

Evoking survival, be that in time or (the flow of) time itself, implies the necessity of directing one's attention toward the future. As the history of mankind has shown many times over, nothing that has been created by humans can last indefinitely and there can be no certainty as to what the future holds for us. If not even the greatest of empires managed to cope with adversities and avoid downfall, then it would be smart for every social entity to brace itself for the challenges of the future. What transpires from the above remarks on the decline and downfall of the Roman and the British Empires, as well as of any other historical empire or nation for that matter, is a profoundly disturbing question of the possible inevitability of such a scenario. In other words, it is necessary to establish whether the latter constitutes the outcome of a string of events resulting from certain objective and, so to speak, "technical" factors (such as geopolitical circumstances, economic condition, or demographic vitality) or is it underpinned by an inexorable fate that befalls all human creations alike?

In the opinion of John Glubb (1976, p. 23), a British military officer and scholar, "The life-expectation of a great nation, it appears, commences with a violent, and usually unforeseen, outburst of energy, and ends in a lowering of moral standards, cynicism, pessimism and frivolity." His assessment corresponds with the findings of Toynbee and Koneczny, two renowned researchers and theorists of civilizations. In their seminal works, Toynbee (1987) and Koneczny (1962) arrived at similar conclusions, according to which the demise of civilizations stems from moral and societal decay. A crucial aspect of that process is neglecting and abandoning one's culture and identity, as demonstrated by Gibbon (2017) and Koneczny (2009) in their accounts of the decline and fall of the Roman Empire. That case proves that the national and state security *sensu largo* hinges, among many others, also on the identity-related aspect of security *sensu stricto*. One avenue through which the latter can be approached is OST.

Consequently, what must be adopted here is a holistic approach to security. This approach rules out the perception of ontological security as negligible next to the overarching category of national security (often equated with physical security, namely the absence of military threats to the state's territory and population) and the survival of the nation-state. According to Steele (2008, pp. 2–3), it is just the opposite. For him:

> While physical security is (obviously) important to states, ontological security is more important because its fulfilment affirms a state's self-identity (i.e. it affirms not only its physical existence but primarily how a state sees itself and secondarily how it wants to be seen by others). The nation-states seek

ontological security because they want to maintain consistent self-concepts and the "Self" of states is constituted and maintained through a narrative which gives life to routinized foreign policy actions.

However, what must also be dismissed is a separation between security-as-survival (physical/military security) and security-as-being (ontological security), as pointed out by Mälksoo (2015, p. 224). The main tenet of the OST as presented above by Steele can be interpreted in a way that presents ontological security not as a separate mode of security but as the condition for the survival of the nation-state.

From the temporal perspective, the critical aspect of the above description of the mechanism of seeking ontological security is maintaining self-concepts. This indicates that national identity is not a predetermined, fixed, and immutable attribute of the nation-state and national community, but it is prone to change and, as such, must be upheld by being reenacted in everyday life social practices (McCrone & Bechhofer, 2015). It does not mean that national identity must be wrapped in cotton wool and no changes to it are to be permitted. Evolution is an intrinsic part of human life and culture, especially in the era of globalization, which poses several challenges to national identity (Scholte, 2005, pp. 232–254, 304–306). However, changes leading to disruption of consistency of national identity, or, in other words, national "self-concept," could prove pernicious to it to the point that they would impinge on and undermine national security itself. According to an international survey on people's willingness to fight for their country (WIN/Gallup, 2015), the lowest level of such willingness is found in the countries of Western Europe, where it ranges from 15% (Netherlands) to 38% (Ireland). At the same time, in a number of those countries, the level of citizens' identification (Eurobarometer, 2021) with their nationality ranks among the lowest in the entire EU, examples being Belgium (52% of citizens saying they identify with their nationality), France (63%), or Germany (64%). Those statistics by no means allow us to infer causality, but seen against the backdrop of the cultural as well as political-ideological tendency in Europe to champion a supranational and civilizational identity associated with the EU (Glencross, 2021; Foret & Trino, 2022) they give rise to an array of questions concerning the interplay between the contemporary European *Zeitgeist* and its evolution, the condition of national identities across Europe and the implications for national security.

The evolution of the national identities within Europe and the EU constitutes a serious challenge to the ontological security of the nation-states, understood as their "consistent self-concepts." The inclination to champion the emergence of the European identity was already signaled in the 90s by Wæver (1993, pp. 68–69), who claimed that when it comes to one of the possible avenues for European integration, "It is (. . .) possible that national identities might be revived in terms of non-state, cultural self-defence. This would help to support Europeanization of political structures, through the evolution of a European political identity, while leaving cultural identity at the national level (*Kulturnation* without *Staatnation*)." Together with Kelstrup (1993, p. 76) he also added that "European integration is a matter of identity, but that integration does not necessarily demand close integration of peoples, shared culture, or homogeneity. It is first a political body that is needed, a political Europe. (. . .) What is needed is a development of political identity." Despite the explicit reassurance that a European superstate is not the ultimate goal of European integration (Kelstrup, 1993, p. 76), the aforementioned split of identity into the national (indeed parochial), cultural, and the European political ones is undoubtedly at odds with the maintenance of the "consistent self-concept" of the nation-state. However, in this context, a puzzle is revealed that confounds the clarity of the temporal dimension of ontological security. As mentioned before, its cornerstone is the duration of the nation-state as a referent object of ontological security. For that object to survive on the physical plane of existence, it is crucial to maintain its "consistent self-concept" that has been established through the course of its history. The rationale for that is, for example, Buzan's (2016, pp. 38, 95, 109, 111) contention that lack of coherence of identity is what undermines societal security and renders states weak. In the face of the unstoppable advance of the European *Zeitgeist*, though, it could be argued that time, in a sense, overrides the intrinsic desire to maintain the national Self intact. If evolution and progress are indeed inscribed in the very nature of Europe and its nations and, as such, inescapable, then it is safe to assume that the strive for the fulfillment of national ontological security needs must allow for the middle ground between preservation and change of national identity.

The outlined challenge concerning the transformation of nation-states and national identities within the EU evolving into a supranational entity sheds light on another aspect of ontological security, which also bears far-reaching implications for the intricate interplay between time, identity, and security. According to Giddens (1991, p. 47), the preservation of ontological security consists in a subject's ability to "bracket out" what he termed "fundamental questions," concerning existence and being, finitude and human life, relations, and autobiography. Among those, it is the one concerning finitude that enables us to realize ontological security does not only cover the "here and now" and the "back then," but also extends to what may loom large in the future, from which the subject of ontological security is shielded as long as the latter remains firm. Ejdus (2020), building upon Chernobrov (2019), lays out a convincing theoretical concept of critical situations, in which subjects of ontological security cannot uphold it due to their inability to bracket out the existential questions and find relevant answers to them. When ontological insecurity transforms into opposition, namely ontological insecurity, uncertainty and anxiety come to the surface, casting a shadow of doubt over the future (Chernobrov, 2019, pp. 33–45; Ejdus, 2020, pp. 12–25). As much as the ontological security needs of an individual or any social entity as well as their pursuit are conservative by nature and oriented toward the past, the readiness to confront the potential threats of the future must be in place to guarantee not only the ontological, but also the all-encompassing security.

Nonetheless, even if the nation-state must embrace the necessity of the pursuit of the future and do its best to keep up with progress taking place in its international environment to secure for itself the most advantageous conditions for prosperity and growth, it cannot disregard and abandon its past as it were no longer relevant and meaningful. That is for at least two main reasons. First, the relevance of national history stems from its impact on the pragmatics of state politics. National history serves as a point of reference, and as such, it plays a part in defining the path for the nation-state to follow, which can be either convergent or divergent from what was done in the past. Also, it makes a valuable source of factual knowledge, which helps avoid the errors of the past and make better-informed decisions. Second, commemoration of national history and saving it from oblivion constitutes a moral duty and imperative for political leaders and citizens alike. This concerns preserving the memory of the most significant historical events and figures, ancestors, myths and legends, customs, and traditions, as well as symbols and values. A failure to do so impedes upholding national identity and ensuring the ontological security of the nation-state by triggering the feeling of guilt, defined by Steele (2008, p. 40) as "a transgression over a recognized principle/law/norm of a community." In terms of ontological security, it should be emphasized that neglecting the memory of national history does not only undermine national identity, that is, national "self-concept" by letting its constituents away, but it also severs the historical continuity of a national community by shutting its ancestors off. Interestingly, this adds a third aspect of the nation-state and the national community that forms it being endangered. As already mentioned, it is threatened by an act of physical aggression, decay of its national identity/self-concept, or severance of the ties between generations.

Importantly, the aforementioned aspects of the history and security of the nation-state do not seem to be mutually separate or incompatible. On the contrary, their intermingling is fairly evident. A striking illustration of that phenomenon is the commemoration of the Warsaw Uprising, an event that is undoubtedly not only among the most tragic ones throughout the entire Polish history but also one that continues to be vastly impactful for contemporary Poland. On the grounds of political conduct, the Uprising embodies the perennial conflict between Polish inclination to political romanticism (though the critics of the former would rather label it as a penchant for martyrology) on the one hand and the lack of the sense of political realism on the other (Tumolska, 2016, pp. 61–75; Gawin, n.d.). Despite being often considered a grave error that led to the destruction of Warsaw and the death of thousands of Polish citizens, it is at the same time treated as a source of patriotic ethos and moral values that fuelled the resolve of Polish democratic opposition during the communist period and eventually gave rise to the Solidarity movement. Some even go as far as to say that without the Warsaw Uprising, the Solidarity movement would not have come into being, and thus Poland would not have regained its independence. In the words of the Polish historian M. Wójciuk who works at the Warsaw Uprising Museum, "Without the Uprising, without the ethos that the Uprising carried (. . .), without the heroism, the will to fight, devotion and solidarity between people, the spirit that enabled people to come together, we would have probably not been able to survive communism as society" (Wójciuk, 2022) (author's translation).

This opinion supports the argument that the appraisal of events that make up national history is not only determined by those events' congruence with the precepts of political realism, out of which survival is "a prerequisite to achieving any goals that states may have" (Waltz, 2010, p. 91) but also by their social-cultural significance that can only manifest itself fully with time. Even though it does not seem feasible to test the validity of the above statement in terms of causality, it is however possible to point to unobvious, however palpable, ways in which the memory of tragic events such as the Warsaw Uprising can contribute to establishing contemporary ontological and national security. Essentially, the narrative concerning the lasting impact of the ethos of the Uprising upon Polish national identity can be considered what Somers and Gibson (1994, p. 61) termed "ontological narratives." Those narratives, the authors claim, "are the stories that social actors use to make sense of—indeed, to act in—their lives. Ontological narratives are used to define who we are; this in turn is a precondition for knowing what to do." It should be stressed that the ability to act—agency—lies at the heart of ontological security (Mitzen, 2006, pp. 342, 344–346). Subjects of it do not only strive to achieve it to avoid psychological discomfort but also to acquire the capability of acting and to satisfy their needs. In other words, ontological narratives are not constructed and deployed to cater to one's fancifulness, but this is done for purposes that are by all means pragmatic. In the words of Innes and Steele (2014, p. 19), "Memory proves central to ontological security. It is used, and even manipulated, to create the basis for action." The aspect of manipulation of national memory will be discussed in detail further in this text. At this point, what must be done is to focus on how and to what effect national memory and ontological security can be manipulated.

By so doing, yet another curious ambiguity is revealed, one that results from the clash between (the passing of) time and the struggle for the security of the national community. To begin with, Somers and Gibson (1994, p. 30) emphasize the temporal aspect of ontological narrative, which "embeds identities in time." This constitutes a crucial (*nomen omen*) memento that points to the aforementioned fact that even the necessity to maintain ontological security that is based on consistency of self-concept cannot be reduced to a siege mentality and must be harmonized with the inevitable passing of time. Even so, ontological narratives can help strengthen ontological and national security by opposing not only the Wheel of Time itself but also the inexorability of progress that is driven by the former (which, in turn, very often winds up crushing the particular desire of the nation-state to preserve its identity and security). As aptly remarked by Deacon (2023, p. 4), "Narratives of national past can provide a sense of collective belonging through which individuals are connected to a history greater than themselves, thereby seeking a secure sense of national Self in the present." From the theoretical perspective of ontological security of the nation-state, this is fundamental as it accentuates the duality of the very notion of self-concept, the two inseparable aspects of which are identity and "We-ness." In other words, there can be no collective identity (be it national or any other) unless there is a deeply embedded, firm, and stable tie between the contemporaries and their predecessors. Ultimately, this facilitates the process of overcoming the stumbling block of tragic events of national history that, from the viewpoint of political realism, should be considered burdens rather than assets.

It seems that what makes it possible is the very mechanism of remembering. As long as there is the collective "We" that (chooses to) remember the common past (made of victories and defeats, successes, and errors alike), the national community is set to endure, strengthening national security in the process. However, it is also worth emphasizing at this point that the errors of the past are not the only thing that must be overcome. Perhaps even more important than that is cementing the feeling of "We-ness," that is, the existence of a (national) community that is on the one hand (to a certain extent) doomed to partake in the vicious circle of Sisyphean Labor of upholding the "consistency of its self-concept," but on the other hand one that is also capable of breaking free from the confines of the flow of time to make its destiny. This can only be achieved by a national community making a resilient effort to be the subject rather than the object against the flow of time by consciously taking control of its national memory. To do so mean to possess what can be termed temporal agency, which is the ability to control one's existence throughout time.

4. National memory, the politics of memory and mnemonical security

"The core meaning of any individual or group identity, namely, a sense of sameness over time and space, is sustained by remembering; and what is remembered is defined by the assumed identity"—these words by J. R. Gillis (1994, p. 3) can be adopted as the departure point for the reflection on the mutual relation between identity and memory, as well as the relation between those and ontological and national security. At this point, it can be assumed that both are mutually constitutive, but the goal of the said reflection is not only to shed light on their relation but also on the peculiarity of how they can either contribute to the overarching national security or diminish it.

Memory, as succinctly put by Subotic (2020, p. 50), "is critical to ontological security." It is so because "Memories serve as temporal orientation devices that make the past meaningful by providing a sense of where 'we' come from and what 'we' have been through" (Berenskoetter, 2012, p. 270). In other words, national identity comprises as much its cultural (values, traditions, customs, artworks, etc.) as temporal constituents (such as, e.g., significant and foundational historical periods, events, and figures). One of the latter, according to Kołakowski (1995, p. 48), is memory. As he forcibly states, "No nation can last without being aware that its contemporary existence is the extension of the one in the past" (Kołakowski, 1995, p. 49, author's translation), which points to the aforementioned societal aspect of the continuity of national existence, which is on the one physical and tangible (contemporaries as heirs to their predecessors) and on the other mediated by the more elusive factor of national memory.

According to Gustafsson (2014, p. 73), "Collective memory provides group members with a feeling of sameness and sense of who they are—i.e., with ontological security." That *sameness*, described by Jacobson-Widding (1983, pp. 13, 24, 35) as the dimension of identity vis-à-vis the second one, namely *distinctiveness*, concerns those elements of identity that knit the members of a community together rather than those that set them apart from different ones. It is therefore legitimate to ask (as mentioned before) not only where, but also *when* "We" come from as a national community. That is to say, what have been the most important periods of our national history, and to what extent have they (and/or still do) shaped our contemporary national identity? How much does the heyday of the British imperial period continue to shape British culture and direct its foreign policy? Are the experiences of partitions and communist regimes the burdens that still hunt Polish society and political elites?

If the answers to such questions imply that the historical legacy of a given nation constitutes a crucial factor in shaping that nation's identity as well as security and foreign policy, then it becomes clear that the national memory is to be defended for the sake of upholding national identity and thus ensuring ontological and national security. As pointed out by Mälksoo (2015, p. 224), "Deconstructing the central historical backbone of the self could seriously disrupt and destabilize the respective identity and hamper its agency as an actor in international affairs." At the same time, however, she also warns against securitization of national memory, which may bring about pernicious consequences such as raising new security dilemmas (Mälksoo, 2015, p. 222) or introducing the undesirable logic of security that is intrinsic in the mechanism of securitization, thereby turning national memory into a source of insecurity rather than security (on the phenomenon of security, its logic and mechanics, especially in the context of the process of securitization see i.e., McDonald, 2008; Balzacq, Léonard, Ruzicka, 2016; Aradau, 2004; Roe, 2012; Williams, 2003).

What makes this outcome possible is constructability as the attribute underlying the existence of a nation, its history and memory, as well as security alike, as they are all, essentially, "what we make of them" (Wendt, 1992). Unfortunately, this leads to politicians being tempted to manipulate national identity to perpetuate enmities and conflicts, both external and domestic, that legitimize the power they wield so that they can retain it, cement it, and also extend it. This mechanism of deliberately (re)kindling identity- and memory-based conflicts to the effect of prevailing in power struggles has been described at length by Campbell (1998). Consequently, there is no reason to think that national memory is exempt from the role of serving as a tool in what Stone (2012) terms "memory wars" because such wars are instrumental in the process of fulfilling the ontological needs of the states involved (Mälksoo, 2015, p. 225). Depending on the political agenda, tapping into the reservoir of national history and memory allows us to discursively frame the wars, conflicts, and enmities of the past as already resolved or, on the contrary, still lingering and in need of being dealt with. As an illustration of how such an approach can serve, the current relationship between France and Germany has been stripped of the resentment since France perceives Germany not as a former mortal enemy and occupant but as the key partner in European politics. Such a practice is to be considered not the politics of memory, but rather the *politics of forgetting*, being also a crucial method in the construction of national identity and security. As far as their interplay is concerned, it must be stressed that to construct a desirable biographical narrative that not only involves all the elements of national identity that are indispensable for ensuring a nation's spiritual survival but is also devoid of unwanted and pernicious feelings of shame and guilt (Steele, 2008), the balance must be struck between what is to be included and what should be left out of national memory (Koonz, 1994).

On the other hand, the relationship between South Korea and Japan has been troubled for decades following the Japanese occupation of Korea between 1910 and 1945 (though recently, in the face of the prospect of China becoming the regional hegemon and imposing its dominance in the process, a rapprochement seems to be to taking shape). What is more, the conflicts referred to above, which can be petrified through the use of memory, can take the form not of a "hot" one but of a more deeply embedded geopolitical and/or civilizational cleavage. An example of that can be the fissure between Western and Eastern Europe (as well as Central Eastern Europe—for more information on the criteria of distinguishing those and other parts of Europe see Moczulski, 2019, pp. 300–317; Halecki, 1994), whose roots can be dated back to the division of the Roman Empire in 285 CE. That fissure, as pointed out by Kuus (2007) and Krasnodębska (2021), bears the mark of geopolitical othering and stigmatization, which is challenged by Sălăjan (2020, p. 74) as unjustified considering the process of "memory boom" that can be observed in Western Europe as well. In (critical) geopolitical terms, constructing and maintaining such breakups amounts to what is termed "chronopolitics" (the politics of time), in a sense the alter ego of geopolitics, which is defined by Klinke (2012, p. 685) as "discursive structure that operates inside (. . .) geopolitical narratives."

The above cases, by embedding the problematique of memory politics in the geopolitical context, add to the image of the overarching category of national security being an "ambiguous symbol" (Wolfers, 1952). It has already been emphasized that on the grounds of the OST, states can pursue actions that might bolster their ontological security (that is to say, the security of their identity, that is, self-concept) and at the same time pose a direct threat to their "traditional security," as convincingly demonstrated by Steele (2008, pp. 94–113) based on the example of Belgian stance toward German threat in 1914. Moreover, within the confines of the OST pursuing conflictual relations by states despite their apparent irrationality is considered justified and legitimate because they serve to cement self-concepts as well as sustain the routines (Mitzen, 2006, pp. 346–347, 352–354) and autobiographical narratives that create the former, it appears yet again that time plays an important role of an intervening variable in devising security and foreign policy. It is so because the flow of time brings about not only changes of the essence of the relation between two particular social entities, such as, for example, the nation-states, but more importantly, changes in the international environment in which such a relation is embedded. It is particularly striking in the context of ongoing hegemonic competition between the United States and China, which has rent asunder the fabric of the post-Cold War international order, prompting its members to reevaluate their geopolitical codes and therefore, also their self-concepts, against the temporal determinants of their relations with "significant others." In other words, the profound shifts in the international order challenge the nation-states' ontological security by raising fundamental questions concerning their self-concepts.

An example of that is found in the bosom of the Western civilization, whose supremacy has been openly questioned by the non-Western powers that are aligning themselves with one another to become strong enough to stand up to the West, which is illustrated, for instance, by the continuous expansion of the BRICS format. The imminent clash of civilizations, prophesied by Huntington (1996), has induced very curious developments among the members of the geopolitical West, especially the Western European states. With the position of the United States weakening and its hegemonic status declining, one can observe undertakings by the aforementioned states that are aimed at a form of "decoupling" and embarking on more independent foreign policy to leverage one's status in the international order. When those efforts target rapprochement with non-Western states that do not seem to be benevolent toward the West to say the least (that is, for instance, China and Russia), the legitimacy of such undertakings becomes questionable from the viewpoint of not only national but also ontological security, of which civilizational identity is also constitutive.

To gain a better insight into this matter, worth considering is (geo)political conduct of France. Based on the knowledge of that country's history of geostrategic preferences, its affinity toward Russia and skepticism of America are hardly surprising. However, what is indeed surprising is France's close collaboration with Germany, despite a long history of conflicts and enmity (Kazanecki, 2012). One could argue that close cooperation with Germany and advances toward China are simply tantamount to *Realpolitik* that informs French foreign policy strategy and initiatives. However, both the historical hardships (a euphemism in light of the common French-German history that used to be fraught with wars and conflicts) and the present divergences (economic-political conquest of Africa by China and, most recently, even more so by Russia) make this *status quo* ambiguous and provide arguments to support the thesis that the case under consideration constitutes an example of ontological security that needs shifting with time.

This is in line with the perception of national identity represented by McSweeney (1999, p. 167), who claimed that "We can be led to perceive ourselves differently— to choose a different position on the continuum of identities—by the opportunities which may be offered to satisfy new interests." Ironically, to invoke the famous passage by Wendt yet again, it could be argued that (the notion of) consistency of self-concepts is what the nation-states make of it. In other words, it is apparently up to them to decide when their national identities are to remain intact and to be defended at all costs or when it pays to alter them deliberately and purposely to achieve goals and fulfill interests that would otherwise remain unachievable and unfulfillable. As a result, what can be and frequently is subject to deliberate change is not only national identity but also national memory.

Delving into the matter of manipulating national identity and memory (and ontological security in the process) must go deeper and further than this. What is important (ironically again) is not to overlook the ontological dimension of national identity and national memory, which is important not only for the sake of adequate understanding of the nature of that memory but also for ensuring national security. As per the words of warning by Kłoskowska (2005, p. 99),

"Nation is not a psychological unit, to which as a whole one can ascribe cognitive, emotional and evaluative functions" (author's translation). This reminds us that, at least in democratic countries, for any designs that involve fiddling with national identity and memory toward political ends, citizens' perception and approach to the former must be taken into account, especially given the possibility of substantial discrepancies between the state-level and the individual-level memory (Rumelili, 2020). One way to do it is to examine how national identity and memory are reproduced by citizens through their everyday social practices (McCrone & Bechhofer, 2015) to become essentially "banal" (Billig, 1995). However, the very term "social practices" indicates that, in a sense, the sociological fly must be added to the so far predominantly political ointment to bridge the gap between the state-level and the individual-level enactment of collective memory. To do so, it is worth adducing the remarks by Bachleitner (2021, p. 29), who explicates that

> Collective memory means that individuals remember as social beings: that is, within social frames. With this in mind, sociologists practically relocated the past into the present (political) space. To research memory, whether that of individuals or collectives, scholars from then on resorted to the contemporary social frames that reflect memory. For countries, these are public symbols, official representations, rituals, speeches and—importantly for our assumptions—also their policy choices and state behaviour.

As far as the social context (i.e., "frames") is concerned, its mediating functioning should be conceived of in a dualistic manner, which happens to be the prevailing theme in the reflections so far. First, as mentioned before, this context is simultaneously constitutive of and constituted by social actors. A part of this process is represented by political discursive that can be used instrumentally to mold any element of what is known as the noosphere, that is, the collective consciousness (Teilhard de Chardin, 2008), including national identity and memory (Wodak et al., 2009). This confirms that national memory, as indicated by Bachleitner (2021, p. 30) "cannot be fixed as a static story about the 'self in history,' but rather is a 'constitutive narrative' that, through remembering, literally re-members (that is to say, constitutes) a group and as such also its identity."

In this vein, one could argue that it is more accurate to speak of (the process of) *memory-ing* rather than of memory as such. Second, the very nature of memory (-*ing*) is one of a process rather than an a priori phenomenon involves the factor of time, which in this context does not refer to the act of reaching out back to the past to recall the events that laid the foundation of a given nation and its identity and to attempt to etch them into that nation's national memory, Instead, it concerns the ensemble of the macro-sociological process that undermine the very concepts of nation-statism and nation-ness as they dissolve peoples attachment and appreciation of the nation-state and nation as a type of community. This is reflected in substitute ideas and identities, such as post-nationalism (Breen and O'Neill, 2010; Wickham, 2021) and cosmopolitism (Booth, 2007).

As far as the interplay between nation and the nation-state, nation identity and memory, as well as ontological security and national security on the one hand and the politics of memory and discursive (re)construction of the entire social reality (covering, but not being limited to, national memory or identity) on the other, is concerned, it is a meta-process comprising innumerable subprocesses that take place on many different levels of social reality, which are in turn characterized by different temporal dynamics. Crucially, to grasp this complexity and intricacy, it is necessary to employ meta-level reasoning. Regarding national memory and its interrelation with security, two levels of analysis can be distinguished.

On the one hand, one could inquire into the very content of national memory and try to determine what elements of it are indispensable for the preservation of consistent self-concept and thus ensuring ontological security. In the case of Germany and its national memory, one could ponder the contemporary relevance of remembering positive (unification of Germany in 1871 and 1991) or negative (the Treaty of Versailles in 1919 or occupation and partitioning of Germany in 1945 and 1949) facts from its history. It could be determined whether and why those and/or other events from Germany's history bear relevance for the national security of contemporary Germany and, upon an affirmative conclusion, how they should be memorized.

On the other hand, though, subject to reflection and concrete actions can be the very concept of (national) *memory-ing*, especially in light of the processes (brought about by the Wheel of Time, propelled by, as many claims, the inexorable *Zeitgeist*) leading to undermining the significance of the nation-state and nation-ness. For, as could be inquired, does it still make sense to uphold the *memory of memory-ing*? That is to say, it is worth considering whether it matters or not to pay attention to *memory-ing* the elements of vernacular German culture, identity, and history in the face of the superior process of forming a new European civilizational polity and universalist identity. What is more, would not holding onto such vernacular identity and memory amount to perverting the new memory and identity of a higher order, thereby posing a threat to the emerging new entity in the form of Europe—as—a civilization? In this context, the very concept of national security is thrown out the window, and the referent object of ontological security is elevated from the national onto the supranational level, both of which are essentially at odds with one another. Noteworthily, what is being considered here is the fact that time (*nomen omen*), at the same time, is used by people to define what counts as a legitimate referent object of ontological security (which, on the meta-level, is no longer the security of a nation, but of a superior entity) and pushes people to rethink the very ontology and essence of fundamental concepts of (relevant) social entities, their security, identity, and memory.

By this point, it has at the very least been established that what daily appears to be of paramount importance and value, namely the preservation of national identity, memory, and security, amounts to but a scrap of social reality thrown against an overwhelming vortex of social and temporal forces that may (and do) drive and hinder, reinforce and undermine, as well as safeguard and threaten them. Those effects depend on those wielding political power that are capable of enacting their agenda the way they see fit, but not less so on the formidable processes of social and civilizational change, taking place working on the basis of the logic of longue durée, that superimpose themselves upon the undertakings by people on a much shorter temporal scale. Ultimately, regarding the security of the nation-state and national community (as well as of individuals and all other conceivable types of human communities), the workings of time can be likened to those of water.

On the one hand (the flow of), time can be benign and allow itself to be used in ways that people can benefit from. But on the other hand, it can also be a fearsome and unstoppable force that wreaks havoc on the world that people live in. That is why it must be borne in mind that for people to survive, it means always not only surviving in time but also surviving time itself.

At this point it has become evident that to achieve that end, however, it is insufficient to rely on the politics of memory alone. Given the fragility of human creations and the fact that time itself, as it passes, does exert adverse effects upon those creations and human beings themselves, the future must not merely be anticipated and awaited, but also designed and implemented through an undertaking referred to as "the politics of the future," which amounts to treating the future as a subject of consciously and deliberately implemented politics (Wenger et al., 2020; Berten & Kranke, 2022; White, 2024; Mazé, 2019). As far as the latter is concerned, by its very nature it is associated with projecting people's hopes and desires as well as anxieties and fears onto the future, which is not meant to be awaited passively but, on the contrary, bent to people's will and aligned with their designs. It is especially important from the perspective of national security, given the unpredictability and unceasing flux of the globalized world, an unforgiving reality in which nation-states must be able to maneuver deftly and steer clear of threats. Because national security, as indicated in this chapter, is underpinned by national identity and ontological security needs, statesmen face the challenging task of, on the one hand, reconciling the necessity to preserve the identity and ensure the said needs of their people and state; and, on the other, pursuing states' policies in a way that involves flexibility sufficient to adjust national identity to the needs that are to be obtained and counter (more or less likely) future threats that are feared.

5. Conclusion

As per the quoted words by Wolfers, national security is "an ambiguous symbol." So too, as it appears, is time. Regarding establishing ontological and national security, time takes many forms, all of which bear different meanings and exert different types of influence on the identity and security of the nation and the nation-state. Those forms include the substance of national identity and memory, a tool capable of yielding power to political leaders and other social actors, a dimension of the world in which social life is embedded, and a powerful force that bends people and their creations to the direction in which it is heading. Therefore, it cannot be reduced to a single factor that is easily mastered by people to their ends. On the contrary, more often than many realize, our designs either fall victim to it or are brought to existence by it rather than by our own will. What is more, the implacable impact of (the flow of) time can either bring harmony into people's lives and help them achieve the much-desired security or it may bring chaos into it and put it in jeopardy. Therefore, more often than not, it is worth thinking of time as a constant and multifaceted challenge that is not always within people's reach to overcome, rather than yet another "factor" or "variable" that is mechanically "accounted for" in the process of determining the interests, setting up the goals and selecting the methods within a vision of the future that is meant to be fulfilled by not only the nation-states, its leaders and citizens, but also any other social entity. Sometimes we, as human beings, succeed in bending time to our will and using it to our ends. But for the sake of our security and well-being, it is crucial to make an effort to become more mindful of situations in which those are not the people that bend time to their will, but it is the time that does it to them. This is why the security and survival of nation-states (and, from a much broader perspective, of people in general) must always be pursued not only through time but also against it.

Considering the above, an adequate politics of national identity, memory, and security is supposed to be formulated in a way that is informed by the intricacies of the interplay between time, identity, memory, and security. Such politics must account for the multiformness of time as well as its meta-level impact on human affairs. This is meant to prevent scenarios in which history and memory, being, in a sense, "by-products" of (the flow of) time, are used instrumentally in a way that provokes conflicts as well as emancipates human beings from constraints imposed on them by time. One way or another, though, it must be borne in mind that the temporal dimension of human efforts to achieve security must at the same time be rooted in history and directed to the future. For it is our past that gives us the strength to cope with the future, and it is the future that constitutes the extension of the past and the present, as well as the ultimate destination for those who strive to cultivate their past.

Without aiming at a desired future and employing national history and memory as means to that end, our collective past is but a collection of artifacts that are only fit for the role of museum exhibits. As such, it is not without a value of some sort but cannot be expected to help people cope with a world that is ever getting more complex and unfathomable and whose future is ridden with ominous threats that we need to either avoid or conquer to survive (in) time.

References

Anderson, B. (2016). *Imagined communities: Reflections on the origin and spread of nationalism*. Verso.

Aradau, C. (2004). Security and the democratic scene: Desecuritization and emancipation. *Journal of International Relations and Development, 7*(4), 388–413.

Bachleitner, K. (2021). Ontological security as temporal security? The role of 'significant historical others' in world politics. *International Relations, 37*(1), 25–47.

Balzacq, T., Léonard, S., & Ruzicka, J. (2016). 'Securitization' revisited: Theory and cases. *International Relations, 30*(4), 494–531.

Beard, M. (2015). *SPQR: A history of ancient Rome*. Profile Books.

Berenskoetter, F. (2012). Parameters of national biography. *European Journal of International Relations*, *20*(1), 262–288.

Berger, P. L., & Luckmann, T. (1966). *The social construction of reality: A treatise in the sociology of knowledge*. Penguin Books.

Berten, J., & Kranke, M. (2022). Anticipatory global governance: International organisations and the politics of the future. *Global Society*, *36*(2), 155–169.

Billig, M. (1995). *Banal nationalism*. Sage.

Booth, K. (2007). *Theory of world security*. Cambridge University Press.

Breen, K., & O'Neill, S. (2010). *After the nation? Critical reflections on nationalism and postnationalism*. Palgrave Macmillan.

Buzan, B. (2016). *People, states and fear: An agenda for international security studies in the post-Cold War era*. ECPR Press.

Campbell, D. (1998). *Writing security: United States foreign policy and the politics of identity*. University of Minnesota Press.

Chernobrov, D. (2019). *Public perception of international crises: Identity, ontological security, and self-affirmation*. Rowman & Littlefield.

Cox, R. W. (1986). Social forces, states, and world orders: Beyond international relations theory. In R. O. Keohane (Ed.), *Neorealism and its critics* (pp. 204–254). Columbia University Press.

Deacon, Ch. (2023). Perpetual ontological crisis: National division, enduring anxieties and South Korea's discursive relationship with Japan. *European Journal of International Relations*, 1–25.

Durkheim, E. (2007). *Zasady metody socjologicznej*. Wydawnictwo Naukowe PWN.

Ejdus, F. (2020). *Crisis and ontological insecurity: Serbia's anxiety over Kosovo's secession*. Palgrave.

Eurobarometer. (2021). *Values and identities of EU citizens*. European Union. Retrieved August 30, 2023, from https://europa.eu/eurobarometer/surveys/detail/2230

Ferguson, N. (2003). *Empire: How Britain made the modern world*. Penguin Books.

Flint, C. (2006). *Introduction to geopolitics*. Routledge.

Foret, F., & Trino, N. (2022). The 'European way of life,' a new narrative for the EU? Institutions' vs citizens' view. *European Politics and Society*, *24*(1), 1–18.

Gawin, D. (n.d.). *Powstanie Warszawskie a powojenne spory o kształt polskiego patriotyzmu*. Ośrodek Myśli Politycznej. Polskie Tradycje Intelektualne. Retrieved August 30, 2023, from http://www.polskietradycje.pl/artykuly/widok/381

Gibbon, E. (2017). *Zmierzch Cesarstwa Rzymskiego, Upadek Cesarstwa Rzymskiego na Zachodzie*. Państwowy Instytut Wydawniczy.

Giddens, A. (1984). *The constitution of society: Outline of the theory of structuration*. University of California Press.

Giddens, A. (1991). *Modernity and self-identity: Self and society in the late modern age*. Stanford University Press.

Gillis, J. R. (1994). Memory and identity: The history of a relationship. In J. R. Gillis (Ed.), *Commemorations: The politics of national identity* (pp. 3–24). Princeton University Press.

Glencross, A. (2021). The EU and the temptation to become a civilizational state. *European Foreign Affairs Review*, *26*(2), 331–350.

Glubb, J. (1976). *The fate of empires and search for survival*. William Blackwood & Sons Ltd.

Gustafsson, K. (2014). Memory politics and ontological security in Sino-Japanese relations. *Asian Studies Review*, *38*(1), 71–86.

Halecki, O. (1994). *Historia Europy—jej granice i podziały*. Instytut Europy Środkowo-Wschodniej.

Huntington, S. P. (1996). *The clash of civilizations and the remaking of world order*. Simon & Schuster.

Innes, A. J., & Steele, B. J. (2014). Memory, trauma, and ontological security. In E. Resende & D. Budryte (Eds.), *Memory and trauma in international relations: Theories, cases, and debates* (pp. 15–29). Routledge.

International Politics. (2015). *WIN/Gallup International's global survey shows three in five willing to fight for their country*. Gallup International. Retrieved August 30, 2023, from https://www.gallup-international.bg/en/33483/win-gallup-internationals-global-survey-shows-three-in-five-willing-to-fight-for-their-country/

Jacobson-Widding, A. (1983). Introduction. In A. Jacobson-Widding (Ed.), *Identity: Personal and socio-cultural. A symposium* (pp. 13–34). Almqvist & Wiksell International.

Kazanecki, W. (2012). *Współczesna francuska myśl geopolityczna: Główne tendencje i ich reprezentanci*. Adam Marszałek.

Klinke, I. (2012). Chronopolitics: A conceptual matrix. *Progress in Human Geography*, *37*(5), 675–690.

Kłoskowska, A. (2005). *Kultury narodowe u korzeni*. Wydawnictwo Naukowe PWN.

Kołakowski, L. (1995). O tożsamości zbiorowej. In K. Michalski (Ed.), *Tożsamość w czasach zmiany. Rozmowy w Castel Gandolfo* (pp. 44–55). Wydawnictwo Znak.

Koneczny, F. (1962). *On the plurality of civilisations*. Polonica Publications.

Koneczny, F. (2009). *Cywilizacja bizantyńska*. Dom Wydawniczy Ostoja.

Koonz, C. (1994). Between memory and oblivion: Concentration camps in German memory. In J. R. Gillis (Ed.), *Commemorations: The politics of national identity* (pp. 258–280). Princeton University Press.

Krasnodębska, M. (2021). *Politics of stigmatization: Poland as a 'latecomer' in the European Union*. Palgrave Macmillan.

Kuus, M. (2007). *Geopolitics reframed: Security and identity in Europe's Eastern enlargement*. Palgrave Macmillan.

Mazé, R. (2019). Politics of designing visions of the future. *Journal of Future Studies*, *23*(3), 23–38.

Mälksoo, M. (2015). 'Memory must be defended': Beyond the politics of mnemonical security. *Security Dialogue*, *46*(3), 221–237.

McCrone, D., & Bechhofer, F. (2015). *Understanding national identity*. Cambridge University Press.

McDonald, M. (2008). Securitization and the construction of security. *European Journal of International Relations*, *14*(4), 563–587.

McSweeney, B. (1999). *Security, identity and interests: A sociology of international relations*. Cambridge University Press.

Mitzen, J. (2006). Ontological security in world politics: State identity and the security dilemma. *European Journal of International Relations*, *12*(3), 341–370.

Moczulski, L. (2019). *Geopolityka: Potęga w czasie i przestrzeni*. Zona Zero.

Morgenthau, H. J. (1949). *Politics among nations: The struggle for power and peace*. Alfred A. Knopf.

Murray, D. (2017). *The strange death of Europe*. Bloomsbury Publishing.

Naylor, H. D. (1922). *Horace Odes and Epodes: A study in poetic word-order*. Cambridge University Press.

Ricoeur, P. (2004). *Memory, history, forgetting*. University of Chicago Press.

Roe, P. (2012). Is securitization a 'negative' concept? Revisiting the normative debate over normal versus extraordinary politics. *Security Dialogue*, *43*(4), 249–266.

Rumelili, B. (2020). Breaking with Europe's pasts: Memory, reconciliation, and ontological (in)security. In C. Kinnvall, I. Manners, & J. Mitzen (Eds.), *Ontological insecurity in the European Union* (pp. 32–47). Routledge.

Sălăjan, L. C. (2020). The political psychologies of "Eastern" and "Western" Europe: Insights from ontological security. *Eurolimes*, *29*(29), 65–78.

Scholte, J. A. (2005). *Globalization: A critical introduction*. Palgrave Macmillan.

Somers, M. R., & Gibson, G. D. (1994). Reclaiming the epistemological "other": Narrative and the social construction of identity. In C. Calhoun (Ed.), *Social theory and the politics of identity* (pp. 37–99). Blackwell Publishers.

Steele, B. J. (2008). *Ontological security in international relations: Self-identity and the IR state*. Routledge.

Stone, D. (2012). Memory wars in the 'New Europe'. In D. Stone (Ed.), *The Oxford handbook of postwar European history* (pp. 714–731). Oxford University Press.

Subotic, J. (2020). Political memory, ontological security, and Holocaust remembrance in post-communist Europe. In C. Kinnvall, I. Manners, & J. Mitzen (Eds.), *Ontological insecurity in the European Union* (pp. 46–65). Routledge.

Teilhard de Chardin, P. (2008). *The phenomenon of man*. Harper Perennial Modern Thought.

Toynbee, A. J. (1987). *A study of history*. Oxford University Press.

Tumolska, H. (2016). *Mity polskiego patriotyzmu w psychologii zbiorowej (perspektywa historyczna i współczesna)*. Wydawnictwo Naukowe FNCE.

Wæver, O. (1993). Securitization and desecuritization. In R. D. Lipschutz (Ed.), *On security* (pp. 46–86). Columbia University Press.

Wæver, O., & Kelstrup, M. (1993). Europe and its nations: Political and cultural identities. In O. Wæver, B. Buzan, M. Kelstrup, & P. Lemaitre (Eds.), *Identity, migration and the new security agenda in Europe* (pp. 63–92). Pinter Publishers Ltd.

Waltz, K. N. (2010). *Theory of international relations*. Waveland Press.

Wendt, A. (1992). Anarchy is what states make of it: The social construction of power politics. *International Organization*, *45*(2), 91–425.

Wenger, A., Cavelty, M. D., & Jasper, U. (2020). *The politics and science of prevision: Governing and probing the future*. Routledge.

White, J. (2024). *In the long run: The future as a political idea*. Profile Books.

Wickham, G. (2021). Post-nationalism, sovereignty, and the state. *Journal of Sociology*, *57*(1), 47–58.

Williams, M. C. (2003). Words, images, enemies: Securitization and international politics. *International Studies Quarterly*, *47*(4), 511–531.

Wodak, R., de Cillia, R., Reisigl, M., & Liebhart, K. (2009). *The discursive construction of national identity*. Edinburgh University Press.

Wójciuk, M. (2022). *The historian: Without the Insurgence we would not have been able to survive communism as society*. Polish Press Agency Studio. Polish Press Agency. Retrieved August 30, 2023, from https://www.pap.pl/aktualnosci/news%2C138746 4%2Chistoryk-bez-powstania-nie-bylibysmy-w-stanie-przezyc-komuny-jako

Wolfers, A. (1952). National security as an ambiguous symbol. *Political Science Quarterly*, *67*(4), 481–502.

6   The changing mood of the world in times of 'polycrisis' and its influence on the post-2015 development spirit

Md Mohaiminul Islam Khan and Reidar Staupe

1. Introduction

The year 2015 marked significant progress and optimism in the field of global development, as well as a significant milestone for multilateral cooperation as a whole. That year, United Nations (UN) Member States adopted four interconnected resolutions outlining the post-2015 development agenda. These four frameworks are:

- The Sustainable Development Goals (UN, 2015a).
- The Paris Agreement (UN, 2015b).
- The Sendai Framework for Disaster Risk Reduction (UN, 2015c).
- The Addis Ababa Action Agenda (UN, 2015d).

These frameworks were met with considerable enthusiasm in 2015 and in the period leading up to their launch, a time which was, for the most part, characterised by hope and positive anticipations concerning the future of multilateralism and global development, including poverty alleviation and climate action. The launching of the SDGs has been referred to as the greatest marketing effort of all time. Of the four frameworks, the Addis Ababa Action Agenda was met with the most scepticism, and media coverage was overall towards the pessimistic side. While the Paris Agreement was met with considerable enthusiasm in most media reports, it also attracted some critical remarks due to the voluntary nature of the so-called Nationally Determined Contributions, the emission reduction targets that governments set as part of the Agreement. The SDGs are by far the best-known amongst the documents that make up what we here refer to as the post-2015 (or 2030) development agenda and will be the main focus of this chapter.

The SDG agenda operationalises global development progress broadly, comprising 17 goals, 169 targets, and 247 indicators. There are two notable differences between the SDGs and the 2000–2015 development agenda, known as the Millennium Development Goals (MDGs). The first difference is that the UN resolutions behind the SDGs explicitly mention their global nature: their applicability to all countries, irrespective of current development status, however defined. The second major difference is the large increase in the number of goals, from eight MDGs to

DOI: 10.4324/9781003537311-7

seventeen SDGs. There are also other differences, such as a broader scope due to the introduction of nine additional goals and adjustments to the ambition level of the targets.

The SDGs have also been met with considerable criticism, despite the fanfare at their launch, both before and after their introduction in 2015. As the MDG reporting period drew to a close, it became increasingly clear that many of the targets would not be met by 2015 (Lomazzi et al., 2014). Yet, as part of the process of defining the post-2015 development agenda, the number of goals more than doubled, with existing targets, such as those for poverty eradication, becoming more ambitious. Many commentators have also voiced concerns about various issues omitted from the SDGs, leading to a discourse around concepts like SDG18 or the 'missing SDG' (Kelman, 2020). Some argue that the SDGs are too ambitious and cannot realistically be achieved globally. Others, however, contend that the SDGs are not sufficiently ambitious. It is important to recognise that perceptions of the SDGs vary widely, encompassing debates over their adequacy and realism. According to Greig and Turner (2024, p. 66), one of the main functions of global development agendas, such as the MDGs and SDGs, is to 'inject' hope into global affairs discourses. As the goals were not on track to be achieved by 2030 by their review in 2019, the UN designated the 2020–2030 period as the Decade of Action (UN, 2019).

A decade into the post-2015 development agenda, the mood of the world has arguably changed significantly. The Covid-19 pandemic and the subsequent 'polycrisis' following the footsteps of the multilateralism crisis have resulted in what is often referred to as the end of the 'neoliberal world order,' from which the development agenda originated. In this chapter, we explore how the post-2020 SDGs literature frames the possibility of still achieving the agenda by 2030. In doing so, we aim to introduce to the global development literature a mooded conceptualisation of global development spirit through an exploration of the notion of 'mood of the world' (Bude, 2018). To this end, we investigate how authors writing on the SDGs between 2021 and 2024 frame optimism or pessimism concerning the realism of achieving the agenda by the 2030 deadline. Phenomenologists and social theorists have a rich tradition of exploring mooded responses to societal crises and offer diverse approaches to analysing epochal moods, zeitgeist, mood of the world, and similar ideas (e.g., Butler, 2022). We work from the assumption that a review of the literature on the SDGs in the post-Covid epoch can attune us to the mood of the authors, which, on aggregate, reveals something about the current mood of the world and its potential implications for the global development spirit.

The text is structured as follows: The next section elucidates the notion of global and epochal moods, including related terms of a phenomenological nature, of which perhaps zeitgeist is the best-known example. Section three then introduces the recent literature on the SDGs, focusing on how they conceptualise optimism or pessimism concerning the possibility of achieving the SDGs. The final section summarises the main insights from the chapter and provides a reflection on the state of the overall global development spirit in light of our close reading of the recent SDG literature and flagship reports.

2.   Mood of the world

In this chapter, we engage the work of Heinz Bude on global and epochal moods, as laid out in his seminal book *The Mood of the World* (2018, [*Das Gefühl der Welt: Über die Macht von Stimmungen*, 2016]). According to Bude, moods of the world are approached as ways of being in the world and in time. They not only shape the conditions for how we experience the world and historicity but are also the 'how' and the 'what' that are registered and picked up as significant. Such moods are not simply reflections of individual feelings or isolated events. Instead, they represent the widespread sentiments that pervade societies at given points in time, influencing how people perceive the world, their place in it, and the future. Bude conceptualises these moods as distinct from private emotions or opinions (e.g., 'public opinion,' which is seen more as an aggregate of individual opinions). The mood of the world or an epoch is taken to be a communal, pre-reflective phenomenon that circulates through interactions, colouring people's outlooks often without one's being aware of it. In many ways, they are a force of their own, with the power to generate realities and influence behaviours, economic decisions, cultural movements, and sway public opinion in ways that are difficult to explain or pin to a single cause. In Bude's words (2018, p. 39), we become affected by the turn of epochs and the mood of the world more as a surprise than as a conscious stance we take:

> The eclecticism of everyday conversations is what makes them so receptive to the feeling of the world and the thoughts of the age. The power of mood is thus expressed though its articulation in people's opinions. No one is behind it, pulling the strings. Instead, it emerges through exchange and stabilizes itself through repetition. We return to it automatically, surprised that a feeling of finality, change, inertia, has again come over us.

The main thesis of this body of work is that moods are fundamental to understanding the dynamics of contemporary global societies because they both reflect and shape the collective experience of historical moments (or epochs). Bude argues that moods are not merely reactions to external conditions, such as crises, but are active, generative forces that condition how societies view and experience such circumstances on a more fundamental level. For instance, the optimism of the 1990s, following the end of the Cold War, reflected a mood of global confidence in liberal democracy, development, and global integration. This mood did not merely arise from specific political or economic events but actively coloured how these historical events were framed. It is thus not that frames necessarily colour moods of the world deliberately, but that the way issues are framed and talked about is indicative of the prevailing mood (or moods, if competing discourses exist). For Bude, understanding changes in the mood of the world is of particular interest, signalling changes in epochal terms.

Bude's notion of the mood of the world is deeply influenced by phenomenological thought but articulated in sociological terms. The phenomenon is conceptualised as inherently dynamic and responsive to social occasions, taken to be of an eventful character. It draws from Heideggerian traditions, emphasising mood as *something we find ourselves in*, a fundamental structure of our being, strongly related to the idea that we cannot choose where to be in history or in time, always coloured by emergent situations in which we find ourselves. An excellent elaboration of such an epochal sense of mood or atmosphere is given by Ben Anderson (2009), who cites Karl Marx's words: 'The atmosphere in which we live weighs upon every one with a 20,000-pound force, but do you feel it? No more than European society before 1848 felt the revolutionary atmosphere enveloping and pressing it from all sides' (cited in Anderson, 2009, p. 77). Fascinated with this question and the notion of 'do you feel it?', Anderson conceptualises this sense of atmosphere, this something that people are perhaps, or perhaps not, feeling (in the words of Kathleen Stewart (2011), due to either being 'attuned' or 'not attuned' to said atmosphere). This goes to the heart of the notion of moods of the world, which refers to the emotional undercurrent that drives how societies see occurrences in the world as they unfold, whether as utopian or dystopian, or as eventful or uneventful. The relationship to the anticipation of disaster is also clear.

The moods of the world are significant because they provide the emotional and existential framework through which societies engage with and make sense of crises. Moods determine how societies confront (or comport themselves towards) the emergent future, and we can face the future either as something to be feared, as dreadful, or as uncertain (something we wish would not arrive so soon). Likewise, our stance towards the future can come to be seen as highly optimistic or even utopian (as something that must be brought about sooner rather than later). Within this framework, such moods do not emerge from objective realities as much as from more fundamental ways of finding ourselves in the world and developing a particular comportment towards the future. As such, moods of the world are not only reflections of the present but also determinants of what becomes possible in the political, social, and cultural realms.

Drawing upon Bude's concept of the mood of the world, we shall now examine whether texts on the progress and crisis of the 2030 development agenda, as spearheaded by the SDGs, demonstrate changes in the mood of the world in the 2021–2024 period. Following Bude, epochal moods are taken to influence how societies interpret challenges and possibilities, framing whether agendas like the SDGs become seen as achievable or unattainable. Bude highlights that these moods are not just abstract forces but can be traced in texts (reflecting the moods of the author, who in a sense embodies the mood at the time they were writing), where the emotional tone of an era is articulated and reinforced. By situating the SDGs literature within this framework, the chapter connects shifts in optimism and pessimism to the broader mood of the time.

3. Optimism and pessimism for the SDGs in 2021–2024 publications

The 2015 development agenda, guided by the SDGs, represented a call to action to tackle critical global challenges like poverty, hunger, health, and education. However, crises like the Covid-19 pandemic and the Ukraine war have significantly altered the development trajectory of many countries. This shift is not surprising, given the urgency and magnitude of these crises. It can be argued that the SDG timeline and scope were ambitious. It can also be argued that they may still be within reach if efforts are massively scaled up. Nonetheless, it also seems plausible that the 2015 development agenda has run out of steam, given the shifts in attention and resource use triggered by geopolitical crises.

The literature presents a host of different views on the possibility of achieving the SDGs by 2030. There is also disagreement on how far off we are and on what it would take to reach them. Disagreement also exists on which goals are the most important to focus on in the years ahead, and which goals are faring the best. We observe that while some researchers remain optimistic, pessimism towards the SDGs is on the rise. In the following pages, we will take a closer look at the 2021–2024 SDGs literature and then discuss whether changes in frames within this literature over the recent years are indicative of a change in the mood of the world. We have, for the most part, excluded the 2020 SDGs literature because the manuscripts were often written prior to the onset of the Covid-19 crises, or at least prior to a mature understanding of its wider global repercussions. The review is sorted by year to help give readers an understanding of year-to-year changes in SDGs discourse.

3.1   A review of 2021–2024 articles attempting to assess SDG progress

In the article 'The Implications of the Covid-19 Pandemic for Delivering the Sustainable Development Goals,' Richard Fenner and Thomas Cernev (2021) sketch out how the Covid-19 pandemic impacts global progress on the SDGs over the medium- and long-term. The article (submitted in July 2020 and revised in January 2021) provides an early view on the anticipated impact of the pandemic on the development agenda and its future. One interesting observation is that, at the time the manuscript is written, the authors note that 'the pandemic may also present an opportunity both for increased motivation towards the completion of such goals and a redefining of future targets to be achieved' (p. 1). Overall, the four scenarios pursued in the article (from the vantage point of 2020–2021) include two potentially positive futures and two potentially disastrous anticipations as likely.

The article identifies four possible scenarios that might positively or negatively impact the possibility of achieving the SDGs: first, a scenario in which global well-being becomes more salient in the post-pandemic world, with increased investment in global cooperation and SDGs funding (described by the authors as the ideal but potentially unrealistic post-pandemic scenario); second, a world in which trade recovers and where 'globalization continues, with borders open and countries preferring to not pursue an isolationist approach' (p. 8); third, a post-pandemic world where poverty gaps continue to widen 'as a result of the countries of the world looking inwards, resulting in diminishing international co-operation and thus an isolation of developing countries from the rest of the world that without the continued development programs from international organizations will experience population growth, increased inequality, lack of services, and events such as disease outbreaks' (p. 8), where the risk is seen as that 'as global inequality grows there will be increased fragmentation with achievements made towards the SDG targets coming undone, and the progress over the previous decades being lost entirely' (p. 8); finally, a post-pandemic scenario is envisioned where Earth systems deteriorate further, as nations look inwards as part of their recovery strategies and 'effective global governance for both climate change, resource control and biodiversity protection [becomes] challenging in an era of economic nationalism' (p. 8) and where 'climate targets such as the 2015 Paris Agreement will be abandoned, and international bodies such as WHO and the UN will be at risk of being dismantled,' which would, as a consequence, lead to the removal of 'any co-ordinated governance and consistent monitoring of progress in the SDGs' (p. 8), throwing these into jeopardy.

Overall, the four scenarios that Fenner and Cernev envision in 2020–2021 suggest a crisis in the real meaning of the word (e.g., Koselleck, 2006) as a time at which critical decisions and outcomes in the present shape the future. The authors envision one scenario where the pandemic crisis leads to a recovery characterised by global solidarity and renewed efforts towards the SDGs. Likewise, the authors imagine a future characterised by isolationism, declining multilateralism, and waning support for international agreements and law. In their conclusion, the authors note that the future at that point in time seems particularly uncertain and that the 'ability to deliver the Sustainable Development Goals by 2030 is in doubt, and will depend on how the world emerges from the COVID-19 pandemic' (p. 11). From the perspective of moods in the world, we can deduce that the moment at which the manuscript is written reflects great uncertainty about which direction the future will take, stressing also the contingency of history.

A hopeful analysis by Kalterina Shulla and colleagues (2021) in 'Effects of COVID-19 on the Sustainable Development Goals (SDGs)' puts forward the view that Covid-19 may be seen as an opportunity rather than an obstacle to achieving SDGs, noting that 'We were already behind on reaching the SDGs before the Covid-19 pandemic started,' driven by such forces as 'digitalization, authoritarian and extreme right tendencies, and growing global inequality' (p. 2). The authors anticipate that the pandemic might act as a catalyst for concerted progress on numerous SDGs, as 'the multilateral system is *enhanced* by the pressures for collaboration brought by the pandemic' (p. 2, our emphasis). The authors stress that the pandemic makes it clear how human health is closely tied to the health of ecosystems and that this could spark the missing momentum, where 'the 2030 Agenda for Sustainable Development, which encompasses sustainability in all forms, can be a useful framework and guideline toward a sustainable future' (p. 12). This, according to the authors (again, we stress that this is based on anticipations from 2021), will happen through leveraging pandemic-induced digital solutions and investments in 'green recovery,' which will simultaneously tackle social injustices and inequality.

Another 2021 chapter by Joe E. Colombano and David N. Nabarro on 'COVID-19 and the SDGs' underlines that Covid-19 and its resulting lockdown measures create 'a formidable challenge in meeting the SDGs and realizing the promise of the 2030 Agenda' (p. 17). The authors observe that 'far from being the great equalizer it was initially thought to be, COVID-19 hits the poor and the most vulnerable the hardest' (p. 29). It is noteworthy here that the chapter refers back to an initial mood centred on the potential for the crisis to be a great equalizer and that the authors become disillusioned by the time of writing. The chapter concludes on a hopeful note, however, noting that:

> The *global reset* triggered by the crisis is an opportunity for a better recovery, to rebound forward toward realizing a sustainable world, rather than backward to the original system with its flaws, as we did, for example, after the 2008 financial crisis. For this to happen, we need to strengthen our commitment to implement the 2030 Agenda and invest in meeting the 17 goals. This is how we can turn this global pandemic into the opportunity to start anew and realize the vision of a fairer and more sustainable world.
>
> (p. 31, our emphasis)

We can read out of the quote above a mood at the time of there both still being hope for reaching the SDGs with greater effort, and a narrative that existed at the time of there being a global reset, or a sense of the pandemic having opened up a window of opportunity for social and environmental transformations. From the perspective of the mood of the world, these sentiments that we can read out of texts from this period are significant, as they have largely disappeared from texts just a year or two later.

The article 'Mapping the Impact of COVID-19 Crisis on the Progress of Sustainable Development Goals (SDGs): A Focus on Global Environment and Energy Efficiencies' by Roopali Fulzele (2022, advance online publication in 2021) sets out to quantify the potential impacts of the pandemic on the SDGs, with a particular focus on its role as a catalyst for transitioning to clean energy. The authors note that the 'SDGs that were adopted in the year 2015 by the UN Member States addressing various global issues, now seem difficult to be achieved by 2030 due to coronavirus pandemic' (p. 873), stressing that even though the Covid-19 crisis has erased much of the progress on the SDGs. The article concludes that 'with the advent of COVID-19 crisis, *the aspirations to achieve 2030 agenda for sustainable development has been jeopardized*' (p. 878, our emphasis). However, the authors also note that there are clear grounds for optimism on the potential for progress on energy transitions (SDG7), where the pandemic might open windows for positive change. They insist that the disruptions caused by the pandemic present an opportunity for countries to focus on renewable energy, improve energy efficiency, and build greener economies, ultimately accelerating progress towards achieving the SDGs as part of the recovery, especially those related to environmental sustainability. The authors conclude on a pessimistic note, however, on the possibility of achieving the SDGs in their entirety.

In the chapter 'Beyond the SDGs: From 2030 to 2050 Agenda for Development,' Muhammad Jameel Yusha'u and Jan Servaes (2021) set out to reflect on the future of the sustainable development agenda towards and after 2030 towards

2050. The authors take an optimistic stance and remain hopeful that the SDGs may be within reach despite major setbacks due to Covid-19, noting that:

> Mobilizing an average of US $2.5 trillion per annum up to 2030 is not an easy feat. But as the optimists for achieving the SDGs would argue, *it is not impossible to do so*. Perhaps when you look at the size of the global economy, and if the 193 UN member states that signed off to be part of the SDGs would see themselves as a single family, working collectively to deliver the 2030 agenda, the future of the SDGs might look brighter. The prospects of achieving the 2030 agenda would look more likely. The global economy is estimated to be worth US $133 trillion in 2019 compared to US $120 trillion dollars two years earlier, though the global economy is expected to shrink due to the impact of COVID-19 by the time the report on the global economy for 2021 is out.
>
> (p. 610, our emphasis)

The chapter concludes with more careful optimism, arguing for the potential need for a revised timeline towards 2050, the importance of increased political will, and a greater focus on risk mitigation and win-win solutions to speed up progress. It should be noted that the chapter is written from the perspective of international development professionals, which might influence the kinds of moods that this chapter embodies.

The literature survey 'The COVID-19 Pandemic and the UN's Sustainable Development Goals: A General Overview' by Ogechi Adeola (2021) reviews the 2020–2021 literature on the potential impacts of the pandemic on the SDGs, noting that the pandemic is still ongoing at the time of the chapter's publication. Adeola reports that the publications reviewed express concern that progress on the SDGs might be erased and threaten the 2030 development agenda by 'significantly exacerbating SDG financing gaps' (p. 23). After a breakdown on progress on each of the SDGs, the author notes that 'the capability to deliver the SDGs by 2030 is in doubt and may depend on how the post-COVID world emerges from the pandemic' (p. 33). Adeola (2021, p. 33) hence concludes that 'the attainment of the sustainability development agenda is less than ten years in the future' and that 'the current stagnation in institutional resource flows to developing countries (as further influenced by the pandemic) poses a daunting task' to their attainment. In other words, similarly to Fenner and Cernev (the first article cited in this section), Adeola's chapter ends with a mix of pessimism and cautious optimism, indicating a sense that the attainment of the SDGs is in strong doubt but within reach should efforts be redoubled.

Overall, this small sample of published works illustrates that 2021 is a year of crisis and great uncertainty, in the sense that commentators find themselves at a precipice of sorts, where the future is open; it could still get much worse or much better. Thinking back, we remember that throughout 2021, Covid-19 maintains pandemic status, and the majority of countries are still under different kinds of restrictions, economies are in pandemic mode, and the global mood is highly focused on this crisis. The sense of crisis for the SDGs deepens further with the Russian invasion of Ukraine in early 2022 and a deepening sense of global geopolitical crisis (only reflected in later 2022 publications), which intensifies in the aftermath of 7 October 2023 (not directly mentioned in most subsequent publications but surely impacting the overall mood of the authors and their analyses). We now shift our attention to how this deepening sense of crisis manifests in the SDGs literature in the period after 2021, where we also wish to underline that through most of 2022 the war in Ukraine is still not reflected in the literature due to the time it takes to get articles accepted for publication.

In the 2022 viewpoint article 'Defining a Sustainable Development Target Space for 2030 and 2050,' Detlef van Vuuren and colleagues offer a middle-ground perspective based on the realisation that 'the 169 targets and 232 indicators used for monitoring SDG implementation cannot be used' (p. 142). The goals are simply 'too many, too broad, unstructured, and sometimes not formulated quantitatively' (p. 142). As an alternative, they propose a streamlined 'target space' which aggregates the SDGs into 36 more precise targets, with 2050 as a more appropriate reference point. While this approach is essentially a vote of no confidence in the SDGs and their likely achievement by 2030—among other factors due to the setbacks caused by the Covid-19 pandemic—it is also a piece that demonstrates faith in the core ideas underpinning the 2015 development spirit and argues for their continued relevance and conceptual, if not operational, feasibility. For example, for SDG four on quality education for all, van Vuuren and colleagues observe that 'considering current enrolment rates in primary education, achieving 100% completion of lower secondary education by 2030 is *practically impossible*, so the target values proposed are 80% in 2030 and 100% in 2050' (p. 149, our emphasis). Here, the authors express hope for reaching the objective but not within the timeline. Other goals are seen as achievable by 2030 but with increased efforts, such as reducing the under-five mortality rate where the 'SDG target level of 25 deaths per 1,000 live births is taken for 2030, further halved by 2050 to increase progress' and 'although this is still far from levels currently recorded in developed countries, it is still *ambitious and achievable*' (p. 149, our emphasis). In summary, this viewpoint article, while not entirely optimistic, demonstrates great faith in the possibility of achieving the SDGs, if not by 2030, then at least by 2050. This constitutes an endorsement of the 2015 development agenda spirit.

The article 'Impacts of COVID19 on Sustainable Development Goals and Effective Approaches to Maneuver Them in the Post-Pandemic Environment' by Rajvikram Madurai Elavarasan and colleagues (2022) sets out to provide a detailed quantitative ranking of how deeply each of the 17 goals has been impacted by the pandemic (note that the study was carried out before the wars). They find that the goals on poverty, hunger, decent work, and inequality have seen some of the greatest setbacks. Yet, this publication takes an optimistic stance on the possibility of achieving the SDGs by 2030, and the authors underline that 'stimulating the progress in the impacted SDGs in the post-pandemic period, the SDGs can be put back on track' (p. 33958), concluding on the note that 'humans should perceive the current situation as an opportunity to tune themselves to impart actions and developments such that it ultimately favors the [SDGs]' (p. 33983). While this is one of the most optimistic anticipations considered thus far, it must be mentioned that the article does consider a number of scenarios where the increases in poverty become more permanent or more temporary (a high-damage scenario, a baseline scenario, and an SDG push scenario).

A 2022 editorial by Paulo Pereira and colleagues, titled 'The Russian-Ukrainian Armed Conflict Will Push Back the Sustainable Development Goals,' argues that 'with this conflict's emergence, several nations' ability to achieve SDGs by 2030 can become unattainable' (p. 286, our emphasis). Moreover, the editorial underlines that 'the escalation of this conflict is imposing severe threats to achieving the UN SDGs not only to the countries directly involved in the conflict but also to other countries' (p. 277), stressing that in a world at war there is no possibility of sustained global progress on the SDGs. As the authors observe:

> The Covid-19 and Russian-Ukrainian armed conflict is affecting global efforts to achieve the SDGs because it is uncertain when Covid-19 will abate and the conflict will end. Before these events, many countries were already struggling to meet the established goals. For many, it was already a race against the time. The challenges to meeting the SDGs by 2030 will be even higher, given current conditions. Uncertain times come ahead.
>
> (p. 278)

As we can elucidate from the quote above, the authors attune to a mood of the world here shaped by great uncertainty about the wider implications of the elusive Covid-19 recovery and a protracted conflict in Ukraine. However, we can also sense that the text is not overly pessimistic, maintaining formulations that suggest hope that the goals might still be within reach in the eyes of the authors at the time, despite great hurdles to be overcome.

In his 2022 essay 'Replacing Sustainable Development: Potential Frameworks for International Cooperation in an Era of Increasing Crises and Disasters,' Jem Bendell argues that 'halfway into the period allocated for those goals, official analyses show that there is *no significant progress*, there is *much regress*, and *the goals cannot be met*' (p. 17, our emphasis). He contends that the time is ripe for replacing the overall framework of sustainable development with 'alternative frameworks that are better suited for our new era of increasing crises and disasters' (p. 1), where disaster risk reduction and disaster risk management are presented as one possible and more focused alternative. Bendell observes that diverse fields have increasingly adopted crisis terminologies and that terms such as 'polycrisis,' 'permacrisis,' and 'metacrisis' are increasingly used in international development cooperation. The author asserts that disaster risk management 'can be improved from recognising that we are entering an era of "metadisaster" due to climate chaos' that will challenge the 'future availability of external support' to disaster-stricken communities (p. 17). Disaster risk management, as an alternative to sustainable development, is thus presented as better suited to the current times, emphasising that 'as times change, it is essential to allow a reconsideration of all assumptions and a refocusing of our future attention, no matter how initially uncomfortable that may be.' This should be read in the context of his argument that, despite three decades of international development professionals identifying strongly with their work as part of a post-Rio Earth Summit agenda centred on the notion of sustainable development, the author believes it is time to reconsider this assumption.

In a 2022 United Nations Department of Economic and Social Affairs (UN DESA) policy brief on *Ensuring SDG Progress Amid Recurrent Crises*, Marcelo T. LaFleur and colleagues argue that 'SDG progress has been set back, and the outlook faces uncertainty given the cumulative and amplified impacts of the COVID-19 pandemic, the war in Ukraine and climate change' (p. 1). The authors observe that progress has slowed due to multiple shocks, causing a funding deficit of over 30 trillion dollars over the medium term. They also note that 'The fragile economic recovery from COVID-19 has been upended by the war in Ukraine' (p. 2). While the brief acknowledges that these multiple shocks 'imperil' the SDGs, the concluding section is overall vaguely optimistic, recommending that efforts be redoubled, interventions be made more efficient, and the lowest-hanging fruits be prioritised for the best results possible in the years towards 2030.

The 2022 viewpoint article 'COVID-19, the Russo-Ukrainian War, the Global Sustainable Development Project and Post-Crises Demography' by Landis MacKellar and colleagues offers a critical perspective based on the realisation that 'the global sustainable development project as currently conceived is foundering, and the twin crises of the COVID-19 pandemic and the Russo-Ukrainian War have driven a stake through its heart' (p. 39). The viewpoint piece argues that 'The resources to bring the project—or its successor, and any other global sustainable development project of similar design and ambition that might emerge—to a successful conclusion do not exist, and never did' (p. 39), presenting a bleak outlook not only for the SDGs but for any notion of the post-2015 development agenda spirit. However, while MacKellar is overall pessimistic towards the goals' initial or current feasibility, he remains unwilling to throw the baby out with the bathwater, as he suggests reform to what he calls the global sustainable development 'project.' In the author's own words, 'The global sustainable development narrative should abandon *grand, hortatory razzmatazz* in favour of goals that have a chance of being achieved' (p. 67, emphasis in original). In short, the proposed course of action is one of simplifying not the SDGs per se but the project of development, focusing on concrete tasks where the track record has historically fared better, such as vaccination, education, climate change adaptation, and rule of law, while remaining sensitive to the forces of demography.

An early 2023 technical input paper to UN DESA by Andreas Antoniades, titled 'Crisis as a Trend and the Achievement of SDGs,' opens with the observation that 'even before the break-out of the COVID-19 pandemic, progress made in SDGs (e.g. poverty, hunger, education) was faltering' and that the crises we have experienced since 2015 are creating 'the most challenging environment for global development that we have experienced in the recent economic history' (p. 3). The author observes that the closer we get to the SDG timeline, the more concern shifts to the inadequate progress towards SDGs. He emphasises that setbacks in the most vulnerable countries underscore the inequitable nature of progress, which further highlights the challenges in achieving a fair and global implementation of the SDGs. Antoniades argues that 'the retreat of SDGs that we mentioned above may quickly turn into a negative domino for the targets of the Agenda 2030, with unforeseeable socio-environmental consequences' and that avoiding this outcome hinges on taking 'immediate global action' to reverse the undoing of development progress (p. 4). He further notes that the issue goes beyond progress or failure on individual SDGs or the SDGs as a whole, as the 2030 development agenda spirit has come under threat, at worst jeopardising the idea of development cooperation overall.

The European Parliament input paper 'Achieving the UN Agenda 2030: Overall Actions for the Successful Implementation of the Sustainable Development Goals Before and After the 2030 Deadline' by Kalterina Shulla and Leal-Filho (2023) argues that a significant transformation in SDG financing is required if the goals are to be met. The authors note that 'global crises, such as the COVID-19 pandemic, the war in Ukraine and climate change, have all effectively reversed progress in achieving the SDGs' and that the funding gap has increased by a trillion dollars (p. i). However, the analysis ultimately stresses that the SDGs are still within reach by 2030 but that 'intensified and integrative collective actions are needed between countries, sectors, disciplines and actors' (p. 1). In summary, while the authors point out that the challenge of achieving the SDGs by 2030 has become more significant due to recent crises, they note that there is still hope for their realisation, which is indicative of a hopeful stance towards the goals in this publication.

Issue four of the 2023 edition of *Nature Communications Earth and Environment* contains two articles on the progress and outlooks of the SDGs. The first, 'Progress Towards the Sustainable Development Goals Has Been Slowed by Indirect Effects of the COVID-19 Pandemic' by Haixia Yuan and colleagues, expresses concern that Covid-19 has fundamentally disrupted progress across multiple dimensions—economic, social, and environmental—affecting nearly all the SDGs in one way or another. They note that the challenge is that these impacts are not straightforward or easily quantifiable, and that the 'indirect effects slowed progress much more than the direct initial disruptions' (p. 1). Further, the authors observe that 'when the SDG Decade of Action began in 2020, COVID-19 broke out and became a global pandemic, significantly impacting progress towards the SDGs, that was already faltering, even before COVID-19,' which 'further undermined countries' ability to achieve them by 2030' (p. 2). As other authors have pointed out earlier, the SDGs were not on track prior to the crises we currently face, which reduces the hope that they may still be within reach. However, as implied by Yuan and colleagues, not all hope is lost, but it remains 'vital to understand how the track of the world towards the SDGs was altered by the pandemic' and 'reaccelerate the pace to rescue the 2030 Agenda from failing' (p. 1). Differently put, the authors acknowledge the persistent impacts that the crises of our time will have on the 2030 development agenda but remain moderately optimistic in tone. The second article in this issue is 'Responses to the COVID-19 pandemic have impeded progress towards the Sustainable Development Goals' by Cai Li and colleagues, who state that 'COVID-19 pandemic responses have brought unprecedented challenges to the United Nations 2030 Agenda' and that 'nearly two-thirds of the SDG targets may be under threat' (pp. 1–2). The article does not address the post-pandemic geopolitical crises and wars or their impacts on SDGs funding or mood. Rather, the article concludes that 'a post-pandemic strategy for the 2030 Agenda requires sustainable pandemic responses across all SDG targets and countries' which 'should not only reduce the inequality between developed and developing countries but also resolve the trade-offs between society, the economy, and the environment' (p. 7). The authors argue that the goals can become within reach, given higher levels of growth and economic development in the coming years.

The article 'Shifting Norms, Multiplying Actors, Turbulent Times: An Emerging Landscape of International Development Cooperation' by Peter Taylor and colleagues (2023) argues that in turbulent times such as ours, it is normal for norms underpinning international development cooperation to change. In the words of the authors:

> Consensus was also central to the near-universal 2015 adoption of the UN global SDGs. Yet, as nations look forward to a world characterized by turbulence, conflict, and uncertainty, how will they navigate the inevitably complex web of relationships and agendas that balance national and global interests? [. . .] the landscape of international development co-operation continues to evolve. Regional agendas such as Africa 2063 are emerging. Sources of funding from emerging donors such as China, India, and Brazil continue to grow in magnitude and diversity; new types of donors are entering the international development community The private sector is playing an increasing role. [. . .] This growing community of development actors has huge potential for diversity and inclusion, but also brings complexity.
>
> (pp. 2–3)

The authors indicate that including new actors and partnerships creates a fresh dynamic that can potentially lead to more innovative and practical solutions to achieve some SDGs in some places, while not necessarily being guided by the SDGs explicitly. This, however, undermines the symbolic role of the SDGs and any sense of a post-2015 development agenda or spirit, making development, yet again a more bilateral phenomenon rooted in geopolitical dynamics. The authors emphasise opportunities for new actors from the belief that greater diversity and broader participation could bring new ideas, resources, and energy into the development sector. The article also highlights that partnerships and collaborations have always been crucial to overcoming challenges in a more connected and turbulent world. Overall, the publication represents a balanced mood that sees a clear undermining of the SDGs as such, as the normative landscape of development cooperation changes. However, it also suggests that progress on SDGs in many countries can still be achieved in the absence of a clear development strategy guided by global goals, such as the SDGs.

In the 2023 special issue editorial 'Enhancing the Achievement of the SDGs: Lessons Learned at the Half-Way Point of the 2030 Agenda,' Philipp Pattberg and Karin Bäckstrand introduce a series of papers that seek to understand the lack of progress and decline on a number of key SDGs. As the authors pinpoint, '2023 marks the half-way point between 2015 and 2030 and could be considered "a make or break it moment" for the achievement of the SDGs' (p. 108). The authors observe that only 12 percent of the targets are on track and that 30 percent of targets show no progress or are regressing. As examples, the authors stress that 'unless action on poverty alleviation (SDG 1) accelerates, 575 million people will still be living in extreme poverty in 2030, and only a third of the countries in the world will meet the target to halve poverty levels' (p. 109). A similar situation is noted for SDG2 on hunger, as '150 million people more suffer from hunger in 2021 compared to 2019, which is [by 2023] further worsened by the food security crisis due to the war in Ukraine' (p. 109). The authors explain that the regression, compounded by global challenges like sluggish Covid-19 recovery, wars, and food price spikes exacerbates a massive implementation gap that had emerged since 2015. As a response to the sluggish and reversing progress, the authors point to UN initiatives such as the 2023 'Rescue Plan for the People and the Planet' (UN News, 2023) and a planned 'SDG stimulus plan,' which aims to streamline SDG progress and monitoring and increase funding. However, these remain elusive, as the authors also point out. From the text, we can read a sense of careful optimism, while the overall tone is coloured by a pessimistic mood.

A 2023 editorial by *Nature Computational Science* titled 'The Next Seven Years' remarks that many of the targets are seriously off track but does not reference either Covid-19 or geopolitical turmoil. It notes that current projections suggest that by 2030 there will still be over 500 million people living in extreme poverty, only one in six countries is likely to have equitable quality education by that time, and that it would take about 140 years until gender equality is achieved in the workplace and in leadership positions. The editorial concludes that, noting the importance of technology, digitalisation, and computational innovations, 'with a concerted and multi-disciplinary approach—we can better move towards reaching these goals in the next seven years, and ensure a more prosperous, equitable and sustainable future for all' (p. 721). This piece stands out for not reflecting a sentiment tainted by crisis, and while it notes the lack of progress on most SDGs thus far, the editorial remains optimistic.

The 2024 study 'Understanding Public Sentiments and Misbeliefs about Sustainable Development Goals: A Sentiment and Topic Modeling Analysis' by Abhinav Verma and Jogendra Kumar Nayak sets out to probe people's sentiments regarding the SDGs by analysing the comments on SDG-related videos on YouTube. One pertinent remark is that the authors note that 'we discovered several new misbeliefs about SDGs that earlier research had not reported' (p. 258) and that 'the public is carrying mostly negative sentiments and emotions toward the SDGs' (p. 269). The authors unearth 'a general sense of negativity and skepticism toward governments, as well as a deep-seated fear of SDGs' (p. 264). They mention the identification of five topics that strongly exhibit scepticism related to the

SDGs: anti-global governance, 'New World Order,' propaganda, depopulation agenda, and World Governing Body (antichrist). One topic indicates that 'the SDGs are the tactics of rich people to make the poor poorer and the rich richer' (p. 267). Another focuses on the impact of global politics, 'mainly represented misbeliefs regarding the political will and actions towards achieving the SDGs' (p. 267). Two more topics concentrate on perceiving pandemics and vaccinations as 'a planned global agenda to depopulate the world through vaccination' (p. 267). Additionally, another topic mines the public discussion about 'the use of conflict as a method to oppose the SDGs' (p. 268). The final topic portrays public views 'about the role of political leadership in achieving or obstructing SDGs.' The authors also find positive and supportive comments, although more general, with some commentators suggesting that they have been inspired by the SDGs. However, the authors observe that sentiments have gradually worsened in recent years based on this sentiment analysis of user comments (though people experiencing neutral or positive reactions to the videos may be less likely to comment). In the context of the mood of the world, we can infer that public perception regarding SDG attainment has become more pessimistic among YouTube viewers consuming SDG-related content, including UN-related content.

The analysis 'Sustainable Development Goal Attainment in the Wake of COVID-19: Simulating an Ambitious Policy Push' by Taylor Hanna and colleagues (2024) aims to take stock of progress and setbacks on the SDGs in light of the halfway point having been passed and recent crises having affected their implementation. As many other authors note, this article also observes that 'even prior to the outbreak of COVID-19, the world was not on track to meet SDG' (p. 6). However, a central argument of the article is that a recovery from the global crisis is possible with an integrated approach, and 'an ambitious global push across issue areas can accelerate progress towards the SDGs' (p. 13). On the whole, the three scenarios portrayed in the article—initially devised in 2021 and revised for this 2024 publication—compare a no-Covid scenario baseline, a current scenario, and a push-strategy scenario for SDG attainment by 2030. The authors conclude with hopeful optimism that the goals are largely attainable given such a concerted push, stating that 'the SDG Push scenario stimulates the results of moving beyond recovery from a global crisis' (p. 13). In a nutshell, the three scenarios outlined by Taylor and colleagues suggest that although the impact of the global crisis has been an immense obstacle for SDG attainment, with global policy changes and cooperation, the SDG goals are attainable—maybe not by 2030, but with an extended timeline till 2050. Considering mood, it is noteworthy that the authors present a global push on the SDGs as a viable option in the current political and financial climate. However, one limitation of this article is that it is only a revised 2021 analysis.

Sebastian H. Schneider and colleagues published a survey in 2024 titled 'Public Opinion of the 2030 Agenda: A Mid-Term Review,' which underscores awareness and attitude changes on the SDG 2030 agenda among informants in Germany since their inception until the present. The survey data show that 'the general public is sceptical as to whether the goals can be achieved by 2030.' Overall, the authors find two interesting observations concerning the SDGs that relate to the mood of the world. The first is that, although it has been eight years since the inception of the SDGs, a clear majority report that they 'had not yet heard of the 17 goals,' meaning that a large portion of the population is still unfamiliar with the SDGs. The second finding is that the general public does not seem to have much faith in the most ambitious goals, such as SDG1 on eliminating poverty. As the authors note, 'the general public is most pessimistic with regard to SDG 1' (p. 3). The brief concludes on a tone of pessimism, noting that the SDGs hold lower-than-expected salience in the population and that those who are aware of them are not optimistic about their potential to be realised by the 2030 deadline.

Junuguru Srinivas and colleagues published a systematic literature review in 2024 on 'The COVID-19 Pandemic and Its Impact on Sustainable Development Goals-2030.' The focus of the review is to understand the influence of the Covid-19 pandemic in the context of the world economy and the substantial outcomes on SDG aspirations. The authors concede that 'COVID-19 had devastated the aspirations of the SDGs' (p. 1). The review draws on three different perspectives in its analysis of the impacts: a general perspective, a liberal perspective, and what they refer to as a realist perspective. From a general perspective, the authors observe that the pandemic impacted people's lives across financial, social, and political considerations. Citing World Bank data, they note that 'the COVID-19 pandemic had struck a devastating blow to the global economy, causing unprecedented effects on the developed world, emerging market economies, and developing countries' (p. 4). Among the direct effects is the greatest increase in poverty 'in the last 20 years' (p. 10) and negative progress on most indicators except environmental ones. As the authors note, indirect effects are harder to quantify as their impacts may endure for a generation, including disrupted education, earlier marriages, and so on. From a realist perspective, the authors find that realist views held true, as cooperation and mutual support between states were challenging. They note that 'the pandemic has shattered the myth of the liberal views of international relations' and that 'instead, a realist perspective prevailed during the pandemic because almost all countries have practised an inward-looking approach and acted like a self-centred actor' (p. 5). However, overall, the article concludes with a hint of positivity, mentioning that 'despite the havoc created by COVID-19 on the global economy and the state of the SDGs, there is still a possibility of recovery and scope and hope for faster planet development.' The authors acknowledge that the war in Ukraine has worsened matters but argue that it is not beyond hope. They end by highlighting the positive ambition of the SDGs for a better world, adding that their success will hinge on enhanced diplomatic cooperation.

Natalia Millán-Acevedo and Diana Gómez-Bruna (2024), through their work 'Contradictions between Capitalism and Sustainable Human Development: Where Is the 2030 Agenda Headed,' undertake to explore the opposing relationship between theoretical and political applications of capitalism and development thought. The most interesting observation noted by the authors is that 'contradictions, which are essential to understanding the logic of power and the limits of progress for the common good, are, however, invisible and denied in the proposals of the 2030 Agenda for Sustainable Development' (p. 2). The article stresses that the 'capitalist dynamic itself is incompatible with the sustainability of life,' thus rejecting the SDGs as a framework for any sensible development agenda at all. The authors note numerous contradictions in the SDGs and pose these against the notion of a sustainable development agenda, stressing that 'the economic and political foundations of capitalism are at odds with equality of opportunity' because it will require 'intervention in the market to promote equity' (p. 14). The authors thus reject the SDGs as a way forward to operationalise the 2030 sustainable development agenda or whichever agenda will replace it due to its alleged promotion of capitalist values through numerous SDG targets. They note that 'real structural limits' underpin the SDGs, making it impossible to use them 'in the construction of a just, safe, and equitable world' (p. 16). While the mood of the world that is painted in this article does not make direct references that enable us to infer how Covid-19 or the war in Ukraine and other aspects of our current polycrisis has affected its conclusions, we see in this article a growing suspicion of the SDGs due to a sense of it perpetuating a sense of contradiction that cannot be resolved without replacing the framework with another.

In the article 'Why SDG4 and the Other SDGs are Failing and What Needs to Be Done,' Steven J. Klees (2024) aims to account for the failure of the SDGs, particularly SDG4. In this publication, Klees opens by exclaiming that the state of SDG4 at the halfway point of the 2030 agenda is 'dismal!' (p. 1), noting that SDG4 is one of a long line of broken promises made by the international community since the 1960s and that 'the most basic goal—universal primary education—has repeatedly been promised and never fulfilled' (p. 1). The reasons for the dismal progress are seen as a lack of financing and political will. On a pessimistic note, the author observes that 'The barriers to achieving SDG4 are very much connected to the barriers to attaining all the SDGs' and that 'we did not achieve any of the MDGs, and we are not on target to achieve any of the SDGs by 2030' (p. 1, our emphasis). The piece stresses that 'We don't have time to waste; climate catastrophe is upon us, war and violence are ubiquitous, and the danger of nuclear confrontation has never been greater' (p. 3). The author identifies a number of solutions, which are seen as inadequate, addressing symptoms rather than the root causes of failure. Simply hoping for better results is not enough, Klees notes, and 'while very difficult, the only way we will achieve the SDGs is system change' (p. 2), adding that:

> Any sober assessment of SDG progress must recognize that we will never achieve these goals without drastic changes in how we live and organize ourselves on this planet. The endeavors mentioned above only scratch the surface of the myriad efforts around the world challenging business as usual. Most directly, we must challenge the assumptions underlying the SDGs that economic growth is the way forward and that the private sector can be the engine of 'development.' We also must challenge the new multistakeholder governance model for the UN and its obscuring of what is actually a corporate takeover. Let me return to my opening argument that the proximal cause of the failure of SDG4 and all the SDGs is the failure to adequately finance them. We must drastically change the ethos and practice behind the current

international financial architecture. The World Bank and the IMF need major reforms or, more likely, to be replaced with new institutions designed for today's world. As alluded to above, the UN itself is in need of major reform or redesign.

We can note in the words of Klees a pessimistic mood towards the possibility of realizing the 2030 development agenda. More of the same is not seen as a solution by the author, and incremental changes are not seen as sufficient. While the author does attempt to come off as hopeful, the overall commentary piece is on a pessimistic note, As captured very well in the quote above.

A 2024 chapter by David Mhlanga and Emmanuel Ndhlovu, titled 'The Russia-Ukraine War and Sustainable Development Goals in Africa,' sets out to assess the prospects of achieving the SDGs in Africa given the Russia-Ukraine war. In opening, the authors state that 'the war has developed into a prescription for an obvious worldwide catastrophe on the social, economic, environmental and political dimensions,' and with few years left to the SDG deadline, their realisation has become 'much more difficult' (p. 364). They note that 'in conjunction with the COVID-19 pandemic . . . ongoing conflict in Ukraine has hindered the global progress towards achieving the SDGs' (p. 369). Not only has the global political and financial will connect to the 2030 development agenda largely dissipated, but the local conditions for development have also been eroded with inflation, rising food and energy prices, as well as nations being forced to take sides in the conflict with political and diplomatic consequences. Mhlanga and Ndhlovu therefore argue that 'the circumstances possess the capacity to exert adverse implications on the attainment of the SDGs,' particularly the social goals, such as SDG1 on poverty and SDG2 on hunger. Whereas earlier publications emphasised the potential for the pandemic to trigger sustainability transitions, the war in Ukraine is seen, at least in this chapter, as detrimental to the environment and also for concern towards global environmental issues. However, the chapter concludes somewhat optimistically by recommending that governments, global organisations, and NGOs 'work towards mitigating the adverse effects of the Russia-Ukraine conflict on the pursuit of the SDGs' (p. 377). Ultimately, the authors note, these goals ought to guide the long-term recovery and development of the affected countries and the world in the years ahead. As such, the chapter remains optimistic about the relevance of the SDGs, despite not demonstrating any confidence that they will be attained by 2030 given current conditions.

4. Concluding reflections

The world arguably looks very different now than it did in 2015, at least from the viewpoint of global development policy. Multiple and intersecting crises related to the global repercussions of Covid-19 and the conflicts in Ukraine and the Middle East have made global cooperation on frameworks such as the SDGs difficult. This chapter set out to analyse the impacts that this 'polycrisis' has had on the spirit of the post-2015 development agenda, recognizing that the SDG reporting period has reached its midway point, with discussions now often centering on its continuation towards 2050. Drawing on a close reading and survey of literature on SDG progress published between 2021 and 2024, this chapter has explored the question of whether and how we can observe a sense of a changing 'mood of the world,' drawing on the work of Heinz Bude, in this body of work. Seven key observations stand out based on our analysis.

First, we find hardly any sense within the literature that global crises have entirely foreclosed the possibility of achieving the SDGs. While setbacks and challenges are universally acknowledged, the underlying ambition of the goals continue to be upheld by most of the authors, with some increase in pessimism in 2023–2024. This reflects an important aspect of the SDGs themselves: in line with Greig and Turner (2024), the development agenda can be seen as a politics of positive anticipation, as having a symbolic role of infusing global politics with hope. Crises such as Covid-19, the war in Ukraine, and the resurgence of economic inequality have tested this. However, the SDGs are still framed by most authors as still worth pursuing, regardless of whether they will be attained by 2030, and that the agenda as such is not one to be abandoned. This persistence reflects hope, as very few authors, despite noting great challenges for the agenda, rarely perceive the future of the SDGs as completely foreclosed and utterly out of reach. Even when they do, their importance as principles is recognised in most of the work surveyed.

Second, authors forwarding pessimistic views on SDG setbacks frequently interpret the failure of the agenda as more fundamental, rooted in systemic flaws that were evident from its inception. These critiques emphasise the structural and political barriers to success, often pointing to the failure of the MDGs as a historical precedent. If even the relatively modest goals of the MDGs proved unattainable, critics argue, how could the far more ambitious SDGs succeed? This perspective underscores a deep scepticism about the ability of the global system to achieve such transformative aims without profound systemic change and a mood that is not directly tied to recent crises. Issues such as inadequate financing, entrenched inequality, and weak political will are not seen simply as obstacles to be overcome—they are seen as indicators of the underlying flaws in the SDG framework itself. These critiques challenge not just the implementation of the goals but the assumptions and aspirations that underpin them, suggesting that the SDGs may have been destined for failure irrespective of the specific crises of recent years.

Third, we note a surprising lack of reflection in the 2022–2024 literature on the global repercussions of the war in Ukraine, particularly in terms of its impact on multilateralism and international cooperation. Given the war's significant implications for food security, energy markets, and geopolitical alliances, this omission is striking. It suggests that academic publishing, constrained by the time it takes to do research and then lengthy peer-review processes, and thus struggles to capture and respond to rapidly evolving global contexts. The lack of responsiveness in academic literature to such developments highlights a broader challenge in understanding and addressing the dynamic nature of global crises, and must also be pointed out as a central limitation in this chapter. Future work should revisit the questions raised in this perspective when the benefit of hindsight has crystalised to a greater degree.

Fourth, the literature from 2021 to 2022 reflects a post-Covid utopian imaginary that appears to have faded entirely by 2023–2024. In 2021, there was a sense of possibility, a belief that the crisis could serve as a catalyst for transformative change across social justice, sustainability, and global governance domains. Authors during this period often framed, as our survey also shows, the pandemic as a critical moment in history and a window of opportunity for radical change. However, as the initial optimism waned and the cumulative effects of overlapping crises (or polycrisis) became clearer, this mood faded and is nowhere to be found in the more recent literature. The shift reflects both the potentiality and generativity of crises but also the fallacy of expecting drastic systemic change in the wake of a crisis, after which many are going to want to go back to old ways of life.

Fifth, despite the bleak outlook painted in much of the literature, a sense of unfaltering hope persists. Many authors continue to express optimism that the SDGs, or at least some of their core objectives, remain achievable under the right conditions. This optimism often hinges on the potential for a 'big push'—a concerted effort involving increased funding, reforms, and global cooperation. Other authors emphasise the possibility of success only in the case of more radical change, arguing that systemic shifts in global governance, markets, the capitalist system, and values could create the conditions necessary for achieving the goals. This hope, while often tempered by realism, underscores the enduring appeal of the SDGs as a vision for a better future. It also reflects a broader tendency of refusing to give up hope, even when none of the data the authors cite point in the right direction. This suggests that empirical observations on their own might not be a sufficient or a necessary condition for changes in mood.

Sixth, we observe that prescriptive conclusions display three kinds of sentiments. The first is a call for more of the same: redoubled efforts, increased funding, and greater political commitment to the existing SDG framework. This perspective assumes that the goals are fundamentally sound and that their failure lies in inadequate implementation rather than flawed design. The second sentiment involves adjusting the timeline, with some authors advocating for a 2050 development agenda and adjusting the "deadline" (or, as some of the authors surveyed note, there is a tendency for wanting to "kick the can down the road"). The third, more radical sentiment involves a view where one should not settle for anything other than replacing the current system with another, suggesting that the current system is incapable of delivering on the SDGs or on global justice concerns, for that matter. These divergent perspectives highlight the tension between pragmatism and idealism in the discourse on global development, and vividly illustrate the need for more work on the role of moods in development discourse.

Last, at this midpoint review, all the surveyed literature points to a sense of overall failure and setbacks for the SDGs, with varying interpretations of the underlying causes and whether to abandon them or simply redouble our efforts. Some authors view the multiple intersecting crises we currently face (i.e., Covid-19, economic disruptions, and a changing geopolitical landscape) as the primary obstacles, while others see them as additional burdens on an agenda that was already faltering. This debate echoes insights from disaster research, which emphasises the non-deterministic nature of crises and the importance of addressing underlying vulnerabilities. The SDGs, in this view, are not failing because of unprecedented challenges but because of long-standing vulnerabilities across the world that have yet to be addressed.

As we look to the future, the persistence of hope remains a striking feature of the literature on SDG progress. The SDGs may or may not be realised by 2030 or even 2050, but the development spirit as such does not show evidence of having burned out. Whether the UN can regain trust and credibility in the face of growing scepticism remains an open question, especially under Trump 2.0 and the slashing of aid budgets. Similarly, the centrality of the SDGs in coordinating global development efforts will depend on their ability to adapt and respond to an increasingly complex and fragmented world. As long as the global development spirit persists, a guiding framework such as the MDGs or the SDGs may turn out to not even be that central to global development efforts. While this chapter has focused on literature explicitly addressing SDG progress, broader analyses of development thought will undoubtedly play a crucial role in shaping the future of global governance and cooperation. Undoubtedly, the present moment will leave its mark on development thought and we must recognise that global cooperation is in deep crisis—but this history is still being written and the mood of our current epoch is only beginning to be articulated.

References

Adeola, O. (2021). The COVID-19 pandemic and the UN's sustainable development goals: A general overview. In O. Adeola (Ed.), *Gendered perspectives on COVID-19 recovery in Africa: Towards sustainable development* (pp. 17–38). Springer.

Anderson, B. (2009). Affective atmospheres. *Emotion, Space and Society, 2*(2), 77–81.

Antoniades, A. (2023). *Crisis as a trend and the achievement of the SDGs.* University of Sussex.

Bendell, J. (2022). Replacing sustainable development: Potential frameworks for international cooperation in an era of increasing crises and disasters. *Sustainability, 14*(13), 8185.

Bude, H. (2018). *The mood of the world.* Polity.

Butler, J. (2022). *What in the world is this? A pandemic phenomenology.* Columbia University Press.

Colombano, J. E., & Nabarro, D. N. (2021). COVID-19 and the SDGs. In N. Kakar, V. Popovski, & N. A. Robinson (Eds.), *Fulfilling the sustainable development goals: On a quest for a sustainable world* (pp. 17–32). Routledge.

Elavarasan, R. M., Pugazhendhi, R., Shafiullah, G. M., Kumar, N. M., Arif, M. T., Jamal, T., Chopra, S. S., & Dyduch, J. (2022). Impacts of COVID-19 on sustainable development goals and effective approaches to maneuver them in the post-pandemic environment. *Environmental Science and Pollution Research, 29*(23), 33957–33987.

Fenner, R., & Cernev, T. (2021). The implications of the COVID-19 pandemic for delivering the sustainable development goals. *Futures, 128*, 102726.

Fulzele, R., Fulzele, V., & Dharwal, M. (2022). Mapping the impact of COVID-19 crisis on the progress of sustainable development goals (SDGs)-a focus on global environment and energy efficiencies. *Materials Today: Proceedings, 60*, 873–879.

Greig, A., & Turner, M. (2024). Policy and hope: The millennium development goals. *Global Policy, 15*(1), 66–77.

Hanna, T., Hughes, B. B., Irfan, M. T., Bohl, D. K., Solórzano, J., Abidoye, B., Patterson, L., & Moyer, J. D. (2024). Sustainable development goal attainment in the wake of COVID-19: Simulating an ambitious policy push. *Sustainability*, *16*(8), 3309.

Kelman, I. (2020). *Sustainable development goal 18: Do proposals for expanding the 17 goals stand up to scrutiny?* https://www.psychologytoday.com/intl/blog/disaster-choice/202007/sustainable-development-goal-18

Klees, S. J. (2024). Why SDG4 and the other SDGs are failing and what needs to be done. *International Journal of Educational Development*, *104*, 102946.

Koselleck, R., & Richter, M. W. (2006). Crisis. *Journal of the History of Ideas*, *67*(2), 357–400.

LaFleur, M. T., Helgason, K. S., Vieira, S., Julca, A., Cheng, H. W. J., Hunt, N., & Mukherjee, S. (2022). *Ensuring SDG progress amid recurrent crises* (Policy brief no. 137). United Nations Department of Economic and Social Affairs.

Li, C., Deng, Z., Wang, Z., Hu, Y., Wang, L., Yu, S., Li, W., Shi, Z., & Bryan, B. A. (2023). Responses to the COVID-19 pandemic have impeded progress towards the sustainable development goals. *Communications Earth and Environment*, *4*(1), 252.

Lomazzi, M., Borisch, B., & Laaser, U. (2014). The Millennium development goals: Experiences, achievements and what's next. *Global Health Action*, *7*(1), 23695.

MacKellar, F. L. (2022). COVID-19, the Russo-Ukrainian War, the global sustainable development project and post-crises demography. *Vienna Yearbook of Population Research*, *20*, 39–81.

Mhlanga, D., & Ndhlovu, E. (2024). Conclusions: The Russia-Ukraine War and sustainable development goals in Africa. In D. Mhlanga & E. Ndhlovu (Eds.), *The Russia-Ukraine conflict and development in Africa: Implications for sustainable development* (pp. 363–379). Springer.

Millán-Acevedo, N., & Gómez-Bruna, D. (2024). Contradictions between capitalism and sustainable human development: Where is the 2030 agenda headed?. *Capitalism Nature Socialism*, 1–20.

Nature Computational Science. (2023). The next seven years. *Nature Computational Science*, *3*, 721.

Pattberg, P., & Bäckstrand, K. (2023). Enhancing the achievement of the SDGs: Lessons learned at the half-way point of the 2030 agenda. *International Environmental Agreements: Politics, Law and Economics*, *23*(2), 107–114.

Pereira, P., Zhao, W., Symochko, L., Inacio, M., Bogunovic, I., & Barcelo, D. (2022). The Russian-Ukrainian armed conflict will push back the sustainable development goals. *Geography and Sustainability*, *3*(3), 277–287.

Schneider, S. H., Gödderz, A., Zille, H., & Bruder, M. (2024). *Public opinion of the 2030 agenda: A mid-term review* (DEval Policy Brief, 1/2024). Deutsches Evaluierungsinstitut der Entwicklungszusammenarbeit.

Shulla, K., & Leal-Filho, W. (2023). *Achieving the UN agenda 2030: Overall actions for the successful implementation of the sustainable development goals before and after the 2030 deadline*. European Union Parliament.

Shulla, K., Voigt, B. F., Cibian, S., Scandone, G., Martinez, E., Nelkovski, F., & Salehi, P. (2021). Effects of COVID-19 on the sustainable development goals (SDGs). *Discover Sustainability*, *2*, 1–19.

Srinivas, J., Kolloju, N., Singh, A., Naveen, S., & Naresh, S. (2024). The COVID-19 pandemic and its impact on sustainable development goals–2030. *Journal of the Knowledge Economy*, 1–14.

Stewart, K. (2011). Atmospheric attunements. *Environment and Planning D: Society and space*, *29*(3), 445–453.

Taylor, P., Macdonald, K., Huckstep, S., & Sun, Y. (2023). Shifting norms, multiplying actors, turbulent times: An emerging landscape of international development co-operation. *Development Policy Review*, *41*(4), e12686.

UN. (2015a). *Transforming our world: The 2030 agenda for sustainable development.* United Nations.

UN. (2015b). *Paris agreement.* United Nations.

UN. (2015c). *Sendai framework for disaster risk reduction 2015–2030.* United Nations.

UN. (2015d). *Addis Ababa action agenda of the third international conference on financing for development (Addis Ababa action agenda).* United Nations.

UN. (2019). *Decade of action.* https://www.un.org/sustainabledevelopment/decade-of-action/

UN News. (2023). *Sustainable development goals require global rescue plan, secretary-general tells political forum, hailing effort to improve developing nations' access to finance.* https://press.un.org/en/2023/sgsm21945.doc.htm

van Vuuren, D. P., Zimm, C., Busch, S., Kriegler, E., Leininger, J., Messner, D., Nakicenovic, N., Rockstrom, J., Riahi, K., Sperling, F., & Soergel, B. (2022). Defining a sustainable development target space for 2030 and 2050. *One Earth, 5*(2), 142–156.

Verma, A., & Nayak, J. K. (2024). Understanding public sentiments and misbeliefs about sustainable development goals: A sentiment and topic modeling analysis. *Journal of Information, Communication and Ethics in Society, 22*(2), 256–274.

Yuan, H., Wang, X., Gao, L., Wang, T., Liu, B., Fang, D., & Gao, Y. (2023). Progress towards the sustainable development goals has been slowed by indirect effects of the COVID-19 pandemic. *Communications Earth and Environment, 4*(1), 184.

Yusha'u, M. J., & Servaes, J. (2021). Beyond the SDGs: From 2030 to 2050 agenda for development. In M. J. Yusha'u & J. Servaes (Eds.), *The Palgrave handbook of international communication and sustainable development* (pp. 605–620). Palgrave Macmillan.

7 Misconstrued anticipations? Disaster politics in the age of disinformation

Miriam Matejova

1. Introduction

The year 2020 wasn't the year of the pandemic; it was the year of disasters. Human life losses, property damage, and environmental destruction followed Australian bushfires, Indonesian floods, locust swarms in East Africa, and several large commercial plane crashes. Europe was one of the worst-affected continents, struck severely by the Covid-19 pandemic as well as by powerful windstorms in the north, one of which—storm Ciara—wreaked havoc as far as Central Europe. Extratropical cyclones and other natural hazards are likely to sweep through the continent more often as temperatures rise due to climate change. This is, of course, a global trend. According to the Intergovernmental Panel on Climate Change's Sixth Assessment report (2021), in the near term, the world should expect increased frequency, severity, and duration of extreme environmental events, among many other things.[1]

Concurrently, another global trend has been on the rise—the creation and spread of various types of misinformation, from hoaxes and conspiracy theories to "fake news" and "alternative facts." While mis- and disinformation in various forms have existed for centuries, the growth of social media usage and influence has enabled a much faster and broader spread of false claims (Allcott et al., 2019). Conspiracy theories in particular have seen a new wave of public interest as the Covid-19 pandemic progressed. The pandemic was a disaster with vast social impacts; it brought home the importance of crisis management, crisis planning, and disaster resilience. The accompanying "misinfodemic," a phenomenon linked to the fast spread of false information on various aspects of the pandemic, revealed the danger of mis- and disinformation that, together with the disaster itself, multiplied damages.

This chapter evaluates the intersection of the above two phenomena—disasters and disinformation—in the context of public risk perception. Underlying the chapter is the argument that disasters are political events, and this *disaster politics* affects both vulnerability (i.e., how people are affected by disasters) and public risk perceptions (i.e., how people perceive disasters and their impacts). Through brief case studies of the Covid-19 pandemic and the Chernobyl nuclear disaster and their respective conspiracy theories, I trace the effect of disinformation on public disaster risk perceptions, highlighting the role of temporality within the context of disaster politics.

DOI: 10.4324/9781003537311-8

2.　Disasters as political events

What are disasters? How do we conceptualize these events in relation to human societies? In what ways are disasters political? In general, disasters are understood as catastrophic events that overwhelm the ability of human systems—whether political, economic, social, or other—to endure external pressures. Environmental disasters in particular are events that either originate in nature or disproportionally damage the environment (or both). They can be brought on by human activities such as industrial accidents from industrial processes (e.g., resource extraction) or by natural phenomena like earthquakes and tsunamis, or a combination of the two like the 2011 Fukushima disaster. Increasingly, however, disasters—even those from natural hazards—are thought to stem from the intersection of human and ecological factors (e.g., Kelman, 2020).

Disasters were long treated as nonpolitical events and thus largely neglected in political science (Hannigan, 2012, p. 8). They are, however, political in at least two aspects. First, disasters are political events in and of themselves because they open space for their own politicization as various groups in a society (e.g., government officials, activists, experts) strive to define or explain the event (e.g., Albrecht, 2022; Olson, 2008). Second, disasters produce indirect or secondary political effects; they tend to open windows of opportunity for various groups to challenge the existing social structures or power arrangements (Pelling & Dill, 2006).

The literature on the politics of disasters has grown over the past decades. Disasters have been studied in light of their electoral impacts and leader survival, effects on preexisting grievances and legitimacy of regimes, social networks and norms of interaction during emergencies, disaster-related governance, and the politics of disaster aid (e.g., Aldrich, 2014; Carlin et al., 2014; Cohen & Werker, 2008; Comfort, 2002; Drury & Olson, 1998; Flores & Smith, 2013; Le Billon & Waizenegger, 2007; Robinson et al., 2013; Wood & Wright, 2015). Among the most widely studied topics is the relationship between disasters from natural hazards and violent conflict. In particular, scholars are divided over whether such disasters mitigate conflict by fostering cooperation among states or various groups (e.g., Kelman, 2006; Kreutz, 2012) or exacerbate it because of their negative effects on scarcity and economic development (e.g., Brancati, 2007; Nel & Righarts, 2008).

Studies of the disaster aftermath also tend to focus either on popular responses such as activist campaigns, protests, and volunteer mobilization or policy responses, including legal changes and international treaties (Birkmann et al., 2010; Elliott, 2013; Macdonald, 1980; Molotch, 1970; Perez, 2003). These types of sociopolitical effects of disasters are, of course, linked to physical damage, but they are also determined by some preexisting sociocultural conditions and social dynamics. These social dynamics are heavily shaped by different framings of the event, including mis- and disinformation. Disaster politics thus has both "objective" and "subjective" elements.

2.1 Hazard and vulnerability as "objective" elements of disaster politics

Disasters occur due to a combination of hazards and vulnerabilities, including an underlying lack of sufficient preparedness. For example, living in a flood zone is a hazard and floods become disasters only if they overwhelm human capacity to respond to them. Hazards and vulnerabilities are "objective" elements of disaster politics in the sense that they are largely out of the hands of individuals but depend on physical exposure and hazard origins, government policies, and broader structural factors.[2]

Hazards simply refer to existing conditions or events that can endanger or negatively affect individuals (e.g., health), their property, or the environment or otherwise anything that people value (e.g., Kates & Kasperson, 1983). Hazards can have natural or human origins. In environmental politics, hazards are frequently discussed in the context of pollution and specifically the contention surrounding different kinds (or sources) of pollution. Such contention tends to involve or give rise to various types of environmental movements. One example is the issue of toxic waste and related environmental disasters in the USA. Perhaps one of the most famous of these disasters is the case of Love Canal,[3] a neighborhood built in the 1950s on top of a toxic waste dump in the state of New York. The site became the center of one of the worst environmental disasters in American history, eventually leading to major changes in US environmental legislation.[4] Other examples of contention surrounding pollution are cases of major oil spills such as the Santa Barbara spill, which triggered large protests in California in the 1960s and eventually led to the establishment of Earth Day (Gephart, 1984; Molotch, 1970). These hazards from industrial processes turned into disasters and subsequent opportunities for societal changes because they interacted with preexisting vulnerabilities (see also Matejova, 2023).

Vulnerability reflects the inability of social, political, economic, or other systems to adapt to disproportionate impacts and sudden changes.[5] Vulnerability to hazards varies over time and space; it embodies a number of different factors, from infrastructure and other built environments to social and economic inequalities to governance systems (Cutter et al., 2003). The interaction of geographic features (e.g., location, topography, climate) and social conditions determine vulnerability to disasters. As Kelman et al. (2015, p. 23) assert, vulnerability is "not only about the present state, but [is] also about what society has done to itself (and especially what some sectors have done to other sectors) over the long-term; why and how society has taken that set of actions in order to reach the present state; and how society might change the present state to improve in the future." For example, the level of urbanization and economic wealth are elements of vulnerability in some coastal countries that may be facing a more frequent occurrence of extreme environmental events due to climate change—yet these elements may be exacerbated or lessened by government policies. Furthermore, disaster impacts are often unequally distributed, with marginalized communities experiencing them more severely. Social injustices like exclusion of communities from policymaking or disproportionate exposure of some communities to hazards are therefore crucial elements of vulnerability, as well (e.g., Schlosberg & Collins, 2014).

(Social) vulnerability determines the physical or material impacts of disasters, but perception plays a role in how we understand these impacts and therefore how they influence our attitudes and subsequent behaviors. The ability to shape those perceptions is therefore a crucial element of disaster politics.

2.2   Risk perceptions as "subjective" elements of disaster politics

The subjective element of disaster politics stems from individual perceptions of disaster risks. Risk can be understood from at least two broad perspectives: objectivist and constructivist. In an objectivist view, for "any given hazard there is one true risk" (Cvetkovich & Earle, 1992, p. 5). This risk is defined as probability multiplied by the severity of impact, and it is possible to assess (and thus mitigate) such risk through analytical risk assessments (e.g., Cutter et al., 2003).[6] In contrast, a constructivist view understands risk as a possibility of adverse effects from hazards where "adverse" is linked to the value of what is affected, and the "possibility" reflects human inability to assess risks with perfect accuracy and certainty (Cvetkovich & Earle, 1992).

Understanding of risk is closely linked to judgments that people make when asked to evaluate hazards—that is, risk perceptions. Risk perceptions are, of course, subjective and they seldom match the objective reality. As a result, public risk perception frequently differs from official (i.e., scientific) assessments of risk. For example, due to various cognitive shortcuts, people tend to overestimate some risks and underestimate others (e.g., Dionne et al., 2007). Frequently, individuals are most concerned with hazards that could have large adverse impacts on human life or those that are largely unfamiliar (e.g., Kahneman et al., 1982). People also tend to assign more credibility to higher risk estimates (Johnson & Slovic, 1995) and in fact often perceive risks as "feelings" (i.e., through an intuitive reaction rather than logical assessment) (Slovic & Peters, 2006).

Risk perceptions are also influenced by broader societal and cultural contexts. Specifically, risk perception evolves over time since the public (e.g., experts, media, nongovernmental organizations) plays an active role in forming specific public perceptions of risk.

At the same time, the language of risk has been an inherent part of the political landscape, as seen in the rhetoric of many state leaders across the world. Different framing of disaster risks—and particularly the same disaster events—by various groups is a common part of disaster politics. For example, the Three Mile Island (TMI) nuclear disaster was framed by diverse actors to influence public risk perceptions of nuclear energy. Public officials and especially US President Jimmy Carter (who was much interested in expanding the US nuclear program) attempted to increase public acceptability of nuclear policy and thus downplay the TMI disaster. The US nuclear industry, with billions of dollars at stake, wanted to reassure the public of the safety of nuclear technology, and the US media, suffering from lack of adequate information, gave in to sensationalism that they then fed to the public

(Nelkin, 1981). Similar framing and counter-framing dynamics concerning disaster impacts and risks occurred after other environmental disasters like, for example, the Exxon Valdez oil spill (Larabee, 2000). Framing—or use of particular language for specific purposes—enables the politicization of disaster events.

3. Disaster framing and disinformation

Political actors frequently use metaphors, targeted phrases, carefully chosen words, or pictures to use disasters for maintaining or advancing their political positions (Albrecht, 2022; Pelling & Dill, 2010). Language and symbols help these actors construct beliefs about the significance of events, issues, policies, and leaders and thus influence shared behavior (Edelman, 1985). In other words, political actors frame disasters. Frames are cognitive shortcuts and framing is a process through which people make sense of the information they receive given some preexisting "schemas" (Benford & Snow, 2000; Scheufele & Iyengar, 2014). To influence behavior, presenting a piece of information in a particular way is much more important than communicating specific content. For example, governments use certain ways to talk about disasters to achieve different objectives: the language of "tragedy" and "devastation" to attract international assistance, the imagery of government competence to boost its popularity, or the rhetoric of "building back better" to initiate domestic social reforms (Chen, 2009; Fan, 2013).

The voluminous framing literature can be broadly divided according to two core questions: What types of frames can we find in the public discourse? Are frames effective? The first group of scholars is interested in "frames in communication" (i.e., what is being said or shown) (Druckman, 2001). They tend to study what frames look like and what they are intended to achieve, from defining problems to making moral judgments to suggesting solutions (e.g., Benford & Snow, 2000; Entman, 2003; Zald, 1996). The second group of scholars is interested in frame effectiveness or the conditions under which the frames achieve what they are intended to achieve (Chong & Druckman, 2007; Gross, 2008; Klar, 2013). The disaster framing literature generally falls under the first category. Examples include the framing of climate change (e.g., Painter & Asher, 2012; Trumbo, 1996; Zehr, 2000) but also of different types of environmental disasters such as chemical spills and floods (Thistlethwaite et al., 2019; Thomas et al., 2016).

The literature on the topic of disaster mis- and disinformation focuses largely on information sharing during crisis (e.g., Brennen et al., 2021; Gottlieg & Dyer, 2020; Sutton, 2010). Disinformation is false information that is created and spread deliberately (as opposed to misinformation, which is simply false or inaccurate information). Theoretically, disaster disinformation can be understood from two broad perspectives. First, at a societal level, anti-science efforts, spread primarily through polarized news media and social media, may decrease the public perception of urgency and thus lessen the need for preparedness when it comes to future disasters. Second, from an instrumentalist perspective, the manipulation of scientific data for political, economic, or other purposes may have a range of social and political impacts, from political polarization to protest movements to regime consolidation.

Some governments are known to have downplayed the existence and/or severity of disasters. For example, after the 1985 earthquakes in Mexico City, the Mexican government downplayed the human losses but exaggerated the economic costs of the disaster (Olson, 2008). Similarly, during Russia's 2010 forest fires, Vladimir Putin's government used the language of intentionally skewed statistics to construct a meaning of the disaster that would convey "a positive idea of the state" (Bertrand, 2012). Other governments have unequivocally denied the existence of disasters within their territories. For example, the state's suppression of information about earthquakes was an established policy in the early history of California (Olson, 2008). Such policies were not limited to the 19th century. As a result of strict Soviet censorship, disasters simply "did not exist" in the Soviet Union (Zavacka, 2006).

Denial of disasters is a type of framing. Political actors such as governments and political parties but also corporate entities and nongovernmental organizations may withhold information for bureaucratic reasons or provide insufficient or delayed release of information on past or potential future events (de Marchi et al., 1996, pp. 97–98). They can also reinterpret disaster events, denying them partially or fully or claiming the event or some aspects of it are not (or will not be) what they seem (Martin, 2007, p. 4). While disaster disinformation has been prevalent in the past in nondemocratic regimes, some empirical evidence suggests that this practice has been present in modern democracies, as well. For example, lack of transparency and various cover-ups have been linked to some nuclear accidents in Japan (Aldhous & Iovino, 2011; Beech, 1999) and oil spills in Australia (Head, 2010). In Central Europe, aside from the Covid-19 pandemic, mis- and disinformation have been observed after the 2010 red sludge disaster in Hungary (Sarlos & Szondi, 2014) and the 2000 Baia Mare cyanide spill, which poisoned Hungary's River Tisa (Greenpeace, 2000). Many disasters are accompanied by a specific type of disaster disinformation—conspiracy theories.

3.1   Disaster conspiracy theories

Conspiracy theories are "beliefs that a group of actors are colluding in secret to reach a malevolent goal" (Imhoff et al., 2022). Frequently, beliefs in conspiracy theories are considered harmful as they tend to go hand in hand with risky behavior such as lack of adherence to public guidelines and rejection of scientific consensus, for example, related to vaccines or climate change (Douglas & Sutton, 2015; Jolley & Douglas, 2014; Uscinski & Olivella, 2017). Such rejection then manifests in activities like searching for alternative medicines (e.g., Oliver & Wood, 2014) as well as a general reduction in trust in experts and science (Galliford & Furnham, 2017). An example is the link between beliefs in conspiracy theories about Covid-19 and public (un)willingness to follow the pandemic measures (Allington et al., 2021; Bierwiaczonek et al., 2020; Stecula & Pickup, 2021). Other health crises (e.g., emergence of the Zika virus in the USA) too have seen negative impacts of conspiracy theories as governments scrambled to communicate accurate information as part of mitigation measures (Sharma et al., 2017).

Disaster conspiracy theories often center on disaster origins, frequently linking those to the malicious intent of some political or economic elites. For example, during the Zika virus disease outbreak in 2015–2016, some people believed that genetically modified mosquitoes were to blame and that governments wanted to intentionally sicken or kill people (Klofstad et al., 2019). Among some conspiracy theorists, the origins of the 2004 Indian Ocean earthquake and tsunami, the 2010 Haiti earthquake, and the 2011 Japanese earthquake and tsunami were attributed to the US High Frequency Active Auroral Research Program (HAARP) (McConnachie & Tudge, 2013, pp. 262–264). Located in Alaska, HAARP is a massive transmitter of 180 antennae designed to observe the processes in the Earth's ionosphere. It is managed by the US Air Force Research Laboratory and the Office of Naval Research and backed by several US universities. Some believe that HAARP is a "mega-weapon" that can alter weather and bring on earthquakes and power outages (McConnachie & Tudge, 2013, p. 259). The Bush administration was also blamed for using HAARP to create disasters like 2008 Cyclone Nargis (to punish Burma's Junta for ruining the US 2008 election) and the 2008 Sichuan earthquake (to punish China for being overly friendly toward India, Russia, and Japan).

Another set of disaster conspiracy theories concerns Hurricane Katrina that devastated New Orleans in 2005. Some believed that Katrina was created to increase oil prices and buy Gulf Coast real estate (McConnachie & Tudge, 2013, p. 261). Suspicions of sabotage emerged as some media and blogs spread the possibility that a levee wall was blasted open with explosives and that the disaster was intentionally made to affect poorer African American communities. Others believed that the hurricane was used to justify more funding for weather altering experiments (McConnachie & Tudge, 2013, pp. 282–284).

While the literature on the negative impacts of conspiracy theories is vast, a few scholars argue that, contrary to popular opinion, conspiracy theories are not simply false beliefs with adverse impacts. They could indeed be beneficial, for example, as "tools of dissent" needed for the healthy functioning of society as they give voice to the less powerful and keep those in power in check (Uscinski & Parent, 2014; Uscinski, 2018). Specifically, conspiracy theories remind the powerful groups that "someone is always watching"; they may also bring to light new information and even help reveal the truth (if the theories are right), as in the case of the Watergate scandal (Uscinski, 2018).

In the following section, I discuss these two different effects of conspiracy theories on public perceptions of disaster risks. Specifically, I trace both the negative and positive effects of conspiracy theories accompanying the Covid-19 pandemic and the Chernobyl nuclear disaster, respectively. These two cases serve as illustrative examples that reveal how information seeking at times of crisis shapes disaster risk perceptions as well as disaster politics.

4.   Everyday disaster politics: the risk perception and disinformation nexus

Both in general and at times of crisis, risk perceptions are influenced by the nature of the hazard as well as the associated emotions (Malecki et al., 2021). These emotions—linked to, for example, the disaster's catastrophic potential or scientific uncertainty—shape the public acceptance of relevant risk mitigation policies. At the same time, uncertainty that surrounds many disasters prompts people to seek more information, including from conspiracy theorists. This dynamic was evident during the Covid-19 pandemic, which illustrates well the negative effects of conspiracy theories on people's behavior.

4.1   From 5G networks to Bill Gates and a Chinese bioweapon: The Covid-19 conspiracy theories

The Covid-19 pandemic began as SARS-CoV-2 emerged in late 2019 in Wuhan, China, and then swiftly spread around the globe. The onset of the pandemic was shrouded in uncertainty and anxiety as the origin, nature, and danger of the virus were unknown (e.g., Huang & Yang, 2020). The diversity of symptoms and impacts, along with the continuing virus mutations, made reducing this uncertainty difficult. Before the roll out of vaccines, government responses included a range of recommendations and policy measures to slow down the spread of the virus, from social distancing and mask mandates to quarantining, travel and business restrictions, and lockdowns. These restrictions generated further economic and social uncertainty, which led to a global recession, food and supply shortages, and cancellation or reduction of social events.

The elements of social vulnerability to the Covid-19 pandemic have been country-specific (and differed even within countries), but some general patterns have emerged. For example, the pandemic exposed inequalities in societies by affecting the poor and marginalized communities the most. Preexisting conditions like poverty, inaccessible health care, lack of quality housing, and even lack of education worsened the impacts of the pandemic on those communities (Kim & Bostwick, 2020). For example, lack of education may contribute to a lesser ability to understand warning advisories (Karaye & Horney, 2020). Employment in the service industry, which generally employs poorer people, has also been linked to lesser adherence to public advisories (de Souza et al., 2020). The public responses to the pandemic and related government policies varied from closely following the guidelines to disregarding the advisories and even spreading various false claims about the virus and the pandemic in general.

Within a few months, several conspiracy theories about the origin of the novel coronavirus were already widely circulating on the Internet. Among the most popular ones were the virus spreading through the 5G networks, Bill Gates causing the pandemic, the virus escaping from a Chinese lab or Chinese scientists creating it deliberately as a biological weapon (e.g., Douglas, 2021; Himelboim et al., 2024; Romer & Jamieson, 2020). Perhaps the most widespread conspiracy theory was that Covid-19 did not actually exist but was made up by the global elites to limit people's freedoms or that it was a plot by Big Pharma. Many people also believed that the virus was no worse than the flu virus and that the number of related deaths was inflated. The mis- and disinformation about the pandemic was helped by the political elite across the world, who downplayed the seriousness of the novel coronavirus (Romer & Jamieson, 2020).

As noted earlier, during crises, conspiracy theories in part fill an informational void but also are linked to the emotions of people affected by the event. According to Malecki et al. (2021, p. 700), emotional aspects of Covid-19 included "catastrophic potential, familiarity, understanding, scientific uncertainty, personal control, voluntariness, trust in institutions, and media attention." These emotional aspects then determined the degree to which people perceived some risks as (un)safe or (un)acceptable, which was then linked to responses to risk mitigation policies.

The lack of information on the virus led to anxiety in some people. While some chose to follow government advisories in coping with the uncertainty, others reduced the uncertainty/unfamiliarity by equating the risk to the common (and familiar) flu, thus downplaying the risk (Malecki et al., 2021). Information seeking behavior was strong during the first few weeks of the pandemic (Huang & Yang, 2020). As more information became available about the nature of the virus, those who saw its risks followed government policies like social distancing and mask mandates (Malecki et al., 2021), while those whose risk perceptions were influenced by other factors (e.g., conspiracy theories) went in the direction of noncompliance.

Conspiracy theories about Covid-19 contributed to a reduced perception of the threat among the believers. In the USA, conspiracy theories were linked to a lowered perception of the risk of the pandemic and the subsequent lowered compliance with government policies such as mask mandates and lowered willingness to get vaccinated (Douglas, 2021; Pummerer et al., 2022; Romer & Jamieson, 2020). However, the adherence to public health guidelines and policies depended on the type of conspiracy theories that people believed. Imhoff and Lamberty (2020), for example, found that people who believed that the pandemic was a hoax were more likely to disregard government guidelines like social distancing. At the same time, those who believed that the virus was manufactured in a Chinese lab were more likely to follow their own protective measures, such as alternative medicine. Therefore, sometimes conspiracy theories increase risk perceptions and lead to self-protective behavior—how beneficial that behavior may be is up for debate.

4.2 American sabotage or Soviet experiment? The Chernobyl nuclear disaster conspiracy theories

The Chernobyl nuclear disaster is an example of this other type of effect of conspiracy theories on public risk perception and subsequent behavior. The disaster occurred in April 1986 at the Chernobyl nuclear power plant in northern Ukraine. During a safety test the power plant operators accidentally triggered a reactor shutdown, which eventually led to a meltdown. During the subsequent explosions and fire, radioactive contamination spread across the Soviet Union and into Europe (e.g., Mara, 2011). The severity of the disaster's health effects is uncertain, but there is some evidence of negative impacts of the disaster on the mental health of the affected people (Bromet & Havenaar, 2007). The immediate disaster aftermath was shrouded in uncertainty and mismanaged by both plant operators and Soviet officials (Mara, 2011, pp. 41–66). While the Soviet Union at the time was afflicted by elements of social vulnerability like poverty and inequality (Slay, 2009), in the context of the Chernobyl disaster, the greatest vulnerability stemmed from the policies governing crisis communication. "Information was the greatest public need," John Lewis (1987, p. 86) writes. The secrecy around the Chernobyl disaster was harmful since people, including the first responders, were not informed early on to take safety precautions.

The invisible nature of radiation has for decades profoundly shaped public risk perceptions of nuclear energy (e.g., Paine, 2002)—in the case of Chernobyl, the invisible threat combined with the lack of official information created a fertile ground for various false narratives, many about human and animal mutations from radiation (Alexievich, 2016). These were accompanied by public fear, which shaped individual behavior in the disaster aftermath (Rahu, 2003). For example, due to fears of birth defects and miscarriages from radiation exposure, many women in Ukraine were choosing not to have children (Mara, 2011, p. 72). At the same time, due to secrecy and cover-ups, various types of rumors and conspiracy theories were considered a better source of information than the Soviet media (Astapova, 2021; Erolova & Tsyryapkina, 2023). For example, people widely shared various folk remedies (like vodka) for radiation poisoning (L.A. Times, 1986). And some, lacking any awareness of the radiation risks, believed that the whole thing was a fraud, a lie with which "the government [was] just trying to take [their] land" (Rahu, 2003, p. 296).

Theories about Western sabotage also began circulating early on. Because it was difficult to believe that the nuclear reactor could fail, sabotage made sense in the eyes of the general public. As Astapova (2021) writes, the USA was blamed for creating the disaster to undermine the USSR economically. Some believed that the Soviet government knew of the sabotage and covered it up so as not to look bad for failing to prevent it. But there were also sabotage theories about the Soviet government creating the disaster as part of an experiment to observe the health impacts of radiation. These types of conspiracy theories had distinct political effects in the Soviet Union. Specifically, the Chernobyl nuclear disaster provided opportunities for dissent against governments in the Soviet republics (Dawson, 1996; Petryna, 1995). Ukraine and Belarus suffered the worst impacts of the radiation contamination, and this disproportionate impact led to some "ethno-national interpretation" of the disaster (Astapova, 2021, p. 36). The Ukrainians, for example, believed that the Russians had built nuclear power plants deliberately on Ukrainian territory to expose Ukrainians to the fallout from any potential accident. Eco-activism in Ukraine was linked to the Chernobyl disaster and subsequent democratic revolution. Similar processes unfolded in Lithuania and Belarus.

5.   Discussion and conclusion

Everyday politics of disasters is about the intersection of objective disaster impacts and subjective perceptions of those impacts. The latter is turning out to be increasingly important in the post-truth era, where the spread of mis- and disinformation is becoming a threat to societies.

Disasters are characterized by high uncertainty, which people tend to experience as feelings of a lack of control or powerlessness. Uncertainty thus prompts people to seek more information (Frewer et al., 2002; Fung et al., 2018; Kahlor, 2010). Conspiracy theories help reduce disaster uncertainty, as people have a need to explain the events in order to cope with them (van Prooijen & Douglas, 2017). Conspiracy theories are therefore attractive to those people whose psychological needs—such as the need to restore a sense of control—are not being met (Douglas, 2021; van Prooijen & Douglas, 2017). As the presence and power of the social media platforms grow in everyday life, conspiracy theories are migrating online (Enders et al., 2021; Stecula & Pickup, 2021). In times of crisis in particular, social media help speed up the spread of false information.

The above examples of two disasters illustrate that disinformation—and specifically conspiracy theories—may, however, have different types of effects on public behavior. False information about a disaster or crisis makes the information environment even more complex and uncertain. The role of emotions is crucial in the post-disaster environment and, to a large extent, determines how people cope with disaster uncertainty. Fear, anxiety, and even anger that tend to be linked to actual or potential damage, lack of familiarity, a sense of control, or institutional responses determine how people perceive danger and thus how they behave. As people seek out more information and as various false narratives spread throughout society, risk perceptions tend to change—they can increase (so people become more risk-averse and follow official guidance) or decrease (so people become more risk acceptant if they fill the information void with disinformation like conspiracy theories).

The false certainty that conspiracy theories entail may be a dangerous effect of disaster disinformation, with potential implications for disaster management and future resilience building. There is a critical time window immediately after a disaster occurrence where disaster uncertainty meets societal vulnerability in an emotional mix that pushes individuals toward different behavioral responses. At this time, the information void is filled with either accurate information or misinformation. This period is, of course, crucial from a crisis communication and disaster response perspective, but from a broader political angle, communication with the public to reduce uncertainty helps increase trust in political institutions and thus weaken the lure of misinformation and conspiracy theories. Our ability to do so will also shape our resilience against future disasters, since how we understand the present influences not only our current behavior but also our future decisions and actions.

Misinformation both decreases future resilience and hinders our ability to anticipate future disasters, especially the complex ones with cascading effects (like, for example, the 2011 Fukushima disaster; see Briggs & Matejova, 2019). This is partly because misinformation, and especially disinformation, may skew people's risk perceptions and behavior in unpredictable ways. Therefore, if we want to anticipate the future in the age of disinformation, we may want to let go of the objectivist idea of risk as "the probability times impact," since such probabilities can hardly be assigned accurately. Focusing instead on "possibilities" and an inter-disciplinary understanding of both natural and human systems may help our antici-pations of the future become better informed rather than misconstrued.

Notes

1 Summary for policymakers available at https://www.ipcc.ch/report/ar6/wg1/downloads/report/IPCC_AR6_WGI_SPM.pdf
2 Although Kelman et al. (2015) argue that vulnerability, too, is subjective rather than ob-jective, because environmental phenomena can be viewed as hazards or opportunities, depending on one's point of view.
3 For a comprehensive account of the Love Canal disaster and its consequences, see Reed (2002).
4 Environmental politics scholars have examined the relationship between hazards and the issues of social and environmental justice—poor, marginalized individuals and communi-ties are disproportionally more exposed to hazardous environmental conditions, whether due to natural or human-caused hazards (e.g., Carruthers & Rodriguez, 2009; Schlosberg, 2004).
5 Some discuss vulnerability with respect to four components: exposure, resilience, sen-sitivity, and fragility (Blaikie et al., 2004; see also Briggs & Matejova, 2019). The rela-tionship between vulnerability and resilience in particular has been debated in the extant literature (see Manyena, 2006).
6 Impacts could be human (e.g., deaths, injuries, population displacement), economic, en-vironmental, and political/social (e.g., public anxiety, violations of public order).

References

Albrecht, F. (2022). Natural hazards as political events: Framing and politicization of floods in the United Kingdom. *Environmental Hazards*, *21*(1), 17–35.
Aldhous, P., & Iovino, Z. (2011, March 18). Japan's record of nuclear cover-ups and accidents. *New Scientist*. https://www.newscientist.com/article/dn20263-japans-record-of-nuclear-cover-ups-and-accidents/
Aldrich, D. (2014). The emergence of civil society: Networks in disasters, mitigation, and recovery. In U. Fra Paleo (Ed.), *Risk governance* (pp. 135–148). Springer.
Alexievich, S. (2016). *Chernobyl prayer: A chronicle of the future*. Penguin Books.
Allcott, H., Gentzkow, M., & Yu, C. (2019). Trends in the diffusion of misinformation on social media. *Research and Politics*, 1–8.
Allington, D., Duffy, B., Wessely, S., Dhavan, N., & Rubin, J. (2021). Health-protective behaviour, social media usage, and conspiracy belief during the COVID-19 public health emergency. *Psychological Medicine*, *51*(10), 1763–1769.
Astapova, A., Colăcel, O., Pintilescu, C., & Scheibner, T. (2021). *Conspiracy theories in Eastern Europe: Tropes and trends*. Routledge.
Beech, H. (1999, October 11). How Japan's accident stacks up next to Chernobyl. *Time*. http://content.time.com/time/world/article/0,8599,2053740,00.html
Benford, R., & Snow, D. (2000). Framing processes and social movements: An overview and assessment. *Annual Review of Sociology*, *26*, 611–639.
Bertrand, E. (2012). Constructing Russian power by communicating during disasters. *Problems of Post-Communism*, *59*(3), 31–40.
Bierwiaczonek, K., Kunst, J., & Pich, O. (2020). Belief in COVID-19 conspiracy theories reduces social distancing over time. *Health and Well-Being*, *12*(40), 1270–1285.

Birkmann, J., Buckle, P., Jaeger, J., Pelling, M., Setiadi, N., Garschagen, M., Fernando, N., & Kropp, J. (2010). Extreme events and disasters: A window of opportunity for change? Analysis of organizational, institutional, and political changes, formal and informal responses after mega-disasters. *Natural Hazards, 55*, 637–655.

Blaikie, P., Cannon, T., Davis, I., & Wisner, B. (2004). *At risk: Natural hazards, people's vulnerability and disasters*. Routledge.

Brancati, D. (2007). Political aftershocks: The impact of earthquakes on intrastate conflict. *The Journal of Conflict Resolution, 51*(5), 715–743.

Brennen, S., Simon, F., & Kleis Nielsen, R. (2021). Beyond (mis)representation: Visuals in COVID-19 misinformation. *The International Journal of Press/Politics, 26*(1), 277–299.

Briggs, C., & Matejova, M. (2019). *Disaster security: Using intelligence and military planning for energy and environmental risks*. Cambridge University Press.

Bromet, E., & Havenaar, J. (2007). Psychological and perceived health effects of the Chernobyl disaster: A 20-year review. *Health Physics, 93*(5), 516–521.

Carlin, R., Love, G., & Zechmeister, E. (2014). Natural disaster and democratic legitimacy: The public opinion consequences of Chile's 2010 earthquake and tsunami. *Political Research Quarterly, 67*(1), 3–15.

Carruthers, D., & Rodriguez, P. (2009). Mapuche protest, environmental conflict and social movement linkage in Chile. *Third World Quarterly, 30*(4), 743–760.

Chen, N. (2009). Institutionalizing public relations: A case study of Chinese government crisis communication on the 2008 Sichuan earthquake. *Public Relations Review, 35*, 187–198.

Chong, D., & Druckman, J. (2007). A theory of framing and opinion formation in competitive elite environments. *Journal of Communication, 57*(1), 99–118.

Cohen, C., & Werker, E. (2008). The political economy of "natural" disasters. *Harvard Business School Working Paper 08–040*, 1–46.

Comfort, L. (2002). Rethinking security: Organizational fragility in extreme events. *Public Administration Review, 62*, 98–107.

Cutter, S., Boruff, B., & Shirley, W. (2003). Social vulnerability to environmental hazards. *Social Science Quarterly, 84*(2), 242–261.

Cvetkovich, G., & Earle, T. (1992). Environmental hazards and the public. *Journal of Social Issues, 48*(4), 1–20.

Dawson, J. (1996). *Eco-nationalism: Anti-nuclear activism and national identity in Russia, Lithuania, and Ukraine*. Duke University Press.

de Marchi, B., Funtowicz, S., & Ravetz, J. (1996). Seveso: A paradoxical classic disaster. In J. Mitchell (Ed.), *The long road to recovery*. United Nations University Press.

de Souza, C., Machado, M., & do Carmo, R. (2020). Human development, social vulnerability, and COVID-19 in Brazil: A study of the social determinants of health. *Infectious Diseases of Poverty, 9*, 124.

Dionne, G., Fluet, C., & Desjardins, D. (2007). Predicted risk perception and risk-taking behavior: The case of impaired driving. *Journal of Risk and Uncertainty, 35*(3), 237–264.

Douglas, K. (2021). COVID-19 conspiracy theories. *Group Processes & Intergroup Relations, 24*(2), 270–275.

Douglas, K., & Sutton, R. (2015). Climate change: Why the conspiracy theories are dangerous. *Bulletin of the Atomic Scientists, 71*(2), 98–106.

Druckman, J. (2001). The implications of framing effects for citizen competence. *Political Behavior, 23*, 225–256.

Drury, C., & Olson, R. (1998). Disasters and political unrest: An empirical investigation. *Journal of Contingencies and Crisis Management, 6*(3), 153–161.

Edelman, M. (1985). Political language and political reality. *Policy Studies, 18*, 10–19.

Elliott, D. (2013). *Fukushima: Impacts and implications*. Palgrave Macmillan.

Enders, A., Uscinski, J. E., Seelig, M. I., Klofstad, C. A., Wuchty, S., Funchion, J. R., Murthi, M. N., Premaratne, K., & Stoler, J. (2021). The relationship between social media use and beliefs in conspiracy theories and misinformation. *Political Behavior*. https://doi.org/10.1007/s11109-021-09734-6

Entman, R. (2003). Cascading activation: Contesting the White House's frame after 9/11. *Political Communication*, *20*, 415–432.

Erolova, Y., & Tsyryapkina, Y. (2023). Local reflections on the Chernobyl disaster 35 years later: Peripheral narratives from Ukraine, Belarus, Russia, and Bulgaria. *Comparative Southeast European Studies*, *7*(1).

Fan, L. (2013). Disaster as opportunity? Building back better in Aceh, Myanmar, and Haiti. *HPG Working Paper*. https://www.odi.org/sites/odi.org.uk/files/odi-assets/publications-opinion-files/8693.pdf

Flores, A., & Smith, A. (2013). Leader survival and natural disasters. *British Journal of Political Science*, *43*(4), 1–23.

Frewer, L. J., Miles, S., Brennan, M., Kuznesof, S., Ness, M., & Ritson, C. (2002). Public preferences for informed choice under conditions of risk uncertainty. *Public Understanding of Science*, *11*(4), 363–372.

Fung, T. K., Griffin, R. J., & Dunwoody, S. (2018). Testing links among uncertainty, affect, and attitude toward a health behavior. *Science Communication*, *40*(1), 33–62.

Galliford, N., & Furnham, A. (2017). Individual difference factors and beliefs in medical and political conspiracy theories. *Scandinavian Journal of Psychology*, *58*, 422–428.

Gephart, R., Jr. (1984). Making sense of organizationally based environmental disasters. *Journal of Management*, *10*(2), 205–225.

Gottlieg, M., & Dyer, S. (2020). Information and disinformation: Social media in the COVID-19 crisis. *Academic Emergency Medicine*, *27*(7), 640–641.

Greenpeace. (2000, April 12). The Baia Mare gold mine cyanide spill: Causes, impacts, and liability. *Reliefweb*. https://reliefweb.int/report/hungary/baia-mare-gold-mine-cyanide-spill-causes-impacts-and-liability

Gross, K. (2008). Framing persuasive appeals: Episodic and thematic framing, emotional response, and policy opinion. *Political Psychology*, *29*(2), 169–192.

Hannigan, J. (2012). *Disasters without borders: The international politics of natural disasters*. Polity.

Head, M. (2010, December 30). Australian government covers up causes of Montara oil spill. *International Committee of the Fourth International*. https://www.wsws.org/en/articles/2010/12/mont-d30.html

Himelboim, I., Borah, P., Lee, D. K. L., Lee, J., Su, Y., Vishnevskaya, A., & Xiao, X. (2024). What do 5G networks, Bill Gates, agenda 21, and QAnon have in common? Sources, distribution, and characteristics. *New Media & Society*, *26*(10), 6019–6039.

Huang, Y., & Yang, C. (2020). A metacognitive approach to reconsidering risk perceptions and uncertainty: Understand information seeking during COVID-19. *Science Communication*, *42*(5), 616–642.

Imhoff, R., & Lamberty, P. (2020). A bioweapon or a hoax? The link between distinct conspiracy beliefs about the coronavirus disease (COVID-19) outbreak and pandemic behavior. *Social Psychological and Personality Science*, *11*(8), 1110–1118.

Imhoff, R., Zimmer, F., Klein, O., António, J. H., Babinska, M., Bangerter, A., Bilewicz, M., Blanuša, N., Bovan, K., Bužarovska, R., & Cichocka, A. (2022). Conspiracy mentality and political orientation across 26 countries. *Nature Human Behaviour*, *6*, 392–403.

Johnson, B., & Slovic, P. (1995). Presenting uncertainty in health risk assessment: Initial studies of its effects on risk perception and trust. *Risk Analysis*, *15*(4), 485–494.

Jolley, D., & Douglas, K. (2014). The effects of anti-vaccine conspiracy theories on vaccination intentions. *PLoS ONE*, *9*(2), e89177.

Kahlor, L. (2010). PRISM: A planned risk information seeking model. *Health Communication*, *25*(4), 345–356.

Kahneman, D., Slovic, P., & Tversky, A. (1982). *Judgment under uncertainty: Heuristics and biases*. Cambridge University Press.

Karaye, I., & Horney, J. (2020). The impact of social vulnerability on COVID-19 in the U.S.: An analysis of spatially varying relationships. *American Journal of Preventive Medicine, 59*(3), 317–325.

Kates, R. W., & Kasperson, J. (1983). Comparative risk analysis of technological hazards (a review). *Proceedings of the National Academy of Sciences, 80,* 7027–7038.

Kelman, I. (2006). Acting on disaster diplomacy. *Journal of International Affairs, 59*(2), 215–240.

Kelman, I. (2020). *Disaster by choice: How our actions turn natural hazards into catastrophes.* Oxford University Press.

Kelman, I., Gaillard, J., & Mercer, J. (2015). Climate change's role in disaster risk reduction's future: Beyond vulnerability and resilience. *International Journal of Disaster Risk Science, 6,* 21–27.

Kim, S., & Bostwick, W. (2020). Social vulnerability and racial inequality in COVID-19 deaths in Chicago. *Health Education & Behavior, 47*(4), 509–513.

Klar, S., Robison, J., & Druckman, J. (2013). Political dynamics of framing. In T. Ridout (Ed.), *New directions in media and politics* (pp. 173–192). Routledge.

Klofstad, C., Uscinski, J., Connolly, J., & West, J. (2019). What drives people to believe in Zika conspiracy theories? *Palgrave Communications, 5*(36), 2–8.

Kreutz, J. (2012). From tremors to talks: Do natural disasters produce ripe moments for resolving separatist conflicts? *International Interactions, 38,* 482–502.

L.A. Times. (1986, May 22). Alcohol no cure for radiation exposure, Soviet official says. *Los Angeles Times.* https://www.latimes.com/archives/la-xpm-1986-05-22-mn-7006-story.html

Larabee, A. (2000). *Decade of disaster.* University of Illinois Press.

Le Billon, P., & Waizenegger, A. (2007). Peace in the wake of disaster: Secessionist conflicts and the 2004 Indian Ocean tsunami. *Transactions of the Institute of British Geographers, 32*(3), 411–427.

Lewis, J. (1987). Risk, vulnerability, and survival. *Local Government Studies, 13*(4), 75–93.

Macdonald, W. (1980). Ixtoc I: International and domestic remedies for transboundary pollution injury. *Fordham Law Review, 49*(3), 404–431.

Malecki, K., Keating, J., & Safdar, N. (2021). Crisis communication and public perception of COVID-19 risk in the era of social media. *Clinical Infectious Disease, 72*(4), 699–704.

Manyena, S. B. (2006). The concept of resilience revisited. *Disasters, 30*(4), 383–507.

Mara, W. (2011). *The Chernobyl disaster: Legacy and impact on the future of nuclear energy.* Marshall Cavendish.

Martin, B. (2007). *Justice ignited: The dynamics of backfire.* Rowman and Littlefield.

Matejova, M. (2023). Silver linings: Environmental disasters as critical junctures in global governance. *Environment: Science and Policy for Sustainable Development, 65*(1), 4–14.

McConnachie, J., & Tudge, R. (2013). *The rough guide to conspiracy theories.* Rough Guides.

Molotch, H. (1970). Oil in Santa Barbara and power in America. *Sociological Inquiry, 40,* 131–144.

Nel, P., & Righarts, M. (2008). Natural disasters and the risk of violent civil conflict. *International Studies Quarterly, 52,* 159–185.

Nelkin, D. (1981). Some social and political dimensions of nuclear power: Examples from Three Mile Island. *The American Political Science Review, 75*(1), 132–142.

Oliver, J. E., & Wood, T. J. (2014). Medical conspiracy theories and health behaviors in the United States. *JAMA Internal Medicine, 174*(5), 817–818.

Olson, R. (2008). Toward a politics of disaster: Losses, values, agendas, and blame. In A. Boin (Ed.), *Crisis Management* (Vol. III). Sage.

Paine, R. (2002). Danger and the no-risk thesis. In S. Hoffman & A. Oliver-Smith (Eds.), *Catastrophe and culture: The anthropology of disaster* (pp. 67–90). School for Advanced Research Press.

Painter, J., & Asher, T. (2012). Cross-national comparison of the presence of climate scepticism in the print media in six countries, 2007–10. *Environmental Research Letters, 7,* 1–8.

Pelling, M., & Dill, K. (2006). 'Natural' disasters as catalysts of political action. *ISP/NSC Briefing Paper 06/01*, 4–6.

Pelling, M., & Dill, K. (2010). Disaster politics: Tipping points for change in the adaptation of sociopolitical regimes. *Progress in Human Geography*, *34*(1), 21–37.

Perez, G. (2003). Early socio-political and environmental consequences of the Prestige oil spill in Galicia. *Disasters*, *27*(3), 207–223.

Petryna, A. (1995). Sarcophagus: Chernobyl in historical light. *Cultural Anthropology*, *10*(2), 196–220.

Pummerer, L., Bohm, R., Lilleholt, L., Winter, K., Zettler, I., & Sassenberg, K. (2022). Conspiracy theories and their societal effects during the COVID-19 pandemic. *Social Psychological and Personality Science*, *13*(1), 49–59.

Rahu, M. (2003). Health effects of the Chernobyl accident: Fears, rumours, and the truth. *European Journal of Cancer*, *39*, 295–299.

Reed, J. (2002). *Love canal*. Chelsea House Publishers.

Robinson, S., Eller, W., Gall, M., & Gerber, B. (2013). The core and periphery of emergency management networks. *Public Management Review*, *15*(3), 344–362.

Romer, D., & Jamieson, K. (2020). Conspiracy theories as barriers to controlling the spread of COVID-19 in the U.S. *Social Science and Medicine*, *263*, 113356.

Sarlos, G., & Szondi, G. (2014). Crisis communication during the red sludge spill disaster in Hungary—a media content analysis-based investigation. *Public Affairs*, *15*(3), 277–286.

Scheufele, D., & Iyengar, S. (2014). The state of framing research: A call for new directions. In K. Kenski & K. Hall Jamieson (Eds.), *The Oxford handbook of political communication theories*. Oxford University Press.

Schlosberg, D. (2004). Reconceiving environmental justice: Global movements and political theories. *Environmental Politics*, *13*(3), 517–540.

Schlosberg, D., & Collins, L. (2014). From environmental to climate justice: Climate change and the discourse of environmental justice. *WIREs Climate Change*, *5*, 359–374.

Sharma, M., Yadav, K., Yadav, N., & Ferdinand, K. C. (2017). Zika virus pandemic: Analysis of Facebook as a social media health information platform. *American Journal of Infection Control*, *45*(3), 301–302.

Slay, B. (2009). *Poverty, inequality, and social policy reform in the former Soviet Union*. UNDP: Regional Bureau for Europe and CIS. https://factcheck.ge/storage/media/other/2021-05-25/3cd5eeb0-bd29-11eb-ace6-831bff4af246.pdf

Slovic, P., & Peters, E. (2006). Risk perception and affect. *Current Directions in Psychological Science*, *15*(6), 322–325.

Stecula, D., & Pickup, M. (2021). Social media, cognitive reflection, and conspiracy beliefs. *Frontiers in Political Science*, *3*.

Sutton, J. (2010). Twittering Tennessee: Distributed networks and collaboration following a technological disaster. *Proceedings of the 7th International ISCRAM Conference*, Seattle, USA.

Thistlethwaite, J., Henstra, D., Minano, A., & Dordi, T. (2019). Policy framing in the press: Analyzing media coverage of two flood disasters. *Regional Environmental Change*, *19*, 2597–2607.

Thomas, T., Kannaley, K., Friedman, D., Tanner, A., Brandt, H., & Spencer, M. (2016). Media coverage of the 2014 West Virginia Elk River chemical spill: A mixed-methods study examining news coverage of a public health disaster. *Science Communication*, *38*(5), 574–600.

Trumbo, C. (1996). Constructing climate change: Claims and frames in US news coverage of an environmental issue. *Public Understanding of Science*, *5*, 269–283.

Uscinski, J. (2018). The study of conspiracy theories. *Argumenta*, *3*(2), 233–245.

Uscinski, J., & Olivella, S. (2017). The conditional effect of conspiracy thinking on attitudes toward climate change. *Research and Politics*, 1–9.

Uscinski, J., & Parent, J. (2014). *American conspiracy theories*. Oxford University Press.

Van Prooijen, J.-W., & Douglas, K. (2017). Conspiracy theories as a part of history: The role of societal crisis situations. *Memory Studies, 10*, 323–333.

Wood, R., & Wright, T. (2015). Responding to catastrophe: Repression dynamics following rapid-onset natural disasters. *Journal of Conflict Resolution*, 1–27.

Zald, M. (1996). Culture, ideology, and strategic framing. In D. McAdam, J. McCarthy, & M. Zald (Eds.), *Comparative perspectives on social movements* (pp. 261–274). Cambridge University Press.

Zavacka, M. (2006). Svet v zrkadle kartoteky utajovanych skutocnosti: K aktivitam ceskoslovenskej cenzury v rokoch 1953–1967. *Historicke Studie, 44*, 121–140.

Zehr, S. (2000). Public representations of scientific uncertainty about global climate change. *Public Understanding of Science, 9*(2), 85–103.

8 Entangled disasters

Relations and vulnerabilities in the transformation and dissolution of Kiruna and Malmberget

Tobias Olofsson

1. Introduction

For the cities in the mineral-rich *Malmfälten* ("ore fields") region in northern Sweden, the relations between themselves and the mines they support and are supported by have reached a breaking point as the mines have started to fracture the ground they sit on. Because of this, the government-owned mining company operating the mines—Luossavaara-Kiirunavaara Aktiebolag (LKAB)—and the affected municipalities, Kiruna and Gällivare,[1] are undertaking a large-scale program of, what they call, urban transformation (*samhällsomvandling* in Swedish). Through this program, Kiruna and Malmberget, the two cities affected by deformations and cave-ins caused by LKAB's mines, are going to be demolished and moved. However, the process and what it means to move a city differ significantly between the two cities. For the people of Kiruna, the transformation means that large swaths of the city center are to be torn down and relocated to a new location east of the old city center. Meanwhile, for most inhabitants in Malmberget, who have long-lived with the knowledge that their homes will one day be consumed by the mine, the transformation means that the city will be dissolved and demolished while its residents are relocated elsewhere.

When I first visited Kiruna in the fall of 2018, I was awestruck when I saw, for the first time, the Kiirunavaara mountain with its flattened top and angled stepped sides, the vast pit that extends toward the city from the mine, and the park that acts as a buffer zone between the mine and the city. At the time, the work to raze Kiruna's city center to the ground and rebuild it out of the way for the mine was just beginning. The old city center was still relatively intact as I walked through it, attempting to shake off some of the road weariness that came from having spent the better part of a day on a bus traveling across Sweden's northern inland. I had come to Kiruna to gather materials for a thesis on how the mining and mineral exploration industry's use geotechnical, financial, and environmental forecasts to justify new mines and mining—a topic of unusual everyday importance in a city so impacted by a mine that simultaneously supported it and consumed its foundations. In this chapter, I revisit Kiruna and Malmberget to explore what the urban transformation and its disaster-like consequences can tell us about disasters in general and about the role that relations—social, economic, geographical, and other—play in

DOI: 10.4324/9781003537311-9

Figure 8.1 View of Kiruna from Luossavaara. Note the deformation zone that stretches from the foot of the Kiirunavaara mountain and the mine towards the old city center (photograph by author).

shaping disasters and their consequences, and I do so through an analysis of documentary films, newspaper articles, scholarly work, and other media representations of life in *Malmfältet* in a time of transformations.

2.   Disasters, vulnerabilities, and politics

As examples of disasters, Kiruna, Malmberget, and other mining-impacted cities in Sweden's northern *Malmfälten* region may seem like a strange choice. After all, the classical view of disaster researchers defines disasters as geographically and temporally distinct dangerous events caused by some form of external hazard that gives rise to adverse impacts to people and property (see, e.g., Fritz, 1961). While the deformations that threaten Kiruna and Malmberget might fit parts of this definition, what is happening in *Malmfälten* is arguably not the product of an external hazard but of social, political, and economic processes and decisions. However, there are benefits to broadening the universe of cases to which the tools of disaster research are applied to include also non-disasters. First, disastrous events and phenomena that are not easily accommodated within existing conceptualizations of disasters offer a venue through which it is possible to critically explore the state of the art of disaster research and the challenges that have been made to the classical view on disasters both from within the discipline and from without. Second, by treating slow-moving man-made disaster-like phenomena, such as those unfolding in *Malmfälten*, as disasters, one is able to contribute to further investigations of other creeping phenomena of human origin that threaten disastrous consequences, such as pollution, biodiversity loss, or global warming.

One of the most fruitful internal challenges to the view of disasters as the products of temporally isolated external events has been that of the vulnerabilities paradigm—an approach that has shifted the focus away from external hazards toward the vulnerability experienced by victims of disasters and the social and political processes that rendered them vulnerable in the first place (Centemeri & Tomassi, 2022). According to the vulnerabilities approach, disasters have histories that stretch back in time, often far from the actual event, and in their inquiries, adherers of the paradigm often seek to unearth the contingent processes through which "human systems place people at risk in relation to each other and to their environment—a relationship that can best be understood in terms of an individual's, a household's, a community's or a society's *vulnerability*" (Hilhorst & Bankoff, 2004, p. 2 (emphasis in the original)).

Other challenges to the classical approach to disasters have come from sociologists and others researching disasters from disciplines outside of disaster research. Such contributions include studies of ambiguous slow-developing disasters such as the environmental disaster at Love Canal (Fowlkes & Miller, 1982) and studies of how organizational culture and interorganizational conflict produce and shape disasters (Clarke, 1989; Vaughan, 1996). One important argument proposed in this line of research is that disasters should not be understood as extraordinary events but as expressions of everyday life. Viewing disasters as extraordinary and isolated events, the argument goes, masks their everyday political nature:

> Disasters, even worst case ones, aren't special. Destruction is no more special than construction. Political struggle is also normal, even when the subject is large-scale devastation. Everyday life is political. So are worst cases.
>
> (Clarke, 2006, p. 127)

Compared to the vulnerability paradigm, this understanding of disasters as part of everyday life and politics forces one to think beyond the limited, albeit important, political dimensions that the former paradigm tends to focus on. That is, while the vulnerabilities approach has highlighted the structures and policies that place people in vulnerable positions, sociologists argue for a deeper and more mundane connection between disasters and the political processes that shape them. According to this sociological approach, what is called a disaster is not an exception to a rule but an expression of an already pathological state. In this understanding, a disaster is not an exogenous event but something that is constructed politically and socially by declaring something a disaster and thereby, in consequence, drawing a line in the sand to declare some forms of suffering abnormal and apart from a kind of "normal" suffering:

> To declare a disaster is a semiotic act that declares certain patterns of suffering and loss abnormal, accidental, an intolerable deviation from society's

desired ends. Other patterns of suffering and loss are then by implication normal and, while perhaps regrettable, an inevitable and tolerable byproduct of the social order.

(Hagen & Elliott, 2021, p. 5)

Accordingly, when something is declared a disaster, some ills are pronounced abnormal while others are determined to be normal and unimportant, and as a consequence of this distinction, only some types of suffering are decided to require remediation while others may be left unaddressed. By understanding disasters as semiotic acts based on claims that some forms of suffering are abnormal and out of place, one is able to ask not only which vulnerabilities existed prior to a disaster but also how these vulnerabilities differ from those deemed to be normal or expected, as well as how the crisis response aimed at addressing only some vulnerabilities might contribute to the reproduction of pre-disaster inequalities—a tendency already highlighted in studies of disasters' unequal impacts in the United States (see, e.g., Elliott & Howell, 2016; Fox Gotham & Greenberg, 2014; Howell & Elliott, 2019; Raker, 2020).

3. Relational disasters and more-than-human suffering

In this chapter, I explore place-based relationality as an additional layer to the broader understanding of disasters developed in the vulnerability paradigm and in sociological studies of disasters. The importance of social relations for how disasters unfold has already been highlighted in studies of catastrophes such as the coal-seam fire beneath Centralia in Pennsylvania, USA, where a fire in the mine and coal seams beneath the town burned for 22 years before the US Congress authorized a plan to dissolve the town and relocate its residents. On the surface, the fire caused several physical and health problems, including cave-ins and carbon monoxide emissions, but it also caused far-reaching social problems as it tore away the social fabric in town, causing severe social conflicts and unrest (Kroll-Smith & Couch, 2009). However, while the experiences of those living in Centralia point to the importance of social relations in disasters, relations, because of the importance they have for how places work, have a broader and deeper importance for how disasters unfold and are experienced still.

The ways in which places have relational aspects to them was a central argument in the work by urban sociologist Henri Lefebvre, who argued that space is socially constituted (1991). According to Lefebvre, places are reproductions of the social relations of production, and as such, they reflect the entanglements between labor and capital in society. However, while viewing places as reproductions of the relations of production can help scholars unpack the ways in which disasters unfold in and are shaped by the economic relations that characterize a disaster-struck area, Lefebvre's theory arguably overstates the importance of cultural factors while downplaying natural factors. To rectify this, I suggest bringing in a Latourian (1993) refusal of the nature-culture divide and an associated focus on hybridity to the understanding of places and the relations they reproduce. Such hybrid relations are explored by science and technology studies scholars who have argued for broadening the study of disasters further and for the inclusion not only of politics and social structure but of the more-than-human world too (see Tsing et al., 2017). Examples of such hybrid relations of relevance here are the geosocial relations described by Palsson and Swanson (2016) and the geosymbioses described by Ureta and Flores (2022).

According to Palsson and Swansson, geosocial relations are the dialectic relations between humanity and geology through which human activities are inscribed in geological matter and geology is inscribed in the human biology—for example, in the silicosis that historically has affected mine workers (Palsson & Swanson, 2016). Geosymbiosis on the other hand, is the many ways in which life forms exist in, often troubled, symbiotic relations with geology. Examples of such a geosymbiotic relation, Ureta and Flores write, include the human communities living downstream of a massive mining waste dam in Chile. Living under the threat of a catastrophic dam collapse, these communities made their homes in the dam's shadow because it offered them access to a reliable, albeit contaminated, source of water (Ureta & Flores, 2022).

Recognizing and acknowledging such more-than-human entanglements have important consequences for how one understands disasters. First, because a relational focus recognizing hybrid entanglements sensitizes research inquiries to the ways in which relations between politics, economy, geology, biology, and geography are made dangerously unstable in the event of a disaster (see Horowitz, 2020 for an example of how long-running entanglements between politics, natural resource industries, and geography shaped Hurricane Katrina). Second, because of how an emphasis on relations in the plural encourages against limiting inquiries into disasters to a few dominant relations. For example, would it be too simplistic to limit an inquiry into the dissolution and transformation of Kiruna and Malmberget to the geosocial relations between the mining company and the municipal actors in charge of the transformation project, as that would overlook other relations in and around the two cities that are also affected by the transformation. Instead, Kiruna and Malmberget are here understood to be nodes that embed the many different relations that entangle residents, organizations, more-than-human entities, and more to each other within distinct geographical locations.

Thinking through a place's relations makes possible a broader approach to crises and disasters that, to some extent, follows the current vulnerabilities paradigm (Centemeri & Tomassi, 2022) but simultaneously adds to it by brining sociology "back in" (Tierney, 2007) by including the multidimensional embeddedness of the places that disasters strike. In brief, by taking account of how disasters stress the entangled relations that bind residents to a neighborhood, a neighborhood to a city, and a city to a wider universe of geographies, organizations, and institutions, it is possible to investigate which and, importantly, who's relations are strained by disasters, as well as which relations are repaired after a disaster, and which relations are allowed to—or even made to—sever.

4. Background: the life and death of Kiruna and Malmberget

While the present transformation and dissolution of Kiruna and Malmberget are extraordinary occurrences in the life of the two cities, the mines beneath them have long caused impacts and forced change. For example, in the 1970s, the Ön neighborhood in Kiruna was torn down to make way for the mine, while in Malmberget parts of the old city center were torn down and the city church moved to a new location that, at the time, put it out of the mine's way. However, these events pale in comparison to the city moves and dissolutions taking place through the urban transformation program. According to LKAB (2022), the transformation of Kiruna affects approximately 6,000 residents, 3,000 homes, and 160 businesses and will include the construction of a new city center to house displaced residents, businesses, and local government functions. Meanwhile, in Malmberget approximately 3,200 residents, 2,000 homes, and 71 businesses are affected by the dissolution of the city and the relocation of residents and municipal services to neighboring Gällivare (LKAB, 2021).

That two cities that grew out of the mining industry in *Malmfälten* are now being wholly or partially consumed by the same mines may seem ironic. However, the current situation is a symptom of the geosymbiotic relations that have shaped the cities and the places they occupy since the latter half of the 19th century. At that time, the unminable deposits at present-day Kiruna and Malmberget were transformed into valuable commodities through the introduction of better infrastructure and new smelting methods (Heckscher, 1954). Before the railroads came to connect *Malmfälten* to more central transportation and financial nodes on the coasts, transports depended on the recruitment of Sámi who, in the winter months, used reindeer-pulled sleds to move the iron across the frozen landscape. Moreover, as the iron deposits in *Malmfälten* often contain phosphor, a pollutant that, unless removed, reduces the quality of the iron produced from the ores, they did not become commercially minable until smelting processes capable of removing the phosphor were introduced in the mid-19th century. Without these factors, the large-scale exploitation of minerals that has since shaped the region would not have been possible.

With the deepened geosocial entanglements made possible through the introduction of the railroad and new smelting processes, new forms of living emerged in *Malmfälten*; ways of living that soon came to encroach on older modes of living and relating to this corner of the Swedish Arctic. The Sámi communities, who have long inhabited the region that today makes up *Malmfälten*, have been severely impacted by the emergence of large-scale industrial mining in the region, and this is especially true of the members of the community who practice traditional reindeer herding. Since the 19th century, a combination of settler colonial policies that forced reindeer owners to choose between traditional herding and access to jobs and homes in the new cities and an ever-growing encroachment of natural resource industries have forced reindeer herders to adapt to the new entanglements growing out of the mines and the neighboring cities (López, 2021). Taking up space, transforming landscapes, and emitting vibrations, noise, dust and other disturbances, the mines—as well as other actors, both governmental and industrial—have significant impacts on reindeer herding (Gallardo et al., 2017; Sörlin & Wormbs, 2010). On top of this, the Sámi's particular embeddedness in the region is often neglected or folded into the general politico-environmental frameworks that regulate mining leases and environmentally impactful industry operations, including into the environmental permitting process, in which the impacts to Sámi interests and culture are often reduced to being just one of many variables in a legal balancing of costs and benefits (Lawrence & Moritz, 2019; Persson et al., 2017).

Thinking through the impacts that the geosymbiotic relations between the mines and the cities have already caused some relations in the region, one is reminded of how the strains that are presently being placed on ways of relating to and through Kiruna and Malmberget are not unique expressions or products of extraordinary events, but merely the latest in a long line of strains felt in the region. After all, at the time of the urban transformations, some entangled relations that once shaped the region had already come under such strain that some versions of what Kiruna and Malmberget had previously been and could have been were already long gone.

5. Death and deformations

Despite the gravity of the present situation and the long history of strains and stresses tearing at the entangled relations that shape the region, no disaster has officially been declared for the cities in *Malmfälten*. One reason for this is that the suffering presently and previously felt in the region has hitherto been accommodatable within a universe of normal suffering. After all, the ongoing fracturing and deformation of the bedrock underneath Kiruna and Malmberget have typically been relegated to the realm of technology, probabilities, and risks—a tendency that follows an established pattern in mining and exploration to approach any social or environmental impacts from mining from a technical viewpoint (Olofsson, 2020). Nevertheless, while the use of language such as risk and probability may give the impression that the fracturing of the bedrock beneath the two cities is exogenous to the mine, they are truly symptoms of the mining methods used by LKAB.

While new smelting methods and the construction of railroads in the 19th century made the deposits in *Malmfälten* commercially minable, the mines at Kiruna and Malmberget have since needed to undergo several waves of modernization to keep them cost-efficient and profitable, and this has at times caused significant strain in the relations between management and workers within LKAB (Eriksson, 1991; Nilsson Mohammadi, 2018). Market factors and the cost-effectiveness of geotechnical and industrial arrangements have therefore always been a factor in the geosocial relations surrounding the mines, and so also today. One of the chief concerns at Kiruna and Malmberget is the cost of following the deposits as they extend toward the deep. Mining underground, as LKAB does in Kiruna and Malmberget, is more expensive than mining in open pits, and it gets more expensive the deeper one goes. To keep costs down, the company has therefore deployed one of the more inexpensive methods available in underground mining, namely sublevel caving, a method through which ore is extracted by making it collapse down into a system of horizontally drilled tunnels from which it can be lifted out and transported to the ground. However, while the method is comparatively inexpensive, it comes with certain costs, the chief of which being that it causes fractures in the overhanging rock in the hang wall.

As explosives and gravity make the ore collapse into the tunnels dug beneath the hang wall breaks and as mining moves deeper, the fractures in the hang wall begin creeping further away from the mine, and in the case of Kiruna, closer to the city center (Stöckel et al., 2012). A similar process is unfolding in Malmberget with the difference that the mining beneath the town has left large empty caverns where the ore once was, and the roof atop these caverns is now breaking. In brief, the choice of mining method and the combination of market factors and geotechnical processes guiding this choice are important factors in the troubled geosocial relations in *Malmfälten* as the affordability of the mining method simultaneously enables and undermines the status quo as it both normalizes and deepens the mines' impacts on the neighboring cities.

6. Strain: representations of fractured relations

The strained relation between the mine and the communities living next to it has been documented in both scholarly and popular reports. In this section, I explore how different ways of living in and relating to *Malmfälten* are actualized in academic texts, documentary films, local government documents, and news media reports on the transformation and dissolution of Kiruna and Malmberget. Paying particular attention to tensions and contradictions in how these accounts describe geosymbiotic entanglements in *Malmfälten*, I highlight the ways in which the normalization of certain relations in Kiruna and Malmberget often overshadows the strain experienced in others.

In a report to the Environmental Court at Umeå, researchers at Umeå University described the impacts that the mine had on the life and well-being of residents in Malmberget. According to the report, people in Malmberget experienced elevated sleep difficulties as well as disturbances from noise, vibrations, and air pollution to such an extent that they found reasons to ask whether it was even possible for the mine and city to coexist within the same geographical area (Pettersson-Strömbäck et al., 2009). Moreover, an ethnographic study of Kiruna in the early years of the urban transformation shows how historical and contemporary conflicts have contributed to the emergence of rifts in the city's social fabric (López, 2021). Some of these conflicts involved different ideas about how and when the transformation was to take place and include conflicts between LKAB and the municipal authorities, who had a significant disagreement as to how the loss of vital infrastructure, including a railroad station, was to be compensated for and by whom. Other conflicts concerned questions of resources and competing interests, or struggles over the loss and memorialization of intangible values. Important to these conflicts were the different ways actors defined that which was to be transformed, replaced, and lost, and in these matters, residents, the local government, and the mining company often held very different views. For example, in the brief inviting architects to a competition for the design of Kiruna's new city center, the municipality highlighted economic values, job creation, and education as central to the city's long-term survival:

> Kiruna's survival as a city stands or falls in the long term by the creation of appropriate conditions for good development, a diversified economy and a place where people want to come and live and, because they like it here, want to stay. New industries and educational opportunities need to be attracted here, to spearhead development.
>
> (Kiruna Kommun, 2012, p. 29)

By framing the city's life and survival in terms of its economic relations, the municipality downplayed other relations of relevance. Moreover, as the brief focuses on the future city's ability to attract new industries and people, the brief also downplays the importance of the relations spun between the city and its current residents. The way that the life of a place is made contingent on economics, while common in discussions on the life and death of rural or peripheral places in Sweden, risks overlooking other relations contributing to the life of and in a place (Olofsson, 2019). For other ways of relating to and experiencing Kiruna and Malmberget exist. López (2021) demonstrates some of these more-than-economic relations when centering the experiences of the Sámi communities in and around Kiruna, and yet still more forms of entangled relations have been made visible in the many reports and documentations that newspapers, documentary filmmakers, and community members have made of Kiruna and Malmberget.

Many of the accounts explored in the continuation of this chapter focus on personal experiences of grief and often reflect on that which has been lost as well as on feelings of uncertainty and apprehension over that which was to come. Meanwhile, other accounts included below depict the events at Kiruna and Malmberget through an exotifying perspective in which the cities in *Malmfälten* are depicted as being alien and apart from the urban centers in southern Sweden. One illustrative example of the former is a report in the local newspaper *Norrländska Socialdemokraten* published in March 2023. In the report, a spokesperson for a local community organization lamented the lack of any official markings of the death of Kiruna's old city center. As the municipality and LKAB had neglected to organize a space for people to remember and reflect on the loss of the old city center, the organization had decided to host their own memorial service to give residents an opportunity to find closure before the center got torn down once and for all. Speaking to a reporter, the spokesperson explained that while the group did not oppose the city's transformation per se, they saw a need to help people move on in a respectful way:

> There is a form of forced cheerfulness over the city's transformation that does not permit one to engage in nostalgia or to grieve, but only to look to the future and say how great everything will be. But that does not feel right.

I think you can compare it to when a person dies. When that happens there will be no one cheerfully telling you to move on.

(Bergström, 2023, p. 10)

In stark contrast to the invitation to grieve and reflect on that which has been stands a short report film published by the Swedish Institute—a government agency whose mission is to spread information about Sweden abroad. In the Institute's short documentary film *This is Kiruna: How to Move a City*[2] Kiruna is depicted through the eyes of two self-described southerners and the city's northern location and distance to the central cities in the south are highlighted repeatedly. In the film, the transformation of Kiruna is described through interviews with a local business owner, the vice chair of the municipal board, an officer at LKAB, and a representative for the architectural firm contracted to design the new city center. Between the interviews, the viewer is served brief clips of the filmmakers being baffled by the darkness of the arctic winter days, stumbling through the snow, participating in a kick-sled race with one of the interviewees, and smelling a vial containing iron ore pellets produced at LKAB's plant before declaring it to be the purest iron ore in the world, so pure that it is worth moving a city for.

The tone of *This is Kiruna* is playful and exotifying. The filmmakers make use of common Swedish tropes such as "the land of Volvo" and Swedish "fika" while simultaneously highlighting how different these common notions of Swedishness are in a place like Kiruna. The Volvos in Kiruna are not just the everyday family cars known to many, but also the heavy wheel-loaders and haulers used by LKAB. Likewise, the Kiruna fika is not just your everyday coffee and cake with family, friends, or colleagues, but something you might enjoy while sitting in a *bivack*—a pit dug into deep snow—on your front lawn. Moreover, while Kiruna is depicted as familiar yet different, its transformation is described as a unique event—"the world's largest urban relocation"—and as a cultural challenge. The question, the architect interviewed in the film explains, is not how one moves a city but how one moves the social and cultural dimensions of a city. Moving the physical infrastructure, he says, is easy; the challenge is to move the "minds of the people and the culture." In one sequence, the architect is even depicted picking up a model of Kiruna's iconic church, placing it next to a model of the new city center, and commenting that "That was easy."

In contrast to the exotifying depictions of *This is Kiruna*, the version of Kiruna depicted in *Kiruna—Rymdvägen*[3] (Kiruna—Spaceroad) is the highly personal yet familiar city of the filmmaker's childhood and adolescence. Throughout the film, the narrator's reconstruction of her own history is juxtaposed with the destruction of the streets and neighborhoods where these histories took place. In the film, the recollections and reconstructions of childhood games, school, and youthful escapades are recalled with an almost feverish urgency as if every memory must be revisited before it is lost in the rubble. Additionally, the film continuously blurs the borders between past and present by inserting depictions of the past in the present while juxtaposing contemporary scenes, recollections, and a recycled slogan from Kiruna's history: "Kiruna is dying . . . Fight!" The slogan first emerged in 1980 when it was spray-painted on the wall of Kiruna *Folkets Hus* (a public venue for meetings and entertainment) as a rallying cry against depopulation and a lack of hope for the future (Linder, 2023) and its recycling in *Kiruna—Rymdvägen* lends itself to the sense that the past has come back to haunt the present. Teetering on the edge of the mine, Kiruna is still dying.

The recycling of history with the view to give meaning to the present is a bearing theme throughout the film. Recycling and reconstruction are here used as tools in the rediscovery of a Kiruna lost. The narrator talks of how she, like many others, left Kiruna for a life in southern Sweden after high school and of how the transformation of the city has led her to wake up to the realization that the city that she in the film describes as "the homeland"—a never-changing place to which she might one day return—was now on the cusp of being lost. "They're tearing down my city. They're tearing down my houses." She laments before asking: "Why didn't anyone tell me that my houses would only live for 50 years? This knowledge came as a shock. The houses crack with the ground underneath. The gap grows larger, inside me as well. It had been going on for so long that I didn't even noticed."

In the space between the sensationalist account of *This is Kiruna* and the hyper-personal accounts of *Kiruna—Rymdvägen* are two films depicting the lead up to the dissolvement of Malmberget. The first, *The Home and the Cavity*,[4] depicts the stressful anticipation residents experienced in the early days of the transformation program. Through a combination of interviews and recordings of town meetings, the film highlights the uncertainty of knowing that one will one day have to move but not knowing when as it follows residents as they watch the deformations caused by the mine creep closer to their neighborhoods. This state of anxious anticipation is visualized both in interviews and in images of the vast pit that divides the city into an eastern and western half. At one point, the camera shows the perimeter fence blocking access to the pit and zooms in on three words written on it with red string. "Home sweet home," it reads.

A dramatic turning point in *The Home and the Cavity* comes as a section of the roof above one of the mineral bodies beneath the city caves in, resulting in the formation of a 200-meter deep and 60-meter-wide sinkhole. Following the cave-in sequence, the film juxtaposes stressed-out residents with statements about how the cave-in was an anticipated consequence of the continued mining beneath the city. Sinkholes, it is made clear, are part of life in Malmberget and will be part of the city's death—or as the municipal commissioner Tommy Nyström phrases it in the film: "(The ground under Malmberget) will turn into something like a Swiss cheese. So, I am confident that the best thing would be for us to dissolve the city as soon as possible."

While most residents are affected by the decision to raze the city and relocate its inhabitants elsewhere, not all residents are included in the plans. Two central characters in *The Home and the Cavity* are Ingrid and Börje, an older couple who feature frequently in interviews and in repeated sequences in which the viewers join them at their kitchen table close to midnight, where they wait for their house to be shaken by the shockwaves from the nightly blast in the mine. Like their neighbors, Ingrid and Börje too live in the shadow of the mine, but because their house lies on a small island of ground that has been deemed not at risk from the expanding mine, they were at the time of *The Home and the Cavity* not part of the transformation program and thereby exempt from the financial or functional compensation available to those living in the sections of Malmberget designated to be given over to the expanding mine.

In the film, Börje verbalizes his anticipations for what life will become like for those few who are to remain whence the rest of the city has been abandoned: "I don't expect there will be a store in town. Or a drugstore, or healthcare center or retirement home. Only the neighbors and I will remain." In the film, Börje and Ingrid's situation becomes an effective contradiction to the uncertainty felt by the other residents, as while others were anxiously awaiting their turn to move, Ingrid and Börje are depicted anxiously pondering what will remain whence everyone else has gone.

The second film, *Den Stora Flytten—En Film om Malmberget*[5] (The Great Move: A Film about Malmberget) documents life in Malmberget some years after the events of *The Home and the Cavity*. At this time, the dissolution of the city has started and people are preparing for their relocation and are struggling with LKAB over what comforts from their old homes—bedrooms for all children or a sauna—will be carried over when they move.

Loss is a central theme in *Den Stora Flytten* as the film records a series of lasts as it documents the final days of several local businesses as well as the end of the local radio station. In one scene, the camera follows hairdresser Annica as she packs up her business, puts equipment, decorations, and her diplomas in boxes before turning out the lights and locking the doors for the last time. The changes brought about by the dissolution of Malmberget is another important theme in the film as people are forced to find new ways when the old ones vanish beneath their feet. This is especially pertinent in the case of Annica who, having closed her saloon, finds herself a job in the mine.

7.   The company and the city

Across all accounts from Kiruna and Malmberget, the focus is with the same group of actors: the municipal government, residents, and the mining company. Despite the extraordinary nature of the processes unfolding in Kiruna and Malmberget, the state is never present except through LKAB, which is a state-owned corporation. The state's absence in Kiruna and Malmberget has been commented on by several actors, who have all drawn attention to this tendency of the government to, so to say, outsource the design and execution of the transformation and dissolvement of the two cities. A report by the National Audit Office (2017, p. 6) found that the government had failed to give the parties involved in the events at Kiruna and Malmberget sufficient guidelines. Moreover, the same report also found that LKAB had neglected to produce "sufficiently developed economic calculations and risk assessments that would allow management to assess the consequences of the investment" in continued mining beneath Kiruna and Malmberget.

Taking a longer perspective, López (2021) finds connections between the government's present absence and *Malmfälten's* history of settler colonialism and a historical tendency by the state to lend LKAB significant influence not only over economic life in *Malmfälten* but political life too; and this strong entanglement between company and city coupled with a weaker entanglement between the government and *Malmfälten* not only shapes the way that the transformation and dissolvement of Kiruna and Malmberget unfold, but also the valuation of the suffering felt by residents.

The strength of the entanglements between the company and the cities is clearly visible in the films discussed above. In *This is Kiruna* the vice chair of the municipality board explains the relation between city and mine, saying that the two have always existed in a symbiotic relation and that "The mine is the reason that Kiruna is placed where it is." Such statements—besides overlooking the long history of other ways of living in and relating to *Malmfälten*—normalize the consequences of mining in the region. Because the mine and city are understood to be two parts of one whole, the strength of that entanglement is allowed to negate all others. That is, while residents may grieve as their personal entanglements are strained and ruptured as a result of the mine's advances, the suffering they experience is a necessary part of a greater whole.

7.1   Bureaucratically defined suffering

One important consequence of the government's absence from the events unfolding in *Malmfälten* is how the process to transform and dissolve Kiruna and Malmberget has been defined by existing rules and regulations and not by new policies or state interventions. Whether they like it or not, everyone living in the region is entangled with the mines and the mining companies through a range of laws and restrictions. Just as part of the mine worker's relation to LKAB is defined through labor laws and collective agreements, residents living above or near minable mineral deposits have their relations to existing and future mines defined through the Swedish Minerals Act, which outlines the rights and responsibilities of mining and exploration companies as well as of landowners and other interests. According to the Minerals Act (The Swedish Riksdag, 1991), properties significantly affected by a mine are to be purchased by the mining company at a compensation equivalent to the market value of the property plus 25% (see: The Swedish Riksdag, 1972). It is this law that has defined the relation between LKAB and the residents affected by the transformation and dissolvement of Kiruna and Malmberget. For example, while Ingrid and Börje in Malmberget were affected by the mine as their home was rocked by the blasting in the mine night after night, the impacts from the mine on their neighborhood were not deemed to be severe enough to warrant any compensation—an assessment that was made based on the environmental permit that the mine in Malmberget was operating under.

According to the environmental permit for LKAB's mine in Malmberget, the company was to purchase any building lying within 100 meters from the deformation zone (defined as areas experiencing surface level movements of 2% vertically or 3% horizontally) as well as buildings experiencing vibrations from seismic events in the mine of 6 mm per second or more during the day or 3 mm per second during nighttime. The majority of Malmberget has been deemed to fall into these categories and have therefore been acquired and compensated for by LKAB, but Ingrid and Börje's neighborhood, Eastern Malmberget, had not. The exclusion of Eastern Malmberget from the compensation scheme has led to a long-standing conflict between the municipality and LKAB. In a recent victory for the municipality, the Norrbotten County Administrative Board (2022, p. 4) expressed support for the municipality's view as it noticed that:

> (T)hat which was originally described as a development area in Malmberget is increasingly looking like an area of decline complete with the challenges this entails. Areas of recreation grow smaller or are lost, playgrounds disappear, Internet access is poorer than for other residents in (the municipality). The County Administrative Board finds that much of the infrastructure in the area is significantly affected, which means that the area can no longer be regarded as a well-functioning and satisfying part of the municipality.

According to the County Administrative Board, residents in Eastern Malmberget experience quakes, vibrations, and ground movement on a near daily basis and have repeated problems with infrastructure, including broken water conduits and sewage pipes. However, what will eventually happen to Eastern Malmberget is yet to be determined. LKAB has filed for a renewed environmental permit for their operations in Malmberget, and whether the new permit will include any changes to whether and how the company is to compensate those who still remain in Malmberget remains to be seen. Until then, the entanglements that bind Eastern Malmberget to the ruins of the surrounding city linger in place.

8. Mines, entanglements, and bureaucratized suffering

The life and death of Malmberget and Kiruna are tightly entangled with the lives of the mines they serve and are served by. Born at a time when advances in ore smelting and a massive investment in railroads made the mineral deposits in *Malmfälten* commercially minable, Kiruna and Malmfältet are marked by the geosymbiotic relations that connect them to the mines that shaped and continue to shape them. However, as López (2021) notes, the places that today make up Kiruna and Malmberget are also entangled in relations that go beyond the extractivist relations of *Malmfälten's* version of geosymbiosis. The two cities are also shaped by a colonial logic in which corporations operating in the northern frontier region have been granted extraordinary freedoms to shape economic and political life in the area. The unusually strong entanglement between company and city and the comparatively weak entanglement between the city and other government actors, I argue, is crucial if one is to understand both how two cities can be made to give way for mines and why the consequences of this do not constitute "an intolerable deviation from society's desired ends" (Hagen & Elliott, 2021, p. 5).

In Malmfälten, the experiences of grief and loss expressed in films such as *Kiruna—Ryndvägen* are accommodated within the geosymbiotic relation between mine and city as well as within bureaucratic visions of what it means to be affected by a mine. However, the consequences of the deep entanglements between mines and cities are not limited to the cities that sprung up out of the minerals rush that hit *Malmfälten* in the late 19th century. Instead, the effects of the strong coupling between the region, the mines, and the economic realities of life in a periphery rich in natural resources spill over and affect places beyond cities such as Kiruna and Malmberget.

On April 29, 2021, a ruling by the Environmental Court in Umeå gave Swedish mining company Boliden permission to expand their operations at the Aitik mine—one of Europe's largest copper mines—by opening a new mining pit 3.5 kilometers northeast of the existing mine. However, before the new pit could open, three villages located within or near the new mining area would first have to be dissolved. Consequently, long-standing entanglements were to be severed, much to the same effect as in Kiruna and Malmberget. In a local radio broadcast, one resident explained what it felt like to be forced to leave her family's home of five generations. In the broadcast, the resident initially recognized the depth and complexity of the geosymbiotic relations between the mines and the communities that have characterized the region since the introduction of large-scale mining around the turn of the 20th century:

When one lives in *Malmfälten*, as I do, you live with this dilemma every day. It's just part of everyday life around here. We know that the metals have a prize—a pretty steep price for those who are affected. It's a double-edged sword. We know that the mine and the steel mills, like LKAB, SSAB, and Boliden, are the reason why our communities exist in the first place.

However, having said this, the resident then proceeded to talk about relations, including her own, that stretch beyond the current geosymbiotic entanglements. The places that today support and are supported by the mines, she said, have roots that go back in time to long before the mining industry began to transform the region. In the broadcast, the resident highlights the importance of these relations for how she experiences life in her village and what it feels like learning that she would soon have to give it up:

Sakajärvi, is mentioned in texts since about the 1700s, and of course the Sámi have traveled these lands since long, long before then. My father's family has lived here since the 1800s. The Aitik Mine, which is now to destroy the village started their operations in 1968. Throughout my childhood I was told that the village would one day disappear because of the mine. And because of that, because I have somehow always known that it would happen, one would have thought that I would have been more prepared for the news we all received at a meeting in the spring of 2016. At that meeting, Boliden told us that the time had come for them to purchase both villages: Sakajärvi and Liikavaara. My future life was suddenly transformed into a dark haze. At the same time as I could hardly think at all my mind was buzzing with thoughts:

Where would we go? Will the company construct a new village for us? When would we have to leave? Will we have to leave (the municipality)? Do we even want to stay in (the municipality)? If we must sell our house, who is to decide what it is worth? Is it possible to put a value on five generations of life? The questions would not rest. And of course, there were no answers to be had at the time.

(Radio Örnsköldsvik, 2021)

In describing her reaction upon learning that she would soon have to move to make way for the mine, the resident offers a window into how the rupturing of the relations that embedded her within a community and a family history becomes akin to a private disaster—a suffering beyond the normal suffering of everyday life—as her life is upended and made uncertain. However, as in Kiruna and Malmberget, the suffering experienced by the residents of Sakajärvi and Liikavara is overshadowed by the dominating geosymbiotic relations that have come to define life in *Malmfälten*.

Together, these examples from across *Malmfälten* highlight how the loss of a home, a neighborhood, a city, and of the memories associated with these places, as well as the uncertainty of what is to come tear at and rupture the entangled relations that connect people both to a place in the world and to their biographies and sense of self. Importantly, while the current wave of changes unfolding in these communities is extraordinary in its consequences, it is but one wave of change among many. Mining in *Malmfälten* has always been a double-edged sword as it has enabled some ways of living while impeding others. For the Sámi, who have long struggled—or resisted—to adapt to and negotiate the consequences of mineral extractivism on their traditional lands, the transformation of Kiruna and the dissolution of Malmberget, Sakajärvi, and Liikavara are merely the latest in a long, and continuing, line of challenges to their way of relation to and living in these places. But the Sámi are not the only ones affected by the expansion of the mines in the region, as the mines cast their shadow over everyone affected by the deep symbiotic relationship between the mines and the cities.

9. The way ahead: relations, disasters, and the Anthroposcene

This chapter has sought to explore the role of entangled relations in disasters and disaster-like events, and it has done so by exploring accounts of the drastic, large-scale changes that unfold in the transformation and dissolution of cities and villages in Sweden's *Malmfälten* region. Paying attention to the ways in which residents are reported to experience the strain and rupture that the transformation and dissolutions of cities and villages cause the entanglements that shape how people relate to their communities and the places they inhabit, and by contrasting them to the deeply entwined geosymbiotic relationship between the mines and the cities in the region, the chapter illustrates how some events may be disastrous in their consequences for not being labeled disasters.

As I noted above, that which is unfolding in Kiruna, Malmberget, Sakajärvi, and Liikavaara are not disasters in the orthodox understanding of the term (see, e.g., Fritz, 1961). Still these events contain several aspects of disasters, including the vulnerability experienced by those who are displaced by the mines, and as scholars working in the vulnerability paradigm would point out, the origin of these vulnerabilities lies in a combination of geological factors and economic and political processes that place people in harm's way. Moreover, when these vulnerabilities are understood to be shaped and mediated through relations, it becomes clear that in *Malmfälten* the vulnerability experienced by those who must see the ground beneath their cities crumble along with the social fabric of what used to be their communities is, so to say, part of the game of living in an area characterized by geosymbiosis. This is why the suffering described in the reports and films discussed here does not spill over to become a suffering out of place. Instead, it is a suffering that is accommodated, however imperfectly, within existing frameworks such as the mining companies' rights and responsibilities outlined in the Swedish Minerals Act.

Importantly, while the transformation of Kiruna and the dissolution of Malmberget, Sakajärvi, and Liikavara may not qualify as disasters under some definitions of the term, a broader relationally informed understanding of disasters that also includes a wider range of disastrous events and phenomena offers avenues for inquiring into the nature of the boundaries implied in calling something a disaster. After all, the processes unfolding in *Malmfälten* offer insights into how not only external hazards but also human-made and bureaucratically managed events lead to disastrous outcomes in how they tear at, stress, and undo the entanglements that connect and shape the way that individuals, communities, natures and cultures, and social structure are embedded in and experienced through a place; and to a large extent they are much alike the processes unfolding in the lead up to, unfolding, and aftermath of disasters such as Hurricane Katrina (Horowitz, 2020) or the PCB dioxin disaster at the Binghamton State Office Buildings (Clarke, 2006).

Moreover, the small acts of resistance depicted in the ethnographies and films discussed above—including the ironizing "Home Sweet Home" graffitied onto the perimeter fence in Malmberget—highlight the role of social movements and activism in disasters and disaster-like phenomena. If successful, victims and social movements may challenge and influence policies and discourses about the origins and consequences of disasters. Examples of how advocacy has influenced the discourse and management of disasters include the sheep farmers who successfully challenged expert opinion on the origin of the radioactive contamination in Cumbria (Wynne, 1998) as well as the long struggle for recognition and compensation by the victims of the Bhopal gas disaster (Zavetoski, 2009). In *Malmfälten* we see examples of how matters such as vulnerability, responsibility, the right to aid, and the politics of the aftermath shape both the present and future of disaster-affected places and for the communities that inhabit, rebuild, or are displaced from them. These are all matters that shape how places live through or die from disasters.

Finally, one may note that while the examples discussed in this chapter are foremost the results of political and economic processes—including extractivism and a settler colonial legacy—the inclusion of such man-made disasters within the greater universe of disasters has consequences for how one approaches researching disasters, especially in the Anthropocene. Disasters such as the Love Canal dioxin disaster (Fowlkes & Miller, 1982) or the explosion of the Challenger Space Shuttle (Vaughan, 1996) were all primarily human in origin, albeit mediated through environmental entanglements, and like the ongoing displacement of communities in *Malmfälten* they encourage disaster researchers to set aside the canonical focus on exogenous events in favor of an approach centering the social, economic, and political relations shape disasters and disastrous processes. Doing so, I argue, will help us better understand disasters as it compels us to ask not only why some people were made more vulnerable in a disaster than are others, but to inquire into the complex and far-reaching entanglements that shape many of the disasters unfolding around us, including the catastrophic impacts caused by anthropogenic climate change (a complex, global entanglement indeed).

Notes

1 Sweden is divided into 290 self-governing lower-level government entities, *kommuner* (municipalities), whose responsibilities include childcare provisions, elderly care, preschools, primary and secondary school, social services, sanitation, and urban planning.
2 Sundberg, J., & Skarstedt, H. (2016) *This is Kiruna: How to move a city*. Swedish Institute.
3 Wajstedt, L. (2012). *Kiruna – Rymddvägen*. Filmpool Nord.
4 Rynéus, A., & Eriksson, P. (2013). *The home and the cavity*. Sveriges Television (SVT).
5 Hillbom, M. (2019). *Den Stora Flytten: En Film Om Malmberget*. Sveriges Television (SVT).

References

Bergström, J. (2023, March 15). Minnesstund för gamla centrum: "Viktigt avslut". *Norrländska Socialdemokraten*, 10.
Centemeri, L., & Tomassi, I. (2022). Disasters and catastrophes. In L. Pellizzoni, E. Leonardi, & V. Asara (Eds.), *Handbook of critical environmental politics* (pp. 232–244). Edward Elgar Publishing.
Clarke, L. (1989). *Acceptable risk? Making decisions in a toxic environment*. University of California Press.
Clarke, L. (2006). *Worst cases: Terror and catastrophe in the popular imagination*. University of Chicago Press.
Elliott, J. R., & Howell, J. (2016). Beyond disasters: A longitudinal analysis of natural hazards' unequal impacts on residential instability. *Social Forces*, *95*(3), 1181–1207.
Eriksson, U. (1991). *Gruva och arbete: Kiirunavaara 1890–1990* [Doctoral dissertation]. Uppsala University.
Fowlkes, M. R., & Miller, P. Y. (1982). *Love Canal: The social construction of a disaster*. Federal Emergency Management Agency.
Fox Gotham, K., & Greenberg, M. (2014). *Crisis cities: Disaster and redevelopment in New York and New Orleans*. Oxford University Press.
Fritz, C. E. (1961). Disasters. In R. K. Merton & R. Nisbet (Eds.), *Contemporary social problems* (pp. 651–694). Harcourt.
Gallardo, G., Saunders, F., Sokolova, T., Börebäck, K., van Laerhoven, F., Kokko, S., & Tuvendal, M. (2017). We adapt . . . but is it good or bad? Locating the political ecology and social-ecological systems debate in reindeer herding in the Swedish Sub-Arctic. *Journal of Political Ecology*, *24*, 667–670.

Hagen, R., & Elliott, R. (2021). Disasters, continuity, and the pathological normal. *Sociologica*, *15*(1), 1–9.

Heckscher, E. F. (1954). *An economic history of Sweden*. Harvard University Press.

Hilhorst, D., & Bankoff, G. (2004). Introduction: Mapping vulnerability. In G. Bankoff, G. Freks, & D. Hilhorst (Eds.), *Mapping vulnerability: Disasters, development and people* (pp. 1–9). Routledge.

Horowitz, A. (2020). *Katrina: A history, 1915–2015*. Harvard University Press.

Howell, J., & Elliott, J. R. (2019). Damages done: The longitudinal impacts of natural hazards on wealth inequality in the United States. *Social Problems*, *66*(3), 448–467.

Kiruna Municipality. (2012). *Program för arkitekttävling: Ny stadskärna i Kiruna/Architecture competition brief: A new city centre for Kiruna*.

Kroll-Smith, J. S., & Couch, S. R. (2009). *The real disaster is above ground: A mine fire and social conflict*. University Press of Kentucky.

Latour, B. (1993). *We have never been modern*. Harvard University Press.

Lawrence, R., & Moritz, S. (2019). Mining industry perspectives on Indigenous rights: Corporate complacency and political uncertainty. *The Extractive Industries and Society*, *6*(1), 41–49.

Lefebvre, H. (1991). *The production of space*. Blackwell.

Linder, A. (2023, March 13). "Kiruna dör. . . Slåss!"—legendariska uttrycket har fått nytt liv. *Sveriges Radio*. https://sverigesradio.se/artikel/kiruna-dor-slass-legendariska-uttrycket-har-fatt-nytt-liv

LKAB. (2021). *Två samhällen blir ett: Samhällsomvandling*. https://samhallsomvandling.lkab.com/sv/malmbergetgallivare/tva-samhallen-blir-ett/

LKAB. (2022). *Vi flyttar en stad: Samhällsomvandling*. https://samhallsomvandling.lkab.com/sv/kiruna/vi-flyttar-en-stad/

López, E. M. (2021). *Transforming Kiruna: Producing space, society, and legacies of inequality in the Swedish ore fields* [Doctoral dissertation]. Acta Universitatis Upsaliensis.

Nilsson Mohammadi, R. (2018). *Den stora gruvstrejken i Malmfälten: En muntlig historia* [Doctoral dissertation]. Stockholm University.

Norrbotten County Administrative Board (Länsstyrelsen Norrbotten). (2022). *Samråd inför tillståndsansökan för fortsatt och utökad verksamhet vid LKAB Malmberget, Gällivare kommun* (Report No. 551–14535–2021). Länsstyrelsen Norrbotten.

Olofsson, T. (2019). The death of place: Exploring discourse and materiality in debates on rural development. In T. Holmberg, A. Jonsson, & F. Palm (Eds.), *Death matters: Cultural sociology of mortal life* (pp. 65–85). Palgrave Macmillan.

Olofsson, T. (2020). *Mining futures: Predictions and uncertainty in Swedish mineral exploration* [Doctoral dissertation]. Uppsala University.

Palsson, G., & Swanson, H. A. (2016). Down to earth: Geosocialities and geopolitics. *Environmental Humanities*, *8*(2), 149–171.

Persson, S., Harnesk, D., & Islar, M. (2017). What local people? Examining the Gállok mining conflict and the rights of the Sámi population in terms of justice and power. *Geoforum*, *86*, 20–29.

Pettersson-Strömbäck, A., Meister, K., & Forsberg, B. (2009). *Rapport om upplevd hälsa och miljöstörning i Gällivare—Malmberget—Koskullskulle: Rapport till miljödomstolen*. Umeå University.

Radio Örnsköldsvik. (2021). Semesterpratare 2021: Katarina Sundelin. *Semesterpratare 2021*.

Raker, E. J. (2020). Natural hazards, disasters, and demographic change: The case of severe tornadoes in the United States, 1980–2010. *Demography*, *57*(2), 653–674.

Sörlin, S., & Wormbs, N. (2010). Rockets and reindeer: A space development pair in a northern welfare hinterland. In P. Lundin, N. Stenlås, & J. Gribbe (Eds.), *Science for welfare and warfare: Technology and state initiative in cold war Sweden* (pp. 131–151). Science History Publications.

Stöckel, B.-M., Sjöberg, J., Mäkitaavola, K., & Savilahti, T. (2012). Mining-induced ground deformations in Kiruna and Malmberget. *ISRM International Symposium—EUROCK 2012*, Stockholm, Sweden.

Swedish National Audit Office. (2017). *Omvandlingen av Kiruna och Malmberget—bristande underlag hos regeringen och LKAB*. Sveriges Riksdag.

The Swedish Riksdag. (1972). *Expropriations Act* (1972: 719).

The Swedish Riksdag. (1991). *Minerals Act* (1991: 45).

Tierney, K. J. (2007). From the margins to the mainstream? Disaster research at the crossroads. *Annual Review of Sociology*, *33*, 503–525.

Tsing, A. L., Swanson, H., Gan, E., & Bubandt, N. (2017). *Arts of living on a damaged planet*. University of Minnesota Press.

Ureta, S., & Flores, P. (2022). *Worlds of gray and green: Mineral extraction as ecological practice*. University of California Press.

Vaughan, D. (1996). *The Challenger launch decision: Risky technology, culture, and deviance at NASA*. University of Chicago Press.

Wynne, B. (1998). May the sheep safely graze? A reflexive view of the expert–lay knowledge divide. In S. Lash, B. Szerszynski, & B. Wynne (Eds.), *Risk, environment and modernity: Towards a new ecology* (pp. 44–83). SAGE Publications Ltd.

Zavetoski, S. (2009). The struggle for justice in Bhopal: A new/old breed of transnational social movement. *Global Social Policy*, *9*(3), 383–407.

9 Cultural resilience in polycrisis

A pathway to suicide prevention

Barbara Schabowska

1. Introduction

Don't fear God.
Don't worry about death.
What is good is easy to get.
What is terrible is easy to endure.

The words of Epicurean *Tetrapharmakos*, as transmitted to us by the ancient historian Diogenes Laërtius (1925) in the 3rd century AD, hold potential as a liberating manifesto resonant with modern culture and Western civilization. With the ongoing process of secularization in Western societies (Casanova, 2007), alongside the proliferation of consumerism within the framework of the "consumer society" (Bauman, 2009, p. 83), we could consider that the first three maxims of the *Tetrapharmakos* have found realization. The fear of deities or the apprehension regarding an afterlife, as well as the dread of death itself, have ostensibly diminished within societies that have come to accept euthanasia by request, a shift exemplified even by figures such as the former Catholic Prime Minister of the Netherlands and his wife who opted for simultaneous euthanasia. These advancements suggest a pathway towards the fulfilment of the fourth tenet of the *Tetrapharmakos*: shielding us from pain, suffering, and the manifold inconveniences of existence.

Meanwhile, reports from the World Health Organization (WHO) (WHO, 2022a) underscore an escalating concern regarding mental health, particularly evident in societies that trace their cultural heritage back to ancient Greek civilization, that is, in the broadly understood West. Available data and projections concerning mental health indicate a significant and expanding global challenge (WHO, 2022b). Depression and alcohol use disorders emerge as the predominant mental health conditions worldwide, with the associated suicide rates remaining alarmingly high, particularly in some developed societies. Consequently, it appears that Epicurus's fourth maxim—what is terrible is easy to endure—proves elusive within contemporary reality, a reality succinctly characterized by Adam Tooze as a polycrisis.

In October 2022, Adam Tooze, a contributing editor at the *Financial Times* and an economic historian at Columbia University, introduced the concept of polycrisis, delineating it as a nuanced and interconnected series of crises. Within this

DOI: 10.4324/9781003537311-10

analytical framework, these crises unfold concurrently across diverse domains such as economics, politics, environment, and health; their interactions often amplify their collective impacts, thereby engendering intricate and formidable challenges. The idea of polycrisis manifests a departure from the four assurances offered by Epicurus, transforming adversities into profoundly arduous circumstances. This transformation is perhaps engendered by the chronicity of the condition and its pervasiveness across various facets of human existence. Indeed, polycrisis stands diametrically opposed to the idyllic notion of a Kantian Garden—a metaphorical construct, conceivably rooted in Kantian philosophy, signifying a utopian realm on Earth. Although the history of the concept of polycrisis is comparatively nascent when juxtaposed with the enduring legacy of paradisiacal gardens, it bears testament to humanity's perennial quest for conceptual frameworks that elucidate and contextualize lived experiences. David Henig and Daniel M. Knight, in their analysis, extrapolate upon the concept of polycrisis, discerning within it an additional layer of significance, which they aptly term "knotted eventedness" (2023, p. 4). They posit that "knotted eventedness" offers an alternative narrative perspective that directs attention to domains of meaning, causal relationships, and the sociopolitical imperative to take action. The initial rupture of crisis, typically construed as a moment of judgement or decisive action, may not unfold immediately. Instead, it fosters novel rhythms and entanglements, intertwining with longer-term temporal dynamics.

Utopian ideals aimed at emancipating humanity, often from its own constraints, which are embedded within political projects (Bartoszewicz, 2014), frequently embody the recommendations of Epicurus, albeit without necessarily conjuring visions of a paradisiacal garden. Historically, the four most perturbing mortal concerns could be assuaged through the practice of philosophy as a spiritual discipline (Hadot, 1995). However, the contemporary portrayal of our world, mired in escalating crises, starkly contrasts with the idyllic imagery of an Epicurean sanctuary. This is evidenced by the mental condition of its inhabitants, especially the growing readiness among increasingly younger individuals to take their own lives.

In this chapter, I endeavour to elucidate why I contend that the flip side of this contemporary milieu—marked by the accumulation of crises and a persistent yearning for salvation—is a descent into existential voids, epitomized, among other manifestations, by suicide (Witkowska, 2021, p. 271). Additionally, I aim to explore how culture, conceived as a repository of distinctive knowledge and universal principles (Scruton, 2007: X), emerges as a resilient force akin to the immune system of our societies, offering solace and moral compass amidst the turbulence of our times.

2. Mental health crisis and suicides

The challenges pertaining to mental health and the pervasive suicide crisis, affecting a significant portion of the populace in developed nations, attained global prominence with the adoption of the 2030 Agenda for Sustainable Development by the United Nations General Assembly in 2015 (United Nations, 2015). While acknowledging the United Nations (UN) limitations and the imperative for its reform, a critique articulated almost since its inception (Gareis, 2012), it is noteworthy that this document represents an unprecedented milestone in human history. With all 193 UN member states pledging to undertake concerted action towards achieving the 17 Sustainable Development Goals (SDGs), this commitment underscores a collective endeavour to secure a dignified existence for all global citizens, foster peace and economic advancement, safeguard the natural environment, and combat climate change. Notably, positioned prominently as the third objective among the 17 goals, SDG 3—"Ensure healthy lives and promote well-being for all at all ages"—is indicative of its paramount importance, following closely on the heels of SDG 1, "End poverty in all its forms everywhere," and SDG 2, "End hunger, achieve food security and improved nutrition, and promote sustainable agriculture." Incidentally, proponents of Epicurean philosophy might draw parallels between the deceitful simplicity of implementing both the *Tetrapharmakos* maxims and the idealistic premise of the first three SDGs unanimously embraced by UN member states. However, the ostensibly utopian character of these objectives does not belittle the fundamental correctness of the direction they delineate.

SDG 3 comprises 13 targets and 28 indicators designed to gauge progress towards these targets. Of particular relevance, SDG 3.4 specifically addresses mental health, aiming to "reduce by one third premature mortality from non-communicable diseases through prevention and treatment and promote mental health and well-being" by the year 2030. Concurrently, the European Union (EU) has mandated that all companies operating within its jurisdiction report on their adherence to Environmental, Social, and Governance (ESG) goals, with the objective of encouraging corporate engagement in socially and environmentally responsible practices. The release of the European Sustainability Reporting Standards in December 2023, as part of the Corporate Sustainability Reporting Directive enacted in January 2023, elicited significant reactions from executives of large corporations. As of the close of the 2024 financial year, these companies are required to disclose the impact of their operations, including on the mental health of employees and the surrounding community. This pragmatic stance by the European community endeavours to establish rational metrics for achieving ESG objectives, including those pertaining to the promotion of mental health. Concomitantly, in June 2023, the EU introduced a new facet to the European Health Union: "a comprehensive approach to mental health." These initiatives underscore the recognition that mental health protection represents both a social and economic imperative, thereby positioning it as a central public policy objective across the EU.

The litmus test of mental health within European societies is evidenced by the concerningly high suicide attempts among young people, which, beyond their tragic toll, also carry significant economic implications for the EU: "Suicide is the second leading cause of death among young people (15–19 years of age) after road accidents. In the EU, the annual value of lost mental health, in children and young people, is estimated at EUR 50 billion" (European Commission, 2023, p. 1). It stands to reason that the European Mental Health Capacity Building Initiative may soon garner a status no less pivotal than the European Green Deal.

WHO member states adopted the Comprehensive Mental Health Action Plan 2013–2030, yet nearly a decade later, the "World Mental Health Report: Transforming Mental Health for All" highlights that the actions taken by member states remain insufficient and inadequate (WHO, 2013).[1] According to the Report, suicide persists as a leading cause of mortality among adolescents. The ultimate impact of the Covid-19 pandemic on suicide rates is still uncertain, as statistical data on this matter is typically subject to understandable delays. Thus far, reports on this subject have yielded mixed findings: while some studies indicate a decline, others suggest an increase (WHO, 2022a). Regardless of whether the numbers remain stable, there have been concerning indicators, as outlined in a scientific brief published by WHO, which highlights widespread suicidal ideation and behaviours, including heightened self-harm among adolescent girls and increased suicidal thoughts among healthcare workers. Globally, more people die by suicide each year than as a result of wars and terrorist attacks. Furthermore, each suicide resonates throughout communities, impacting up to 135 individuals who were acquainted with the deceased, thus posing a potential risk factor for their own susceptibility to suicidal ideation (Cerel et al., 2019).

The escalating expenses associated with treating the repercussions of mental health crises, as underscored by both the WHO and the EU, along with their ramifications for national economies, have spurred European countries to implement national preventive programmes targeting, among other issues, suicide crises.

2.1 The cases of Norway and Poland

Suicide prevention is not the sole realm necessitating support; for every suicide, statistics reveal approximately 20 suicide attempts, emphasizing the imperative of extending care to individuals following such attempts and to their families. Nevertheless, preventive activities have proven to be more efficacious, a strategy adopted by various nations in recent years. In this regard, an instructive comparative case is provided by Norway, which has actively pursued preventive measures in response to suicide crises for nearly three decades. In contrast, Poland is in the nascent stages of implementing such initiatives, marking its initial forays into this critical domain.

According to the Organisation for Economic Co-operation and Development (OECD), "In 2020, the suicide rate in Norway stood at 12 per 100,000 population—slightly above the EU average of 10.24 and aligning with rates reported by other Nordic countries" (OECD/European Observatory on Health Systems and Policies, 2023). In response, the Norwegian government unveiled a comprehensive action plan for suicide prevention spanning 2020–2025, under the rallying cry of "zero suicides." Notably, Norway has embarked on establishing a specialized suicide register, leveraging collaborations with the Norwegian Cause of Death Registry and the Norwegian Patient Registry. The Norwegian Surveillance System for Suicide in Mental Health and Substance Misuse Services, initiated by the Norwegian Directorate of Health, has been established through the collaborative efforts of the National Centre for Suicide Research and Prevention at the University of Oslo. Drawing on methodologies developed by the National Confidential Inquiry into

Suicide and Safety in Mental Health at the University of Manchester in the UK (National Center for Suicide Research and Prevention, 2019), this system is poised to revolutionize suicide surveillance practices.

Empirical research highlights the pivotal role of mental disorders in precipitating suicidal behaviour, with such conditions identified in over 90% of individuals who die by suicide (Cavanagh et al., 2003). Given the nexus between mental health facilities, addiction centres, and the suicide crisis, these institutions emerge as natural arenas for preventive interventions. Nevertheless, there exists a dearth of comprehensive knowledge regarding individuals who succumb to suicide during or after their engagement with these services in Norway. Hence, the overarching objective of the Surveillance Suicide System is to facilitate the systematic collection of national data on suicides among individuals who have had contact with specialist mental health services in the preceding 12 months. This initiative aims to enable continuous monitoring of suicide incidents, elucidate their contextual nuances and contributing factors, and furnish valuable insights to inform the design, implementation, and evaluation of effective preventive measures.

On the other hand, despite being less advanced in suicide prevention measures, Poland exhibits a comparable suicide rate per 100,000 inhabitants to Norway. Moreover, what Norway shares with Poland are a substantial population of immigrants of Polish origin residing in Norway, numbering over 124,000 individuals (Statistics Norway, 2024). Similar to Norway, men in Poland exhibit a significantly higher suicide rate compared to women. However, there are notable disparities between the two nations. Norway's proactive approach to suicide prevention is evidenced by the Norwegian Board of Health's publication of the first national suicide prevention strategy already in 1995. In contrast, Poland only introduced its first National Program for the Prevention of Suicidal Behavior in 2021, implemented by the Ministry of Health as part of the National Health Program, spanning the years 2021–2025 (Polish Ministry of Interior, 2021) This programme, delineated across 10 objectives, aims to enhance access to assistance for individuals experiencing suicidal crises, bolster the competencies of those rendering aid, and enhance surveillance of suicide attempts and fatalities. Unlike Norway, Poland has yet to endeavour to establish a centralized suicide registration system to refine psychiatric services based on medical facility data. Presently, statistical data in Poland are collated from reports furnished by the Central Statistical Office (with suicide-related data subject to a three-year delay) and from records maintained by the Police Headquarters (issued in annual reports).

Although nationwide suicide rates in Poland have remained relatively stable for several years, the escalating suicide crisis among children and adolescents mirrors concerns observed in Norway. A recent report, released on February 23, 2024, by the Life Worth Conversation Association and the Polish Suicidological Society on the World Day for Combating Depression, sheds light on this pressing issue. Drawing on data from the Police Headquarters, the report reveals that teenagers in Poland are making an average of six suicide attempts per day. However, these figures likely represent an underestimation, as not all suicide attempts are reported to authorities

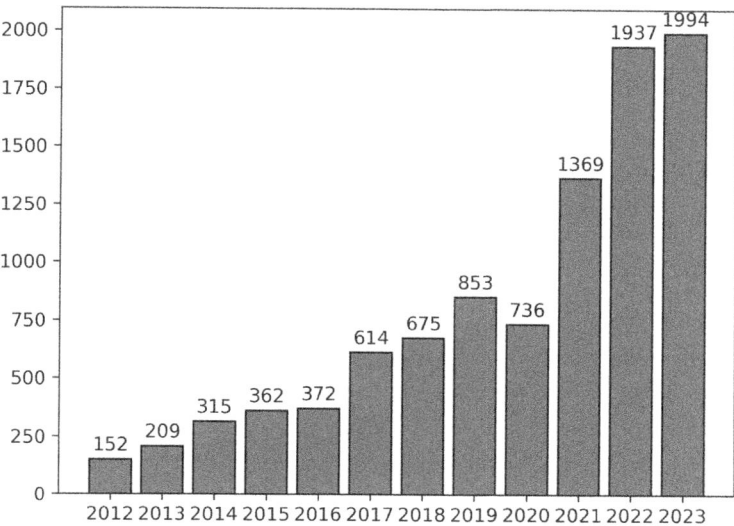

Figure 9.1 Number of suicide attempts among children and adolescents up to 19 years of age in Poland (based on Witkowska et al., 2024).

(Witkowska et al., 2024). The data presented in Figure 9.1 suggest that while there has been a concerning rise in suicide attempts among children and adolescents in Poland, the alarming trend has shown signs of abatement, with an increase of only 2.9% compared to the previous year. This contrasts with the staggering surge observed at the turn of 2021 and 2022, which saw a remarkable 41% spike.

The authors of the report attribute the reasons for this shift to environmental and social factors, highlighting the rise in peer violence, shifts in alcohol consumption patterns, and increased social isolation stemming from the Covid-19 pandemic. Additionally, they underscore the influence of the internet, which has filled voids in relationships and introduced new challenges.[2] Factors such as exposure to suicide-related content online, the impact of social media algorithms on self-destructive behaviour, the potential for forming suicide pacts with peers, the dissemination of information about suicide methods on online platforms, and the romanticization and glorification of suicide all directly shape the behaviour of adolescent internet users.

2.2 Beyond ordinary crisis

Just as contemporary crises manifest as multilayered and simultaneous phenomena, the endeavour to mitigate suicide crises also necessitates multi-vectoral policies, interorganizational efforts, and an interdisciplinary approach. Disciplines pertinent to the study of suicide, especially psychology, psychiatry, and sociology, offer diverse models elucidating the aetiology of suicidal behaviours. While the clinical perspective, anchored in medical studies indicating the overwhelming prevalence of mental disorders in individuals who die by suicide (90%), holds significance, it fails to comprehensively address the complexity of the issue. Indeed, while a majority of suicides occur among individuals diagnosed with mental disorders, at the same time we cannot say that the majority of those afflicted by mental illness succumb to suicide. Hence, the identification of additional risk factors—social or individual—is imperative. Ultimately, suicide is a rare event, which implies that even complex risk models may not fully account for individual motivations. Nevertheless, these models enable the identification of recurring factors and patterns that coincide with suicidal ideation and behaviour, including suicide attempts, thoughts, tendencies, and the act of suicide itself. Within the interdisciplinary framework of suicidal behaviour aetiology, as proposed by Witkowska (2023), such factors can be categorized into five domains:

- individual factors (e.g., somatic diseases, mental illnesses, traumas, interpersonal difficulties, addictions),
- situational factors (e.g., significant life events such as bereavement, divorce),
- environmental factors (e.g., family dynamics, internet influence),
- social factors (e.g., economic conditions, access to support, and education),
- religious-cultural factors (e.g., cultural attitudes towards suicide, portrayal of suicide in media, religiosity).

This comprehensive approach prompts a broader examination of the suicide crisis while avoiding premature recourse to metaphysical conjectures. Whereas philosophy, as a non-applied science, may not provide practical solutions, it offers a conceptual framework to discern underlying connections and foster novel interpretations. However, this broader horizon of issues, transcending the confines of our known reality, offers insight into alternative connections and prompts fresh interpretations.

In the contemporary milieu, this framework extends beyond traditional ontological inquiries to encompass the concept of polycrisis—is this not akin to an anthropologically informed perspective of Henig and Knight (2023, p. 5) who elucidated the interconnected layers of reality shaping economic, political, demographic, and social shifts? If polycrisis serves as a framework for comprehending economic and political transformations, migration, demographic shifts, and social behaviours, then it is pertinent to factor it into discussions surrounding mental crises and suicides. As Henig and Knight (2023, p. 5) assert, the complexity inherent in polycrisis, characterized by its propensity for non-linearity, emergence, exponentiality, scalarity, and unpredictable outcomes as proposed by, parallels the intricate nature of culture—a system replete with meanings, symbols, and interactive content. The only comparably intricate system of meanings, symbols, and interactive content that I can identify is culture. Consequently, in the ensuing discussion, we will first delve into the intricacies of polycrisis before exploring the role of culture as a sanctuary from its ramifications.

3. Polycrisis

The third chapter of the Global Risk Report 2023 delineates how the interconnections among emerging multiple risks may collectively culminate into a phenomenon termed "polycrisis," with natural resource shortages projected to be its focal point by 2030. Citing Adam Tooze, the report defines polycrisis as "a cluster of related global risks with compounding effects, such that the overall impact exceeds the sum of each part" (Global Risk Report, 202: 57). This term, ubiquitous during the 2023 World Summit in Davos, has not only gained traction among publicists but has also increasingly permeated the discourse of political and social sciences in recent years. Crises have historically played an integral role in shaping world events, often serving as a litmus test for Europe's response and fostering greater integration of EU institutions, as highlighted by researchers (Jones et al., 2016). However, the efficacy of this approach appears to have reached its limits, necessitating a fundamental re-evaluation of the European project. Moreover, the rapid advancement of technology introduces entirely novel "man-made existential risks" (United Nations Development Program, 2022), such as the potential loss of human control over artificial intelligence or the emergence of man-made pandemics caused by genetically modified viruses. These new technologies are poised to generate unprecedented forms of existential risk, not only in terms of scale but also due to their unique complexities and their reflection of evolving planetary dynamics and social disparities. Failure to consider the new factor of the polycrisis in risk management could lead to a situation in which we face a "global polycrisis—a single, macro-crisis of interconnected, runaway failures of Earth's vital natural and social systems that irreversibly degrades humanity's prospects" (Homer-Dixon et al., 2022).

The earliest known usage of the word polycrisis can be attributed to Edgar Morin and Anne Brigitte Kern in their book *Homeland Earth*, where they posit that the world confronts "no single vital problem, but many vital problems, and it is this complex intersolidarity of problems, antagonisms, crises, uncontrolled processes, and the general crisis of the planet that constitutes the number one vital problem" (1999, p. 74). This overarching predicament, which they identify as the crisis of the planet, frames the ecological sphere. Drawing upon this, Mark Swilling, a South African sociologist and sustainable transitions' theorist, employed the term to characterize a "nested set of globally interactive socio-economic, ecological, and cultural-institutional crises that defy reduction to a single cause" (2013, p. 98). Today, a decade later, "polycrisis" has evolved into a concept denoting a specific state in world history, wherein processes of globalization have engendered an interdependent and interconnected world, traversed by intertwined crises that amplify each other's effects.

This condition represents a novel state, exacerbating societal discomforts and necessitating a re-evaluation of the decision-making processes of political leaders. Furthermore, crises exhibit distinct paces and intensities, leading to their classification as either fast- or slow-burning crises, hence prompting an examination of their actors, reactions, and expectations (Seabrooke & Tsingou, 2019, p. 476). Such an approach may facilitate a better understanding and communication of crises, potentially mitigating social tensions. However, it remains undeniable that mutually reinforcing crises can yield far graver consequences than the mere summation of their individual negative effects. Examining their dynamics, intersections, and repercussions for those affected as well as the environment may elucidate the mechanisms underlying their proliferation and aid in the management of polycrisis in the future. The latter is of pivotal importance, as drawing insights from the Global Risk Report, it is conceivable to argue that polycrisis will persist for the foreseeable future, potentially marking the onset of a polycrisis era for humanity. This perspective goes beyond superficial intellectual trends that suggest substituting the "Anthropocene Epoch" with another, even broader concept. Instead, let us consider an apocalyptic vision of our future that aligns with both the empirical evidence of the current state of affairs and all modelled forecasts.

The analogy of synchronizing metronomes captivates the imagination with its elegance and offers a compelling cognitive perspective. As referenced by (Homer-Dixon et al., 2022, p. 7), it illustrates how seemingly disparate elements can interact in unforeseen ways.[3] When placed on a platform with slight lateral movement, randomly set metronomes quickly synchronize their oscillations, showcasing the facilitation of invisible interactions within the system. Furthermore, the phenomenon demonstrates positive feedback, whereby the synchronization of more metronomes results in the transfer of greater kinetic energy to subsequent devices. Homer-Dixon et al. propose an additional distinction between "conduits" and "signals," which collectively enhance the interactions between systems. The intricate interplay of conduits and signals, manifesting in various configurations, serves as a basis for the authors' formulation of four hypotheses within this conceptual framework. Particularly noteworthy is the incorporation of cultural and institutional dimensions, a facet often overlooked in conventional global crisis management discourse (Mitroff et al., 1987; Harwati, 2013; Bundy et al., 2017). While this proposition necessitates further elaboration, it resonates with our intuitive sense of the interplay between culture and polycrisis, a connection largely absent in existing scientific literature on polycrisis.

These hypotheses refer to grievances generated by economic dislocations, cross-border migration, the global climate food production system, and—last but not least—spreading nihilistic worldviews. Let us note that the latter hypothesis puts culture at the centre of influence and recognizes its impact on the economy, even pointing to the "contagion of pathogenic idea" (Homer-Dixon et al., 2022, p. 8). This is where their analyses end. Meanwhile, a positive verification of this hypothesis could be the mental crisis spreading in Europe and the increase in suicidal behaviour among children and adolescents in Europe.

3.1 The spirit in (poly)crises

There is little merit in seeking simplistic and hastily implementable solutions for a malady as severe and intricately rooted as polycrisis, given its multifaceted and elusive causes. Nonetheless, the progenitor of this concept, Edgar Morin, offers a clue as to where to begin the search: "Faced with the polycrisis humanity is going through, the first resistance is that of the spirit" (Morin, 2024). The grim portrayal of humanity's future that he conveys operates on two distinct levels: the looming spectre of a global polycrisis encompassing political, environmental, economic, and civilizational realms, alongside the profound erosion of humanity's moral fabric. In his view, the notion of progress, propelled by Enlightenment rationality and driving societal advancement, is portrayed as myopic and emotionally sterile, fostering a culture of self-interest and egoism. "The result is a return to dogmatism, fanaticism and a crisis of morality in a context of surging hatred and idolatry," he puts it succinctly (Morin, 2024).

How can we understand this resistance of the spirit? There is an Epicurean note in this call—according to this philosophy, individuals with fortitude were expected to confront challenges without fear, even in the face of death. Translating this idea into practical implementation suggests envisioning a scenario where, in the coming years, global leaders—perhaps prompted by the realization of the inadequacy of existing crisis mitigation strategies such as those proposed by the World Bank, the forced resettlement of immigrants in the EU, carbon emission reduction efforts, or subsidies for organic agriculture—begin to explore alternative approaches, given that current methods of crisis management have not yielded tangible benefits. In their unconsidered concern for the 2030 Agenda and with a focus on "general human values," much can be done to seemingly help while actually causing more harm, like establishing a UN agency dedicated to defining universal values, taking into account cultural disparities and diverse traditions. One can imagine the creation of 'spiritual cosmetology institutes' (Noica, 2023, p. 29), aimed at cultivating inner balance and tranquillity to restore the beauty of life. These scenarios, though somewhat grotesque, align with the logic typically embraced by the UN, the EU, and the problem-solving approaches adopted by political leaders. However, it must be acknowledged that such measures are unlikely to offer substantive assistance. In addition to knowledge in the form of scientifically systematized information, we require an understanding of "how" to act and "what" to do. This latter aspect is a virtue that cannot be acquired solely through specialized, even the most prestigious, EU programmes, but rather through engagement with culture. Therefore, it is perplexing why culture has not been incorporated among the primary Sustainable Development Goals.[4] Care for the world's cultural heritage warrants attention following mental health, especially considering that culture constitutes a significant and lucrative global market sector.[5] Even more so, since culture can be monetized, its absence in the 2030 Agenda is surprising.

4.   Culture as an emergency exit: navigating the polycrisis

Destructive processes linked to societal decay and civilization crises also infiltrate culture, often rendering it infantile. Furthermore, the entertainment industry has a tendency to diminish cultural value, often reducing it to the level of trumpery (Finkielkraut, 2023). This phenomenon is a consequence of globalization's influence on culture (Barber, 1996), coupled with the legacy of Enlightenment reason

(Delsol, 2020). However, this critical perspective on culture, which suggests a need for a paradigm shift in the era of postmodernism (Derrida, 2017), aligns with the framework of the polycrisis and reinforces it. Yet, fortunately, it is not the sole perspective on culture. The pathway out of the polycrisis, or the means to alleviate its adverse impacts, particularly concerning mental health, lies within culture. Culture serves as a reservoir of moral knowledge, comprising value judgements and facilitating their transmission across generations. This perspective aligns with the argument put forth by Roger Scruton: "culture has become not just precious to us, but a genuine political cause, the primary way of conserving our moral heritage and of standing firm in the face of a clouded future" (Scruton, 2007, p. 10). Indeed, this assertion holds true for what is often referred to as "Western high culture" (Crane, 1992), which imparts its essence through images, myths, and symbols that permeate popular culture. Of particular significance in the context of resilience amidst crisis is a unique form of knowledge offered by culture construed in this manner— an "*emotional* knowledge, concerning what to do and what to feel" (Scruton, 2007, p. 10). Hence, culture serves as a means of appraising reality, accessible to all, and moreover, these assessments are grounded in the realm of values, thereby elevating individuals' lives to ethical contemplation. This is precisely what Edgar Morin implored of us—an ethical examination of polycrisis reality. As Scruton contends, there exists a correlation between moral worth and cultural advancement: the cultivation of proficiency in moral discernment stems from engagement with culture, encompassing literature, theatre, film, philosophy, and the fine arts. This establishes a specific frame of reference, a cultural cosmos that structures thoughts and the art of living, serving as an "architecture of meaning" (Delsol, 2020, p. 316). Possessing such a frame of reference is crucial for evaluating reality—our attitudes towards it and the appropriateness of our expectations. Hence, I expanded Scruton's argument regarding the relationship between cultural development and morality to encompass mental well-being.

Culture, when conceived in this manner, is grounded in a particular worldview, akin to what Kuhn would term a paradigm (2011), which is gradually losing its dominance. Certain trends in the evolution of thought, culture, and history cannot be reversed. Nonetheless, it is plausible to posit that the perspective on culture proposed in this chapter holds such utility across social, individual, and global realms that it merits consideration in the quest for solutions to the polycrisis.

4.1 Cultural resilience

It can be claimed that under certain conditions, culture becomes a security policy (Bartoszewicz, 2018). Among the developed approaches to societal security, the Copenhagen school recognizes the important role of culture and allows for systematizing societal security elements as existing independently of state security (Wæver et al., 1993). Currently, none of the attributes assigned to social resilience (Folke, 2016) refer explicitly to culture. The normative dimension of resilience links it with culture, which is a challenge for researchers, because both are seen as "slippery concepts" (Panter-Brick, 2015, p. 233). Several authors have highlighted culture's role in individuals, social and ecological systems, and community resilience, which has given rise to the idea of cultural resilience (Ungar, 2008; Crane, 2010; Maclean et al., 2014). There are two ways of approaching this concept: as one of the layers of social resilience, drawing from culture, and cultural resilience relating to culture itself. Following Bousquet and Mathevet, the notion of distinctness is at the heart of cultural resilience (2019). However, I consider the conclusion of their very conscious look to be incomplete. Therefore, I argue it is insufficient to ask resilience "from what" and "for what" and then superficially attribute the findings to politics. It would rather be appropriate, by analogy, to Berlin/Taylor's two definitions of freedom to ask about negative and positive distinctness (Szahaj, 2011). Negative, "from what," is easy to describe by contrasting with another culture and "the other." The positive one requires looking at the culture itself and its surroundings, and above all, it involves giving meaning and value. Merely pointing to distinctness is too narrow a definition of cultural resilience and not descriptive enough analytically. The attributes of cultural resilience should be closely studied to further elucidate the causal mechanisms of cultural resilience and its impact on mental health and societal security.

The application of cultural resilience strategies to enhance well-being over the long term will allow strengthening mental health, thereby directly helping EU member states to tackle Target 3.4 of the UN Sustainable Development Goals: "Reduce by one third premature mortality from non-communicable diseases through prevention and treatment and promote mental health and well-being." The potential economic impact could be significant given that "Mental health is linked to each of SDGs" (WHO, 2022b, p. 96). Considering the substantial strain on the European budget caused by escalating costs associated with mental health and suicide crises, alleviating this burden could directly reduce these expenditures. Furthermore, improving mental health outcomes can enhance workforce participation among affected individuals, thereby positively influencing gross domestic product growth. Such arguments are likely more convincing to European technocrats than the assertion that culture as a source of specific knowledge can be used as a tool for assessing reality, naming feelings, and a reservoir of moral attitudes.

This chapter shows that when we look closely at the cultural factors that contribute to suicidal behaviour, the direct correlation between culture and our well-being becomes increasingly apparent. The role of culture in fostering a meaningful existence and imbuing our actions with significance is paramount, especially in light of the fact that one in six people in the EU grapple with a mental health condition, and antidepressant consumption has more than doubled in the last two decades (OECD, 2023). This underscores the imperative of elevating culture to a global goal. Today, as humanity grapples with its expulsion from the Garden of Eden and seeks a pathway back to paradise, it finds itself unable to halt even at the outskirts of Athens, within the tranquil confines of Epicurus' vegetable garden. In the tumultuous landscape of the polycrisis, the notion of an "unnoticed life," lived in harmony with nature and sheltered by the garden's shade (Plutarch, 2005, p. 1128d), remains entirely elusive and beyond our grasp. Practicing values divorced from the realm of symbols, imagination, and cultural richness proves challenging. Cultural transmission, along with the capacity to assess and articulate emotions that it facilitates, erects a protective barrier around individuals, shielding them from the contemporary epidemic of nihilism perpetuated by the polycrisis.

Acknowledgements

I would like to express my most profound gratitude to Professor Monika Gabriela Bartoszewicz, whose belief in the power of thought and wise counsel made this chapter possible.

Notes

1 The WHO initially adopted a plan covering the years 2013–2020, which was subsequently extended to encompass the period until 2030. In 2019, the organization adopted a supplementary document to formally extend the timeline of the plan, thus covering the 2013–2030 period. Consequently, while the cited source may appear unusual with a 2019 date referencing the 2013–2030 timeframe, it reflects the chronological evolution of the WHO's mental health action plan.
2 According to the report "Teenagers 3.0," prepared by NASK, Polish Research and Academic Computer Network (NASK—National Research Institute, 2021), a Polish child under 18 years of age spends on average 5 hours and 36 minutes a day on the Internet. This time significantly increased in 2021–2022. However, the average daily time spent using social media among teenagers is 4 hours and 12 minutes. If we assume that teenagers spend 8 hours sleeping and the same amount for school, meals, and hygiene activities, we can see that they spend the remaining time on the Internet.
3 It calls for the Cartesian metaphor of the world as a clock—an intricate and meticulously crafted mechanism believed to be engineered by a divine and flawless watchmaker (Descartes, 1960). However, contemporary reality no longer resembles the smooth and orderly workings of a clock. Instead, it evokes the image of numerous metronomes, each out of sync with the others, symbolizing the complexity and discordance inherent in our modern world.
4 In May 2020, the Council of the EU introduced the priority "Culture as a driver for sustainable development" to the cultural work plan 2019–2022. This addition was prompted by the realization that the 2030 Agenda inadequately acknowledges the role of culture in advancing the SDGs. It is important to note that the recommendations stemming from the report resulting from this initiative are not binding on member states (EU, 2022). UNESCO's response has been similarly delayed and sluggish in addressing this issue. However, progress was made with the adoption of the MONDIACULT 2022 Declaration during the UNESCO World Conference on Cultural Policies and Sustainable Development. This declaration represents a significant step forward as it acknowledges culture as a global public good (UNESCO, 2022). The declaration emerged as a result of the collective agreement among individual countries to develop a joint action plan aimed at enhancing public policies in the realm of culture for sustainable development.
5 According to UNESCO data, the creative sector is one of the most important drivers of development in the world. Based on an analysis of LinkedIn, which boasts 762 million users worldwide, it was found that in January 2021, 51.2 million people globally self-registered as working in some capacity (full-time, part-time, intern) in the cultural and creative industries. This number accounted for 6.7% of all global LinkedIn users at the time and represented 48.4 million full-time equivalent jobs. Moreover, it is the sector that employs the largest number of young people under 30 years of age (UNESCO, 2021, p. 4).

References

Barber, B. R. (1996). *Jihad vs. McWorld: Terrorism's challenge to democracy*. Ballantine Books.

Bartoszewicz, M. G. (2014). European identity: Europe as its own "other". *Horyzonty Polityki*, *5*(10), 31–49.

Bartoszewicz, M. G. (2018). *Festung Europa*. Ośrodek Myśli politycznej.

Bauman, Z. (2009). *Konsumowanie życia*. Wydawnictwo Uniwersytetu Jagiellońskiego.

Bousquet, F., & Mathevet, R. (2019). Cultural resilience as the resilience of a distinctness. Distinctness from what? For what? In B. Rampp, M. Endreß, & M. Naumann (Eds.), *Resilience in social, cultural, and political spheres* (pp. 305–322). Springer.

Bundy, J., Pfarrer, M. D., Short, C. E., & Coombs, W. T. (2017). Crises and crisis management: Integration, interpretation, and research development. *Journal of York Management*, *43*(6), 1661–1692. https://doi.org/10.1177/0149206316680030

Casanova, J. (2007). Rethinking secularization: A global comparative perspective. In P. Beyer & L. Beaman (Eds.), *Religion, globalization, and culture* (pp. 101–120). Brill.

Cavanagh, J. T. O., Carson, A. J., Sharpe, M., & Lawrie, S. M. (2003). Psychological autopsy studies of suicide: A systematic review. *Psychological Medicine*, *33*(3), 395–405.

Cerel, J., Brown, M. M., Maple, M., Singleton, M., van de Venne, J., Moore, M., & Flaherty, C. (2019). How many people are exposed to suicide? Not six. *Suicide and Life-Threatening Behavior*, *49*(2), 529–534.

Crane, D. (1992). High culture versus popular culture revisited: A reconceptualization of recorded cultures. In M. Lamont & M. Fournier (Eds.), *Cultivating differences: Symbolic boundaries and the making of inequality* (pp. 58–74). University of Chicago Press.

Crane, T. A. (2010). Of models and meanings: Cultural resilience in social–ecological systems. *Ecology and Society*, *15*(4), 19.

Delsol, C. (2020). *Czas wyrzeczenia*. Państwowy Instytut Wydawniczy.

Derrida, J. (2017). *Inny kurs*. Polskie Wydawnictwo Naukowe.

Descartes, R. (1960). *Zasady filozofii*. Polskie Wydawnictwo Naukowe.

European Commission. (2022). *Stormy times. Nature and humans: Cultural courage for change. 11 messages for and from Europe*. https://op.europa.eu/en/publication-detail/-/publication/0380f31c-37c9-11ed-9c68-01aa75ed71a1/language-en

European Commission. (2023). *Communication on a comprehensive approach to mental health*. https://commission.europa.eu/strategy-and-policy/priorities-2019-2024/promoting-our-european-way-life/european-health-union/comprehensive-approach-mental-health_en

Finkielkraut, A. (2023). *Porażka myślenia*. Polski Instytut Wydawniczy.

Folke, C. (2016). Resilience (republished). *Ecology and Society*, *21*(4), 44.

Gareis, S. B. (2012). *The United Nations: An introduction*. Palgrave Macmillan.

Laërtius, D. (1925). Epicurus. In *Lives of the eminent philosophers* (Vol. 2, p. 10). Harvard University Press.

Hadot, P. (1995). *Czym jest filozofia starożytna?* Aletheia.

Harwati, N. L. (2013). Crisis management: Determining specific strategies and leadership style for effective outcomes. *Crisis*, *2*(2), 170–181.

Henig, D., & Knight, D. M. (2023). Polycrisis: Prompts for an emerging worldview. *Anthropology Today*, *39*(2), 3–6.

Homer-Dixon, T., Renn, O., Rockstrom, J., Donges, J. F., & Janzwood, S. A. (2022). *A call for an international research program on the risk of a global polycrisis*. Cascade Institute. https://cascadeinstitute.org/wp-content/uploads/2022/03/A-callfor-an-international-research-program-on-the-risk-of-a-global-polycrisis-v2.0.pdf

Jones, E., Kelemen, D., & Meunier, S. (2016). Failing forward? The Euro crisis and the incomplete nature of European integration. *Comparative Political Studies*, *49*(7), 1010–1034.

Kuhn, T. (2011). *Struktura rewolucji naukowych*. Aletheia.

Maclean, K., Cuthill, M., & Ross, H. (2014). Six attributes of social resilience. *Journal of Environmental Planning and Management, 57*(1), 144–156.

Morin, E., & Kern, A. B. (1999). *Homeland Earth*. Hampton Press.

Morin, E. (2024). Faced with the polycrisis humanity is going through, the first resistance is that of the spirit. *Le Monde.* https://www.lemonde.fr/en/opinion/article/2024/01/24/edgar-morin-faced-with-the-polycrisis-humanity-is-going-through-the-first-resistance-is-that-of-the-spirit_6460205_23.html

Mitroff, I. I., Shrivastava, P., & Udwadia, F. E. (1987). Effective crisis management. *Academy of Management Perspectives, 1*(4), 283–292.

NASK—Naukowy Instytut Badawczy. (2021). *Nastolatki 3.0. Raport z ogólnopolskiego badania uczniów.* https://www.nask.pl/pl/raporty/raporty/4295,RAPORT-Z-BADAN-NASTOLATKI-30-2021.html

National Center for Suicide Research and Prevention. (2019). *The Norwegian surveillance system for suicide in mental health and substance misuse services. Project draft.* https://www.med.uio.no/klinmed/english/research/centres/nssf/norwegian-surveillance-system/publications/reports/annualreport_2019-2020_english_summary.pdf

Noica, C. (2023). *Dziennik filozoficzny*. Państwowy Instytut Wydawniczy.

Organisation for Economic Co-operation and Development. (2023). *Health at a glance 2023: OECD indicators.* OECD Publishing.

Panter-Brick, C. (2015). Culture and resilience: Next steps for theory and practice. In L. Theron, L. Liebenberg, & M. Ungar (Eds.), *Youth resilience and culture, Vol. 11: Cross-cultural advancements in positive psychology* (pp. 233–244). Springer.

Plutarch. (2005). *Żywoty równoległe*. Prószyński i S-Ka.

Polish Ministry of Health. (2021). *Narodowy Program Zdrowia na lata 2021–2025.* https://www.gov.pl/web/mswia/narodowy-program-zdrowia-na-lata-2021-2025

Scruton, R. (2007). *Culture counts: Faith and feeling in a world besieged*. Encounter Books.

Seabrooke, L., & Tsingou, E. (2019). Europe's fast- and slow-burning crises. *Journal of European Public Policy, 26*(3), 468–481.

Statistics Norway. (2024). https://www.ssb.no/en/statbank/table/05183/

Swilling, M. (2013). Economic crisis, long waves, and the sustainability transition: An African perspective. *Environmental Innovation and Societal Transitions, 6.*

Szahaj, A. (2011). Charles Taylor o wolności. In C. Garbowski, P. Hudzik, & J. Kłos (Eds.), *Charlesa Taylora wizja nowoczesności* (pp. 201–212). Wydawnictwa Akademickie i Profesjonalne.

UNESCO. (2021). *Cultural and creative industries in the face of COVID-19: An economic impact outlook.* https://unesdoc.unesco.org/ark:/48223/pf0000377863

UNESCO. (2022). *Declaration: World conference on cultural policies and sustainable development—MONDIACULT 2022.* https://www.unesco.org/en/articles/unesco-world-conference-cultural-policies-and-sustainable-development-mondiacult-2022

United Nations. (2015). *Transforming our world: The 2030 agenda for sustainable development.* https://sdgs.un.org/sites/default/files/publications/21252030%20Agenda%20for%20Sustainable%20Development%20web.pdf

United Nations Development Programme. (2022). *UNDP RBAP foresight brief: Polycrisis and long-term thinking.* https://www.undp.org/sites/g/files/zskgke326/files/2022-09/UNDP-RBAP-POLYCRISIS-AND-LONG-TERM-THINKING-2022.pdf

Ungar, M. (2008). Resilience across cultures. *British Journal of Social Work, 38*(2), 218–235.

Wæver, O., Buzan, B., Kelstrup, M., & Lemaitre, P. (1993). *Identity, migration, and the new security agenda in Europe*. Pinter Publishers.

Witkowska, H. (2021). *Samobójstwo w kulturze dzisiejszej. Listy samobójców jako gatunek wypowiedzi i fakt kulturowy*. Wydawnictwo Uniwersytetu Warszawskiego.

Witkowska, H. (2023). Etiologia z różnych perspektyw zachowań samobójczych wśród dzieci i młodzieży. In H. Witkowska (Ed.), *Zapobieganie samobójstwom. Zachowania suicydalne dzieci i młodzieży* (Vol. 3). Difin.

Witkowska, H., Kicińska, L., Palma, J., & Łuba, M. (2024). *Zrozumieć, aby zapobiec 2024—zachowania samobójcze wśród dzieci i młodzieży.* ZWJR. https://zwjr.pl/artykuly/ zrozumiec-aby-zapobiec-2024-ii-edycja-raportu

World Health Organization. (2013). *Comprehensive mental health action plan 2013–2030.* https://iris.who.int/bitstream/handle/10665/345301/9789240031029-eng.pdf?sequence=1

World Health Organization. (2022a, March 2). *Mental health and COVID-19: Early evidence of the pandemic's impact: Scientific brief.* https://iris.who.int/bitstream/handle/10665/352189/ WHO-2019-nCoV-Sci-Brief-Mental-health–2022.1-eng.pdf?sequence=1

World Health Organization. (2022b). *World mental health report: Transforming mental health for all.* https://iris.who.int/bitstream/handle/10665/356119/9789240049338-eng. pdf?sequence=1

10 Understanding natural hazard phenomena and risks from the perspective of 'instrumental realism'

Examples from Geiranger and Lyngen, Norway

Leikny Bakke Lie and Reidar Staupe

Vignette 1: Åknes, the active and unstable rockslide in Geirangerfjord, Norway

In the picturesque UNESCO site of Geirangerfjord, located in the south-western part of Norway, an invisible risk looms. Hidden from the spectators who immerse themselves in the spectacular view of mountains reflecting in the calm fjord, the active and complex rockslide Åknes poses a serious threat to surrounding villages. This slow-moving landslide (Jaboyedoff et al., 2011; Blikra, 2012; Hungr et al., 2014) has the potential to trigger a rockslide-induced tsunami (Blikra et al., 2006). The locals have been aware of a crack in the mountain for years (Hammer, 2021), attempting to bring the issue to the public's attention in the 1960s (Sandersen et al., 1996) and again in the early 1980s (Sandersen et al., 1996; Hammer, 2021), claiming that the crack was widening. Since an initial field inspection of the area in 1986 (Sandersen et al., 1996) the Åknes rockslide has been the subject of numerous studies (e.g., Ganerød et al., 2008; Kveldsvik et al., 2009; Jaboyedoff et al., 2011) aimed at understanding the hazard and estimating the likelihood of a tsunami and its potential consequences. The active area of the Åknes rockslide is estimated to be 30–40 million m³ (Jaboyedoff et al., 2011) and it has been classified as a high-risk object (DSB, 2016) due to the combination of a high annual probability of an event and the severe potential consequences. The area has been under continuous monitoring since 2004 (Jaboyedoff et al., 2011).

Initial surveillance involved manual measurement equipment (Sandersen et al., 1996), such as tension rods installed onsite to measure movement across small cracks. Since the early days of monitoring, more instruments and technology have been deployed to monitor the Åknes rockslide. Tension rod measurements are now complemented by an extensive network of instruments, making it one of the most monitored rockslides in the world (Ganerød et al., 2008; Blikra, 2012). Digital equipment includes position measurements using navigation satellites to track how the terrain shifts, laser equipment to measure distance, and various radar systems recording movements in the rockslide. Instruments have also been installed in boreholes 150 metres deep within the rockslide, providing data on movement,

DOI: 10.4324/9781003537311-11

temperature, and groundwater levels, while geophones and seismometers record seismic events such as tremors and small rockfalls. A meteorological station at the site provides additional data on precipitation and snow depth. All the data collected for the Åknes rockslide are continuously transferred to a monitoring office (Blikra & Kristensen, 2013; Kristensen et al., 2020; NVE, 2024), where the interpretation of the data is used to assess the level of risk and issue warnings to emergency response actors and residents if necessary.

Vignette 2: three high-risk rockslides in Lyngen, Norway

In the mountainous Lyngen region in Northern Norway, we find no less than three of the seven identified high-risk rockslide objects (Kristensen et al., 2020). The active, slow-moving rockslides Jettan, Indre Nordnes, and Gámanjunni 3, located in Kåfjord municipality, are all under continuous surveillance. A rockfall from the unstable area of Jettan with a potential volume of 17 million m³ (Blikra & Christiansen, 2014) or from Indre Nordnes estimated to have a volume between 10 and 20 million m³ (Henderson et al., 2007) into Storfjorden, has the potential to trigger tsunami waves (Storrøsten & Glimsdal, 2023) that will have large consequences for villages in four surrounding municipalities. Due to its more inland location, Gámanjunni 3 will not trigger a tsunami, but, with a potential mass of 26 million m³ (Böhme et al., 2016), it threatens nearby housing and infrastructure and has the potential to dam the River Manndalselva, leading to a subsequent risk of flooding.

Active rockslides are the result of long-term geomorphic processes, formed by slow, gravity-driven movements along weak zones in the bedrock (Hungr et al., 2014). Although these three rockslides were not discovered and mapped until more recent years (Jettan and Indre Nordnes in 1999 and 2005, and Gámanjunni 3 over a period from 2009 to 2012), residents in Kåfjord and surrounding municipalities have lived, knowingly or unknowingly, with the risk of rockslides from these unstable mountain areas for decades. Since the discovery of these high-risk objects, several surveys and field visits (e.g., Henderson et al., 2007; Böhme et al., 2016; Storrøsten & Glimsdal, 2023) have sought to uncover the processes driving these rockslides, resulting in all three rockslides being categorised as high-risk. A variety of instruments and monitoring systems have been implemented to cover the three areas, including tension rods, electronic tiltmeters, web cameras, weather stations, and lasers measuring the distance between cracks, as well as GPS antennae, receivers, and both ground-based and satellite-based radars measuring continuous movement in the unstable area. Adding to the risk are processes related to the presence of permafrost, where temperature increases and fluctuations can further impact the stability of these rockslides (Blikra & Christiansen, 2014). This issue could potentially be exacerbated by global warming (Böhme et al., 2019).

The ever-present risk from these three active rockslides impacts daily life in Kåfjord and the surrounding municipalities (Stav, 2013; Høyer, 2024). Wave height calculations and hazard zones place limitations on where and what can be built, imposing strong restrictions and limiting the possibilities for further development of the surrounding areas (Hoe, 2023).

Vignette 3: the 1934 Tafjord disaster

On the night of 7 April 1934, the inhabitants of villages surrounding Tafjorden in Møre og Romsdal, Norway, experienced a disaster (Furseth, 1985). In the middle of the night, the rockslide Langhammaren fell into the fjord beneath, triggering a deadly tsunami. The maximum wave height was estimated to be 62 metres (Furseth, 1985; Sandersen et al., 1996) and waves as high as 15 metres washed over the nearby villages of Fjørå, Tafjord, and Valldal. 40 residents lost their lives that night, the oldest victim being 79 years old and the youngest only 2 years old (Furseth, 1985). The additional material damage to houses and infrastructure was immense.

For years, the locals had spoken of a known crack in the mountains above Tafjorden, fearing the consequences if the unstable rock formation were to fall into the fjord (Furseth, 1985). With limited technology available in 1934, there were no discussions about implementing a system for monitoring the unstable mountain area, and few anticipated that the consequences would be as disastrous as they were on that fateful night. Testimonies and photographs documenting the event make up a valuable portion of our knowledge and understanding of what happened during this event. With the introduction of increasingly sophisticated modelling techniques, we are now also able to back-calculate the rockslide-triggered tsunami (Harbitz et al., 2014) and visualise its movement through animated simulations. Both the collected statements and photographs from 1934 (Furseth, 1985), as well as more recent calculations (Blikra et al., 2006; Harbitz et al., 2014), provide us with a greater understanding of how the rockslide triggered a tsunami, how the waves propagated through the fjord, and how the villages along the fjord were impacted. This knowledge further contributes to our understanding of slow-moving landslides and can aid in designing monitoring programmes and disaster management schemes. After all, the 1934 Tafjord disaster is often used as an example when discussing how an event could unfold if the Åknes rockslide were to release into Geirangerfjorden (Blikra et al., 2006; Harbitz et al., 2014), or if Indre Nordnes or Jettan were to collapse into Storfjorden (Storrøsten & Glimsdal, 2023).

1. Introduction

As illustrated by the three vignettes above, the contemporary experience of disaster risk is increasingly mediated by technology and technical instruments. This chapter concerns the significant role that technology plays in shaping not only our knowledge of disaster risks but also the lived experience of them, which we explore by bringing the perspective of instrumental realism (Ihde, 1991, 1998; Kvasz, 2022) in contact with disaster scholarship. Instrumental realism is a perspective that emphasises 'the importance of scientific instruments for the acquisition of scientific knowledge' and that the extent to which 'we have epistemic access to reality . . . is often indirect, mediated by means of instruments' (Kvasz, 2022, p. 165). It introduces a concern regarding how technical instruments mediate our experience of emergent phenomena. Philosophers of technology often define technology generously, where the technological includes more than the kinds of tools scientists use but also knowledge connections used by laypersons across different cultures or contexts (Ihde, 1990; Verbeek, 2005).

Through this examination of the influence of technology on our ability to be concerned about issues beyond the realm of direct perception, we are motivated by a desire to better understand how technological tools and instruments condition our ability to perceive, anticipate, and respond to actual and potential disasters. This is especially pertinent in regions exposed to catastrophic risk scenarios, such as Geiranger and Lyngen in Norway, where the integration of advanced technological systems is both a necessity and a challenge. Through an exploration of key ideas from instrumental realism, we aim to clarify conceptually the ways in which technology can both reduce and exacerbate vulnerabilities, offering new insights into the complex relationship between human societies and the risks that concern us in an increasingly technological (and risky) world.

It is important here to stress that the themes discussed in this chapter are of worldwide relevance. Global crises like climate change, antimicrobial resistance, biodiversity loss, and pandemics, along with more localised manifestations like rising sea levels, extreme weather events or geological hazards, serve as vivid examples of the central role that technology plays in detecting and forecasting hazards. All over the world, communities are grappling with slow calamities (Staupe-Delgado, 2019, 2021), including environmental changes, melting glaciers and glacial lake outburst flood risk, as well as other catastrophic menaces that threaten the future existence of communities (Lacroix et al., 2020; Taylor et al., 2023). One commonality between all these examples is that they contribute to a sense of uncertainty about the future and a demand for more and better simulations and analyses.

Our ability to comprehend and anticipate hazards and risks on a broader scale—whether linked to climate, geology, hydrology, or pathogens—largely depends on sophisticated technological tools and instruments (Ihde, 1998; Hepach & Lüder, 2023). For example, satellite images allow for the monitoring of deforestation or glacial retreat over time, and advanced sensors allow us to detect even slight seismic activity. While our direct, sensory experiences and local knowledge can often provide sufficient understanding of hazards in the immediate landscape, the complexity and scale of contemporary risks (in combination with a growing expectation of safety) drives forward a demand for ever-more sophisticated methods of detection and prognostication. Tools such as real-time monitoring systems and computer simulations are increasingly employed to track the emergence of slow-onset hazards and project their future development trajectories (Granjou et al., 2017; Mathews & Barnes, 2016).

Technology also plays a significant role in learning from the past. By systematically collecting historical data for analyses, it becomes possible to reconstruct and simulate how past disasters, such as avalanches and tsunamis, unfolded (which in turn is often done with the purpose of obtaining knowledge that may help us to mitigate and prepare for future disasters) (Harbitz et al., 2014). Consequently, disaster planning involves a complex temporal dynamic where the past, present, and future are opened to scientific exploration through instrumentation. These tools enable us not only to understand and manage disaster risk in the present but also to project what potential future disasters might look like. This in turn greatly impacts what it feels like to inhabit places where prognostic forms of risk knowledge bring distant but disastrous futures into the palpable realm of the present.

The chapter is structured as follows: The next section provides an introduction to instrumental realist thought, a body of work that remains largely disconnected from natural hazards and disaster scholarship. The third section considers the implications and insights from the instrumental realist perspective for the hazards mentioned in the vignettes above. The fourth and concluding section reflects on implications and recommendations for hazard and risk communication with the exposed populations.

2.   Instrumentation and access to knowledge concerning natural hazards

In his work on the relationship between humans and their environment and the role of instrumentation in the context of science and technology, Don Ihde (1990, 1991, 1998, 2009) identifies a number of different kinds of connections between a person and their world, which have important implications beyond the immediate context of the human-technology relations themselves (see Table 10.1):

In this chapter, we reflect further on these human-technology-world relations (see also: Rosenberger & Verbeek, 2015; Aagaard et al., 2018) in the context of people who inhabit places exposed to considerable disaster risk. As Nørskov (2015) points out, these relations are not mutually exclusive or exhaustive categories but should be seen as a continuum. We identify and discuss four generative aspects of human-technology-world relations that we explore (see Table 10.2):

Table 10.1 Human-technology-world relations

Embodiment relations	A piece of technology becomes an extension of the body and the senses
Hermeneutic relations	A piece of technology provides a reading about the world for interpretation
Alterity relations	A piece of technology is interacted directly with as a thing in itself
Background relations	A piece of technology operates in the background

Table 10.2 Generative aspects of human-technology-world relations

Ingenuity	A piece of technology can give rise to new perspectives and innovations
Transcendentalism	A piece of technology can open new realms of experience
Reflexivity	A piece of technology can shape our understanding of ourselves
Safety and security	A piece of technology can affect our sense of safety and security

These human-technology-world relations can best be understood as attempts at conceptualising different ways in which technology mediates human experience and how instrumentation provides access to knowledge about natural hazards-related phenomena. Importantly, Ihde emphasised in his work the role of technological artefacts in extending perception or the senses in various ways, where unmediated perception is direct observation of the world, and a mediated perception is one where a piece of technology is positioned 'between' the user and the world, in a human-technology-world relationship (Verbeek, 2001).

Knowledge of natural hazard exposure is a precondition for having lived experience of related disaster risk. The human-technology-world relations serve to illustrate how various technologies provide access to such knowledge and shape our interaction with, understanding of, and response to natural hazards like earthquakes, hurricanes, volcanic eruptions, and so on. It is important to emphasise here that 'World' in this context does not necessarily refer to the Earth, nature, or the natural environment per se. It should not be taken to refer simply to an object but to the world we inhabit. Similarly, the 'human,' or a person, a self, is not simply a subject without a feeling, thinking, and sensing body. Rather, existence happens in places and is embodied, as well as existential and reflexive, as phenomenologists have long emphasised. In the following, we provide a brief explanation of each human-technology-world relation, illustrated with examples from a natural hazard context.

2.1   Human-technology-world relations

2.1.1   Embodiment relations

Embodied relations with technology are characterised by technologies (or tools) functioning as an extension of the human body and its sensory apparatus (Ihde, 1990, 2009; see also Verbeek, 2001). Embodied technology relations are what Ihde refers to as 'transparent,' meaning that the technology recedes into the background and becomes almost invisible if we are accustomed to interacting with the world through it. When a technology relationship is of an embodied nature, the technology itself fades from view, and the focus shifts to our experience of the world (although as mediated by the technological artefact). The technology thus acts as a mediator between us and the world, allowing us to perceive or enhance certain aspects of experience.

In the case of monitoring slow-moving landslides, the installation of onsite web cameras can exemplify how instruments can assume a form of embodied relation. These web cameras allow the operators to 'have eyes' on the site without being physically present, representing a form of extension of the body. The focus of the operator is not on the instrument itself, but rather on the access to the world achieved through the provision of real-time images from the web camera.

Another example is how, through the use of instruments, a person can sense imperceptible levels of seismic activity, radiation, or changes in atmospheric pressure. Although the human sensory apparatus cannot directly detect these phenomena, they become accessible through tools that enable us to perceive their presence in the world. As Ihde notes, seamlessly sensing the world through instrumentation depends on developing a form of literacy—an accumulated familiarity with the tool that allows us to interpret its outputs so fluently that the instrument feels like an extension of our primary senses (Ihde, 1990). While instruments that provide data readings are typically considered part of hermeneutic relations (explored in the next section), there are arguably instances where they can take on embodied characteristics as well. When interaction with instruments becomes so intuitive and seamless that the interpretation feels almost like direct perception, these may be experienced as extensions of the senses, as in embodied relations. In this way, the instrument can be seen as an extension of the body. Importantly, the usage of the instrument is what enables the experience, in an embodied sense, of the presence of phenomena that would otherwise remain beyond human grasp (or that would not appear to us the same way without the instrument).

This process highlights how technology in embodiment relations works to mediate and expand human senses and faculties. Instead of being separate from us, technologies become part of our bodies and embodied practice as tools, both through and with which we experience the world. This relationship can open new aspects of reality to experience or enhance existing ones. Ihde's example of eyeglasses is one tool that does not allow access to imperceptible phenomena, but, when seeing through the eyeglasses, our vision becomes enhanced without the eyeglass-wearer being conscious of their presence during practical tasks like reading a book. Through embodied relations, a piece of technology not only augments the sensory apparatus but also becomes part of the body schema, thus altering the human-world relationship.

This aspect of embodied technology relations makes clear what is meant by the invisibility of the tool in embodied relations. Familiarity with a tool inevitably makes us less conscious of its presence as we focus increasingly on its reading—on sensing the world through it. Rather than working to understand or master the tool through conscious effort, experience with the tool gradually results in the ability to sense with the tool as part of our practical engagement with it. The more habitual the use of a tool becomes, the more integrated it is into our embodied experience. When the habit is disrupted (e.g., if it malfunctions), we suddenly become aware of the tool again, and the seamlessness of embodiment is broken. Also, immersed practical engagement with tools requires being literate in whichever instrumentational output the technology produces. Instrumentational literacy makes clear how embodied technology relations are closely tied to the second, hermeneutic, relationship to technologies.

2.1.2   *Hermeneutic relations*

Hermeneutic relations with technology are characterised by the process of reading or interpreting instrumentational outputs of any form. In this mode, the world is engaged with through representations, often emerging from instrumentational outputs or through the use of tools that either enhance or go beyond the primary senses.

It differs from embodied relations (although it partially overlaps, as shown in the previous section) in that, in hermeneutic technological relationships to the world, we do not experience the world through an instrument or tool but rather sense the world through interpretation of representations of it (Ihde, 1991). These representations are often outputs or readouts about the world (Ihde, 1998). The difference can be exemplified by reference to the experience of observing a planet through a telescope and 'observing' a planet through more abstract forms of instrumentation, such as a spectrometer (Ihde, 2009). In this context, technological artefacts work as mediators, transforming (often imperceptible) phenomena—or specific aspects of phenomena—into readable output data such as graphs, images, or numbers (Ihde, 1998). The focus of the experienced user of the instrument is then on interpreting the readout and understanding the implications. One example is how earthquake magnitude readings represent earthquakes in terms of a number indicating comparability on a scale. Instrumentational readings are often for specific uses, intended to represent precisely a particular aspect of the phenomenon rather than multiple dimensions of it.

There are some overlaps with embodied relations in that the interpretive process becomes more intuitive with an increase in the level of literacy involved in working with the representational mode of a said tool. Just as in embodied relations, the tool becomes more transparent with experience and skill, and the focus increasingly shifts from the tool itself to its skilled use. When an experienced meteorologist forecasts an extreme weather event, they will be less concerned with the inner workings of the instruments and simulations and more focused on skilfully using these for specific purposes, such as understanding its severity or whether to issue a warning. Similarly, experience with the hermeneutic process will make the interpretative work increasingly intuitive, meaning that readouts will be read more as situations or in terms of their implications rather than raw data outputs to be examined closely. Adept users in this way 'read' the world through instruments but without focusing on the instrument or the raw data as such.

In this way, hermeneutic human-technology relations are strongly dependent on a specific form of literacy in reading and interpreting the outputs from instruments or in otherwise using tools that enhance the human sensory apparatus (Ihde, 2009). Immersion with tools over time gives a sense of specialisation and competence. Developing the skill to see outputs not as data but as situations or information takes time. Ultrasound is one example of how a layperson needs the help of a skilled user of the instrument to read what is shown on the instrumentational output. If the operator of this device (such as a nurse) were to observe something concerning, further testing with other instruments would be carried out, demonstrating how different instruments are used for specific purposes and have their own affordances regarding the 'epistemic access' they can provide (Kvasz, 2022). As the user becomes increasingly literate in interpreting the instrumentational output (which is often visual but can also be in the form of numbers, sounds, clicks, etc.), they also develop the skill to 'sense' the data in a more embodied way, for example in the form of a 'hunch'—a comparative sense of something being 'off,' abnormal, or atypical in a particular reading (Ihde, 1998). This ability to see outputs as situations will also vary in clarity. Some outputs might be seen quite clearly as indicating a specific result, while other readings might simply be concerning on a more general level, indicating that further examination is needed. Here, technology mediates our understanding hermeneutically, transforming imperceptible or otherwise elusive phenomena (such as annual millimetre advancements in very slow-moving landslides) into standardised representations suitable for scientific and systematic enquiries.

In hermeneutic relations, technology does not merely present data in raw form. Rather, it transforms how we understand the world by offering new ways to see and analyse phenomena and by opening up to experience (and scientific research) entities that would otherwise be beyond sensory reach (Ihde, 1991). This shift changes our relationship with the world and potentially opens completely new aspects of reality in a more fundamental and paradigmatic way. Examples include the worlds revealed by the microscope (the microscopic world of cells and bacteria), the telescope (distant cosmic phenomena invisible to the naked eye), radiometer (access to wavelengths beyond the human senses), or seismic imaging (revealing aspects of the subsurface) (Ihde, 2009). In other words, advancements in instrumentation provide ever-expanding means of gaining epistemic access to different aspects of the world, revealing patterns, trends, and risks that inform how we mitigate and prepare for disasters. The hermeneutic or interpretive aspect of this human-technology relation stresses how technology does not simply provide raw observational data equal to direct sensory observation (as through the primary senses) but provides a mediated understanding (carefully prepared for scientific enquiry in the Latourian sense (Latour & Woolgar, 1986)) that requires active work on the part of the user to obtain new insights about the world.

In contrast to embodiment relations, where the focus is on how our primary senses are enhanced or otherwise extended or mediated through technology (such as glasses or telescopes), a focus on the hermeneutic emphasises indirect forms of experience. Here, the technology acts as an intermediary that not only translates the world into a more accessible format but also requires a human interpreter, literate in the instrument's representational mode, to extract meaning, making the relationship between technology, user, and world inherently interpretive in nature. However, there may be overlaps between hermeneutic and embodied relations, for example, if an adept user has come to experience that they are sensing through the instrumental output.

2.1.3 Alterity relations

Alterity relations with technology are characterised by direct interaction with a piece of technology as an entity in itself, rather than as a tool we 'sense' through or with, either in an embodied sense (as in embodied technology relations) or through more abstract readings (hermeneutic relations). In alterity relations, the technology is interacted with as an 'other,' retaining a sense of separateness from the user (Ihde, 1990, 2009). The focus shifts from what the technology mediates or the kinds of experience or observations it affords to the technology itself as an item rather than a tool in the praxeological sense. Alterity relations closely resemble the tool analysis in Martin Heidegger's *Being and Time* (2010/1927), which emphasises that, when tools break down and our active and embodied engagement with the tool and the task at hand is interrupted, our attention is drawn to the tool itself as an item. Common examples of alterity relations include situations where we diagnose a tool that is broken, attempt to fix it, or tweak it to better serve our practical purposes. In such situations, our focus shifts from praxeological usage to achieve tasks to a focus on the tool itself.

A more sophisticated example from the context of disaster risk management is how instruments often need careful calibration and tweaking to serve the purpose at hand. The user does not merely focus on the natural hazard in question or their immersion in instrumentation readings or embodied use of the tool but, rather, engages with the tools themselves, manipulating them, adjusting parameters, and running and rerunning computer simulations (ultimately making sense of the results, which relates back to the hermeneutic relation again) (Ihde, 1998). A tool like a simulation programme is not a transparent mediator that can be sensed with or through seamlessly; it demands direct interaction as an independent entity, often requiring considerable tweaking and adjustment. The user is very much aware of the technology involved, mindful of its functionality and limitations. The interaction is explicitly with an external instrument that is not embodied but requires fine-tuned work with the tools themselves without directing these at the world as such.

In this sense, alterity relations emphasise the object-like nature of technological artefacts, which requires a type of interaction disconnected from the world that the technology can reveal aspects about. Proper operation of a piece of technology may require specific skills as part of its use, involving complicated tasks like calibration, troubleshooting, inputs, or tweaking. This is especially evident in complex tools involving multiple instruments working in tandem (Ihde, 2009). In such situations, hours, days, weeks, or months might go into instrumentational tweaking and calibration (alterity relations) before the tool is ready to generate an instrumentational reading (hermeneutic relation). Such processes may also involve a long chain of activities, where a multitude of fine-tuned instruments provide various inputs or time-series data that require additional preparation as inputs to a computer simulation, modelling, or other complex analysis processes. For early warning systems, for example, the focus might sometimes be on ensuring that the sirens are functional, that the sensors are accurate with minimal measurement error, that backup systems are working properly, and that hazard scenarios are based on models reflecting the latest insights. These are distinct technological relations, standing in contrast to relations that concern forms of world disclosure, such as the sensing of a hazard phenomenon through instrumentation.

As we have shown, alterity relations often involve explicit attention to the functionality and inner workings of technological artefacts. The piece of technology does not fade into the background, as it does in embodiment relations. It also does not provide representations about the world, as in hermeneutic relations. Instead, it has a presence that requires active attention, interaction, and engagement with the technology itself, as what Don Ihde calls a 'quasi-other'—as another being or entity. As a user becomes increasingly proficient in working with a specific piece of technology, they become increasingly adept at its use, aware of its limitations, and skilled at troubleshooting when it breaks down. Yet, alterity relations do not overlap closely with embodiment relations. As far as alterity relations overlap with hermeneutic relations, this is mainly because alterity relations are characteristic of the tasks often required as part of the preparation of instruments to generate readings. The technology is engaged with not as an extension of oneself (or as something to be read intuitively based on a kind of literacy) but as a separate entity, external to the user. The piece of technology assists the user or is otherwise part of the work context, requiring operation in a direct and conscious sense (e.g., a computer). In this way, alterity relations represent one mode through which users approach their engagement with technological artefacts, where the piece of technology has a stronger presence, as opposed to working as an extension of the human sensory apparatus.

2.1.4   Background relations

Background relations with technology are characterised by the functioning of technologies at the periphery of human experience, operating outside the realm of direct conscious attention or interaction, yet still shaping our relationship with the world in subtle ways. In contrast to other technological relations (where the user actively interacts with the technology), background relations involve devices discreetly operating in the background, where they might influence how we experience and find ourselves in the world without becoming the focus of our attention. Philosophers of technology have explored this idea by drawing on familiar examples such as thermostats, which regulate the temperature of our homes without direct engagement by the user (except perhaps when changing the settings, after which the device fades out of direct consciousness as we go about everyday life) (Verbeek, 2005; Ihde, 2009). Such technologies are often not noticed at all. Rather, they act as part of the environmental context.

Background technologies are often applied to monitor disaster risks, such as sensors that monitor the onset of a slow rockslide. These instruments continuously record data about a phenomenon without human involvement. Attention is not on the numerous instruments that transmit data throughout the monitoring system, but rather with the output produced. Only rarely will the instruments need to be engaged with directly (entering into an alterity relationship with the user), such as when they malfunction or require recalibration. Under normal circumstances, the instrument remains at the periphery of human experience, autonomously recording and transmitting data, which can influence decisions or be analysed when needed.

It follows that background relations are not limited to monitoring technologies but extend to more static forms of critical infrastructure. For instance, communication or warning systems facilitate the transmission of warnings to exposed communities, providing safety despite rarely entering consciousness, except perhaps during drills when the sirens become active. There is also a wide network of background technologies in operation almost everywhere, consisting not only of phone and internet services but also emergency networks and frequencies, satellite communication technologies, and other layers of technology that ordinary citizens are rarely conscious of. Inhabitants may go months or years without thinking about such safety infrastructures, yet they subconsciously trust in their functioning on a daily basis. This highlights one fundamental characteristic of background relations: their dependability. Background relations with technology often emphasise the seamless integration of technology into contemporary everyday life. In many ways, the effectiveness of background technologies depends on their reliability and transparency (we appreciate them the most when they 'just work'). A background technology principally requires human interaction when the settings need to be changed or when it malfunctions, at which point its presence moves from the background to the foreground. This shift in attention shows how background relations depend on the continuous and autonomous functioning of these systems, but also how they can enter back into an alterity relation when malfunctioning or needing adjustment. The result is a technologically embedded way of life in which our well-being, comfort, safety, and security are largely taken care of by specialists and instruments that most beneficiaries are hardly aware of in everyday life.

2.2   Generative aspects of human-technology-world relations

2.2.1   Ingenuity

Technology is often used to create or reveal new aspects of the world, enabling new ways of understanding or interacting with reality. As a generative aspect of human-technology-world relations, ingenuity emphasises how technology is not merely a tool for perceiving or interpreting the world but becomes a key force in the creative transformation of our interaction with it (Verbeek, 2005). Ingenuity, as the capacity for creative innovation through technology, is one generative aspect of human-technology-world relations. Unlike the technology relations discussed in the previous section, considering ingenuity in terms of its generativity in connection with technology helps us glean how humans use technology as a means of thinking about and solving practical problems in new ways. In this context, technology is approached not in terms of its role in extending the senses or establishing epistemic contact with phenomena, but in the way it opens new ways to engage with the world.

While the work of Don Ihde and Peter-Paul Verbeek has emphasised the mediating role of technology, we want to extend these insights to consider how technology relates to ingenuity and creativity, which enables new connections with the world in a less direct form of mediation. In this sense, technology not only mediates human experience but also expands the scope for human ingenuity, by allowing new solutions to real-world problems, and for innovative ideas and ways of thinking.

Whereas embodied relations with technology extend the sensory or physical reach of the human body, advances in this respect ultimately hinge on creative processes that bring technologies into new areas of application to solve specific tasks at hand. This is particularly evident in how technological systems allow for experimentation and explorative problem-solving, whether in the arts, natural or social sciences, or more applied domains such as the disaster risk management context. In the context of Norwegian fjord tsunami scenarios, simulation technologies illustrate ingenuity as a generative aspect of human-technology-world relations. These tools allow for the modelling and visualisation of potential disasters before they have occurred. By manipulating variables such as rock mass and wave propagation, simulations offer new insights into potential future disasters. Moreover, these models integrate knowledge from landslides worldwide, enriching the predictive capacities of the simulations and expanding the scope of geological inquiry as a whole. Here, ingenuity emerges through the creative application of technological tools to generate knowledge that goes beyond natural cognitive limits, opening new pathways for action and understanding.

An important aspect of ingenuity is the literacy required to engage with technology creatively, as we have also explored in the context of embodied and hermeneutic relations. In the case of ingenuity, this literacy involves the ability to navigate and manipulate technological systems in a way that allows for the generation of innovative ideas or solutions. The creative potential of technology hinges on user proficiency. While ingenuity shares similarities with other aspects of human-technology relations, its emphasis on the production of new forms sets it apart. Rather than simply extending or interpreting the world, technology applied for ingenuity becomes a medium for innovation, shaping and transforming the world in ways that go beyond natural human capabilities.

2.2.2   *Transcendentalism*

Technology can also shape the underlying conditions of experience, enabling new ways of understanding or interacting with reality and the structures that shape how technology mediates and even conditions our experience of the world. As a generative aspect of human-technology-world relations, a transcendentalist perspective emphasises how technology functions not only to perceive or interpret the world but, rather, to become a key force in structuring our experience of it and interaction with it. The capacity of technology to shape the preconditions for experience is one generative aspect of human-technology-world relations. Unlike the technology relations discussed in the previous section, considering this ontological dimension allows us to see how technology conditions our way of existing in the world, shaping what can be known, thought, felt, and experienced. This aligns with the 'monolithic' or more fundamental and ontological views on technology of the kind that Martin Heidegger (2013/1954) warned against in *The Question Concerning Technology*, where he mentions the danger of technology becoming the sole world-disclosing power, eclipsing all other ways of interacting with the world (such as indigenous, local, or artistic knowledge). In the words of Verbeek (2001, p. 122), 'His questioning is not about "technologies" but about "Technology"' as a monolithic force characteristic of the human way of existing in the world today.

In this context, technology is not approached in terms of its role in extending the senses or establishing epistemic contact with phenomena but in how it creates new conditions for engaging with the world, affecting how reality itself is opened to us (often as in need of intervention). It may also be limiting, in the sense that science might become the only acceptable way to approach the natural environment, eclipsing other epistemologies (i.e., scientism). Transcendentalism in this sense refers not to technology as a tool for merely interacting with the world or solving practical problems but, rather, to its role in shaping the conditions of possibility for such interactions. Drawing on instrumental realist insights, we note that technologies are not neutral instruments (Ihde, 2009). Rather, they play a key role in shaping how reality appears to us in the first place.

Closely tied to the hermeneutic relation, an important aspect of transcendentalism as a generative element of human-technology-world relations is its capacity to reveal new aspects of reality that were previously inaccessible to us. Whereas embodied relations focus on extending the human body and hermeneutic relations focus on interpreting abstract instrumentational readings about the world, a transcendentalist view concerns the way technologies open entirely new domains of experience.

A transcendentalist view stresses the ontological shift that occurs when new aspects of the world are disclosed. In the case of disaster scenarios, models and simulations do not simply provide representations of possible futures but also define the horizons of those futures. Contingencies that can be anticipated or planned for are shaped by the limitations and affordances of technologies. Through processes of ingenuity, the scope of what is possible to know or predict also evolves. This, in turn, creates new conditions that shape human scope for action and calls for intervention. The literacy required to advance technologies, and their application, is not merely technical but also ideological. Understanding how a piece of technology can disclose the world anew requires a kind of reflexivity or an awareness of the frameworks that steer our engagement with the world and our epistemological stances.

2.2.3 *Reflexivity*

Technology shapes our relationship with the world reflexively, enabling new ways of understanding and adjusting our engagement with the world in ways that allow for introspection and new perspectives on our modes of existence. Technology (or science and technology—technoscience) provides both direct and subtle inputs to self-awareness (e.g., through new discoveries), influencing our sense of self and our place in the world. Unlike the human-technology relations discussed in the previous section, considering reflexivity in terms of its generativity allows us to see how technology facilitates existential engagement with the world. In this context, technology is approached not in terms of its role in augmenting the human sensory apparatus but in how it can inspire questions about the human condition, critical reflection on our place in the world, and its wider effect in shaping our understanding and actions. This shapes not only how people interact with the world but also how we understand ourselves in relation to the world (and our place in it, as well as our role, and limitations).

In terms of generativity, the reflexive element here emphasises how technology and its world-disclosing power enable self-examination as new knowledge with ontological implications is encountered. This may be knowledge on the micro scale (such as knowledge concerning the human body or the place that we call home) or on the macro scale (such as the future implications of climate change for ourselves and our children, or our place in the universe). Through technology, we not only gain new ways of perceiving or acting but also reflect on the impacts of these actions and the technologies themselves. Reflexivity involves a continuous process of adjustment to new observations and knowledge, often with strong implications for how we think about human truths (in the deeper humanistic sense) and our role in the bigger scheme of things.

In the context of disaster risk management, technologies can generate reflexive questions that are often of an existential nature. Technological instruments and tools may detect the existence of previously unknown hazardous exposures in the immediate environment, casting the future of a place into jeopardy. Similarly, a new and improved computer simulation might suggest that a known hazard is potentially far more severe than expected. These examples illustrate some of the existential reflections that new knowledge on disaster risks may trigger in exposed populations.

Another important dimension of reflexivity is the ethical and social implications involved. As technologies mediate our relationship to the world, it remains important to be reflexive about how we interpret and draw conclusions from mediated forms of knowledge and the actions we take in response. Technologies that prognosticate future disaster scenarios may not only serve disaster risk management aims but also raise deeper existential questions, such as whether populations should be allowed to stay in place or whether they should be uprooted from their homelands and resettled. Technologies in this sense also require a deeper form of literacy in interpreting the readings instruments produce—as in hermeneutic relations, but a more fundamental scientific literacy involving being conscious of the limits of technologies and their ideological underpinnings. Reflexivity in this sense also involves the moral responsibilities that come with the use of technology and the worlds it can disclose.

2.2.4   *Safety and security*

Technology is often used in safety and security systems, enabling people to inhabit places exposed to considerable disaster risk. As a generative aspect of human-technology-world relations, safety and security emphasise how technology is not merely a tool for protecting against disaster risk but becomes a key force in shaping people's sense of stability and ontological security.

Ontological security refers to a person's fundamental sense of being safe in the world, the confidence that life will continue predictably and with minimal disruption (Giddens, 1990; Harries, 2017). The feeling of being safe and secure (e.g., due to early warning systems) is one generative aspect of human-technology-world relations and illustrates how technology influences our existential condition, providing a sense of stability or, alternatively, feelings of insecurity. Unlike the technology relations discussed in the previous section, considering safety and security in terms of their generativity in connection to technology helps us grasp how humans use technology to manage uncertainty and create a sense of safety in the face of risks. However, as Ulrich Beck (1992) reminds us, knowledge does not necessarily bring reassurance, as the more we know, the more we realise the sheer multitude of risks we are exposed to, and we become far less accepting of contingencies. In this context, technology is approached not in terms of its role in augmenting the senses or facilitating immediate engagement with the world but in how it is employed to detect and mitigate disaster risk, shaping our perception of vulnerability.

The effect that technology has on experiential safety and security is not limited to disaster risk directly. It also shapes how human beings perceive their place in the world—the very conditions of safety and security (which is what people who have treated risk and safety as more ontological and abstract cultural entities, such as Beck and Giddens, emphasise in their understanding of these terms). This goes beyond the instrumental use of technologies, such as in early warning systems or monitoring instruments. Technology (as a cultural force, a form of world disclosure in the Heideggerian monolithic sense, not as specific instruments) transforms our engagement with risk, creating a sense of trust in the systems we rely on but also deep existential insecurities, often attributed to this secularised approach, manifesting in, for example, ever-increasing reflexivity concerning risks and existential insecurities. Safety regimes in the Norwegian fjords explored in the introductory vignettes, for example, enable people to continue to inhabit these places, by reducing their experience of radical contingency, but also open up existential questions due to the continuous monitoring of those risks. The relationship between technology and security is complex, and, while technology can enhance feelings of safety, its presence (e.g., highly visible instruments monitoring the slow onset of an impending catastrophe) can also generate feelings of insecurity, especially if the effectiveness of those systems is brought into question. This awareness can lead to a paradox of phenomenological safety and security; while the systems provide a sense of safety, they hinge on trust in the authorities. In this way, the generative aspect of safety regimes involves more than just the practical addressing of risk. It encompasses how these technologies shape lived experience, structuring inhabitants' relationship with the world in terms of ontological (in)security.

Thus, ontological security is not just about mitigating immediate risks but about reducing senses of contingency at a more fundamental and existential level, without which everyday life would become paralysed in high-risk environments. While ontological security will always remain fragile, as it is built on trust (in specialised systems and technologies), people also actively seek out coping strategies that allow them to live with contingencies. Giddens (1990) outlines how habits and familiarity with the environment build ontological security over time—described as a cocoon effect, where individuals demonstrate a propensity to bracket out contingencies on a daily basis, as part of our practical engagement with the world.

Building on this work, Harries (2017) notes how people often actively avoid distressing information and cues and often opt out of retrofitting their homes or taking other mitigative actions because they are culturally inclined towards feeling safe in their homes already (also, visible mitigation infrastructures would bring hazards into closer experiential proximity, reminding inhabitants of disaster risks, which is something many choose to avoid). Disaster risk management technologies arguably work at their best when they are invisible and seamlessly integrated into everyday life to reduce distress. Visible safety regimes may create a double-edged experience of safety. On the one hand, these systems may operate quietly in the background, allowing everyday life to proceed without interruption. On the other hand, their effectiveness becomes most evident only in moments of imminent disaster (or breakdown), which can reduce trust in their effectiveness or functioning. We also know that having too frequent drills or particularly having frequent false alarms can erode trust and severely undermine the effectiveness of early warning systems and other safety systems. Thus, the very presence of these technologies can intensify awareness of potential risks, which is something people have a propensity to avoid based on the idea that human beings seek to feel ontologically secure.

To summarise, technologies serve a significant role in mitigating disaster risks and thus contribute towards a sense of ontological security, enabling life in hazardous environments. At the same time, dependence on technology can also produce feelings of insecurity if trust is eroded. This dynamic interplay between security and insecurity, structured by the technologies we use, reflects the complex role of safety technologies in mediating our relationship with the world, shaping the experience of inhabiting places exposed to considerable disaster risk.

3.   Instrumental realism in the context of impending fjord tsunamis

As elaborated on in the previous section, technology plays a significant role in providing access to knowledge about hazards but also in shaping how we perceive, experience, and live with such risk. In this section, we apply the perspective of instrumental realism to discuss disaster risk management in the context of the slow-moving landslides and the subsequent threat of tsunamis in Geiranger and Lyngen, Norway.

The unstable rock formations in Geirangerfjord were initially "discovered" by locals hiking in the area (Sandersen et al., 1996). With local knowledge of cracks forming in the mountains and the recognition of how the cracks appeared to be expanding over decades, locals had a form of lived experience with the risk of slow-moving landslides threatening their communities (Sandvik et al., 2015). For more than 60 years, the locals had feared the consequences of a landslide from Langhammeren in Tafjord, and in 1934, their fear became reality when the unstable rock formation fell into the fjord and triggered a deadly tsunami (Furseth, 1985). In the neighboring fjord, locals had tried to warn about widening cracks in the mountain range Åkerneset since the 1960s (Sandersen et al., 1996; Sandvik et al., 2015). Despite the local awareness and attempts to gain public attention to the presence of slow-moving landslide risk, a national responsibility for landslide risk was not established until 2009, with the Norwegian Water and Energy Directorate assigned as the national authority (NVE, 2024). Up until this point, smaller, less coordinated mapping and monitoring projects were carried out in areas with identified unstable rock formations, and the risk of slow-moving landslides appears to have been treated more as a local, or to some extent, regional issue.

The locals assessed the landslide risk based on recognizable movement determined by how much the cracks had widened since the last visit, often in terms of centimetres or metres over a time span of years or decades (Sandersen et al., 1996; Sandvik et al., 2015; Hammer, 2021). With the introduction of technological advancements in the form of various measuring and monitoring instruments, we are now able to detect much smaller movements in the rock formations than what is visible to the naked eye, in the matter of millimetres over a time span of hours or days (Blikra & Kristensen, 2013). Thus, the phenomenon is experienced differently due to the implementation of monitoring technology. The monitoring process has been sped up, with technology now providing access to imperceptible levels of movement in unstable rock formations. This, in turn, can form the basis for the implementation of a disaster risk management regime in response to the risk of a landslide-induced tsunami in exposed areas such as in Geiranger and Lyngen. But this exercise requires a careful translation, or interpretation, of data collected and accessed through such sophisticated monitoring technology. In other words, sensing the world through technology requires a certain level of literacy. This is a possible explanation for why data collected from instruments monitoring slow-moving landslides is not publicly available (Sugawara, 2023). Instead, this data is interpreted by experts before a translated version is conveyed in the form of daily early warning bulletins displaying a number and a color to communicate a specific risk level to the public. This implies that the use of technology and the interpretation of data gathered are available only to a limited number of people, namely professionals with education and experience in this exercise. While the local population a few decades ago was the 'owner' of this interpretative exercise by physical assessments onsite, they are now increasingly dependent on interpretations made by 'experts.' In a sense, this adds another layer of hermeneutic relations between humans and the world: human—technology—experts—world. Decisions to act, for instance, to evacuate in case of an imminent landslide are based on expert interpretation of a representation of the world provided by carefully collected graphs and numbers indicating movement in unstable rock formations.

Unstable rock formations and the threat of landslides are not a new phenomenon. But monitoring and simulation technology has enabled calculations of hazard zones and real-time early warning systems, providing us with access to information about slow-moving landslides that can be used to make decisions about how to manage the risk and avoid disasters. This generative aspect of human-technology-world relations illustrates how technology can influence both our experiences and our behaviour towards the risk of slow-moving landslides. The installation of a continuous monitoring system that is linked to an early warning scheme intended to reach the exposed population in a matter of seconds, as opposed to just 'wait and see' (Hamza et al., 2024) or passively blaming it on 'Acts of Nature' (Quaran-telli, 2000), transforms how we engage with risk. It exemplifies how technological inventions have allowed us to think about and solve an age-old challenge in a new way. As such, technology is not solely an embodied extension of our sensory or physical reach, but also a tool that fosters creativity and innovation. At the same time, it can also heavily influence our ontological security and our sense of safety. As mentioned, the monitoring process has been sped up. But does having access to real-time information about landslide risk levels, accessible whenever and wher-ever in the form of a subscription to natural hazard alerts, make us feel safer? In the case of Geiranger and Lyngen, the hazard is formed by slow-moving geologi-cal processes. Still, with a real-time broadcast of the risk levels, it could enhance a feeling of living with an imminent threat. And the presence of visible monitoring equipment and early warning systems can act as a constant reminder of the loom-ing threat they are living under, resulting in a heightened sense of insecurity and instability.

Living in close proximity to an unstable rock formation that has been placed under a national, continuous monitoring scheme, provides opportunities for reflec-tion upon our own existence (e.g., 'should I stay, or relocate?'). On a more systemic level, it could spark discussions about governance, spatial planning, and commu-nity development in relation to living with natural hazards. Where can and should development and housing be encouraged or discouraged, should relocation be an option, and are physical protection measures a feasible option to allow for further development? These are all issues that are discussed in the local communities in Geiranger (Hole, 2021) and Lyngen (Elvestad & Haug, 2024; Høyer, 2024), com-munities that are advocating for development and growth to ensure their existence. At the same time, this opens the door to a broader, more existential discussion relating to ethics and values. What should our communities look like in a world that faces the risk of natural hazards? How we understand ourselves in relation to the world, and our place in it—can we control nature through use of technology, or should we remove ourselves from hazards?

However, technology provides a tool to manage uncertainty and risk, enabling communities to continue to thrive despite natural hazards. The implementation of hazard zones with building restrictions, and early warning systems to alert the pub-lic about the heightened risk of a rockslide from Åknes or Indre Nordnes, is an example of how technology can be utilized to protect the population. In a genera-tive sense, these measures can also influence how the population feels about the risk. For some, knowing that the area is continuously monitored could enhance a sense of stability, of feeling safe at home, knowing that in case of increased risk, they would be alerted in time to evacuate to safety. But for the monitoring scheme to provide ontological security, it is dependent on the level of trust in the system, including the technology forming background relations. The communities need to trust that the monitoring equipment is working as intended, that the operators pos-sess the necessary literacy level to interpret the data correctly, that the early warn-ing system will function and reach the population seamlessly, and that the local authorities have evacuation plans in place. This also requires local authorities to have a conscious relationship with communication technology and other forms of technology operating in the background, ensuring the reliability of means of communication to be operational and ready to transmit early warning alerts and information about potential events.

Malfunctions, false alarms, and poorly executed evacuation drills are elements that can erode the public's trust in the system. Similarly, lack of openness when it comes to embedded uncertainty in these prediction technologies and the interpretation and usage of data can reduce public trust not only in the monitoring process itself but also in the hazard zone maps developed, early warning alerts issued, or advice on evacuation or building restrictions provided by the authorities. Technology, and the new knowledge it produces through generating data that can be interpreted by experts, form a basis for continuously assessing what we know and if and how we should adjust to the new knowledge. For example, the development of updated wave height calculations from Jettan and Indre Nordnes in Kåfjord implies that the surrounding municipalities need to update spatial plans and building restrictions, as well as emergency preparedness plans. For the public, this is also a mental exercise affecting their sense of self and sense of safety as they adjust to new knowledge about areas that previously had been considered safe from the impact of a rockslide-induced tsunami, suddenly being placed under development restrictions. The new restrictions on development in these communities are also a source of frustration that can erode trust in the system, as some can perceive this measure as a lack of confidence in the early warning system functioning as intended. This illustrates how technology shapes our relationship with the world reflexively, and it also serves to illustrate Ihde's statement of how technology is not neutral. Technology is value-laden, generative, and mediates our (human) relationship with our world, in this case, it shapes how the locals interact with and understand their communities. New knowledge developed by sophisticated technology has ethical and social implications, and it requires a conscious relationship with the technology we apply to anticipate, cope with, and adapt to living with the risk of natural hazards. What knowledge is created (or not created), what are the limits to the available technology, who has access to the data and holds the power of translation, and to what extent are those most impacted by the updated knowledge allowed a seat at the table to voice their concerns and co-create appropriate solutions? What we can anticipate and know something about, is also what we can prepare for and respond to.

As seen in this chapter, technology impacts what we can know something about, what we think, feel, or experience about something, by providing certain access to a given phenomenon. Technology can reveal or enhance certain parts of the world, but it can also hide other parts or limit us in certain aspects. One example is how technology appears to have taken precedence over local and traditional knowledge. We trust official early warning alerts over a local resident's assessment of weather and historical conditions in defining the risk level for an unstable rockslide. As we remember from the cases in Geiranger, locals knew about and tried to warn about the potential for displacement of unstable rock formations. Despite this, it still took decades before these areas were placed under continuous monitoring, based on instrumentational measurements, not local knowledge. Perhaps there are several other unstable rock formations in Norway than those already placed under a continuous monitoring scheme. Perhaps these are already known to local communities. A society that places a strong emphasis on technological artefacts and their expert interpretations illustrates that what technology gives us access to know about and experience, to a large extent, determines what gets the priority in local preparedness schemes. And maybe rightfully so, but this calls for a closer examination of the relationship between modern, technology-mediated knowledge and more local, traditional knowledge and how these are utilized in disaster management and climate adaptation schemes.

4.   Concluding reflections and implications

Interaction between humans, technology, and the environment can create new possibilities, behaviours, understandings, or realities. Technology is not just a passive tool but an active participant in shaping and transforming human experience with the physical world. New realms of experience, for instance, moving from physical onsite monitoring of slow-moving landslides to technological measurements that can detect millimetres of movement, provide new opportunities for developing disaster management schemes to safeguard exposed populations. But as technology is not neutral, we find that it can both reduce and amplify the perceived sense of safety. To some, a continuous landslide monitoring programme may represent increased safety and a continued existence in the risk-prone communities, while to others, this may have contributed to bringing the risk closer to home. Some may even choose to ignore the risk as a form of coping strategy that safeguards their ontological security while living in a high-risk environment. As people have an embedded need to not only be safe, but also to feel safe (Giddens, 1991), how the use of technology and the risk uncovered is communicated is of utmost importance to support a sense of safety and a certain level of trust in the system.

A stringent emergency preparedness regime that conflicts with further growth and development of local communities may erode people's trust in the technology, the knowledge produced from it, and the decisions made based on this new knowledge. With a strong dependence on literacy in interpreting data collected from sophisticated monitoring technologies, trust and openness are crucial for the functioning of the disaster management scheme that relies on such technology. This dependency on literate professionals to interpret the risk of landslides and fjord tsunamis underlines the importance of being aware of how technology mediates both what we know about the risk and how we experience it, and this awareness should be taken into consideration when communicating about landslide risk to the population. Including local knowledge in the disaster management process can contribute to facilitating trust and adherence to the emergency preparedness plans in place. While technology informs local disaster management, knowledge about how local communities perceive and live with the risk—their knowledge, concerns, and capacities—provides valuable insights that could and should inform local emergency preparedness plans. Applying local knowledge in formalized plans and processes can contribute to the identification of more appropriate actions based on local vulnerabilities, as well as access to necessary resources found in the communities (Lie et al., 2023; Heidenreich & Næss, 2024). And while complex monitoring systems require translation by experts, openness and transparent communication about risk will enable local populations to make their own, informed decisions, freeing up formal preparedness resources to be directed towards more vulnerable groups or areas during an event of heightened landslide risk. Simultaneously, it is important to be conscious of the potential for both deliberate and unintentional misunderstandings, as these monitoring technologies primarily have been designed to provide advice to decision-makers and professionals, not the general public.

To sum up, technology has provided us with access to enhanced knowledge about natural hazard risk, shaping current disaster management schemes. While this has provided us with a sense of control over nature and the risk of slow-moving landslides, the sense of safety among the population is heavily reliant on a certain level of trust in the technology and the interpretations provided by experts. Open communication about how technology mediates our experience of the world, the embedded uncertainty in the knowledge produced, and the inclusion of local knowledge are elements that should be considered within a disaster risk management context.

References

Aagaard, J., Friis, J. K., Sorenson, J., Tafdrup, O., & Hasse, C. (2018). *Postphenomenological Methodologies: New ways in mediating techno-human relationships*. Rowman and Littlefield.

Beck, U. (1992). *Risk society: Towards a new modernity*. SAGE Publications.

Blikra, L. H. (2012). The Åknes rockslide, Norway. In J. J. Clague & D. Stead (Eds.), *Landslides: Types, mechanisms and modeling* (pp. 323–335). Cambridge University Press.

Blikra, L. H., Anda, E., Høst, J., & Longva, O. (2006). *Åknes/Tafjord prosjektet: Sannsynlighet og risiko knyttet til fjellskred og flodbølger fra Åknes og Hegguraksla*. NGU Norges geologiske undersøkelse.

Blikra, L. H., & Christiansen, H. H. (2014). A field-based model of permafrost-controlled rockslide deformation in northern Norway. *Geomorphology*, 208, 34–49.

Blikra, L. H., & Kristensen, L. (2013). Monitoring concepts and requirements for large rockslides in Norway. In C. Margottini, P. Canuti & K. Sassa (Eds.), *Landslide science and practice: Vol. 2: Early warning, instrumentation and monitoring* (pp. 193–200). Springer Berlin Heidelberg.

Böhme, M., Bunkholt, H., Dehls, J., Oppikofer, T., Hermanns, R. L., Dalsegg, E., Kristensen, L., & Eriksen, H. Ø. (2016). *Geologisk modell og fare- og risikoklassifisering av det ustabile fjellpartiet Gamanjunni 3 i Manndalen, Troms*. NGU Norges geologiske undersøkelse.

Böhme, M., Hermanns, R. L., Gosse, J., Hilger, P., Eiken, T., Lauknes, T. R., & Dehls, J. F. (2019). Comparison of monitoring data with paleo–slip rates: Cosmogenic nuclide dating detects acceleration of a rockslide. *Geology*, 47(4), 339–342.

DSB. (2016). *Risikoanalyse av varslet fjellskred i Åknes (Krisescenarioer 2016)—analyser av alvorlige hendelser som kan ramme Norge, Issue*. Direktoratet for samfunnssikkerhet og beredskap.

Elvestad, A. B., & Haug, I. (2024, May 23). Får 28 millioner for å flytte skredutsatt fjøs. Men NVE «glemte» parets bolig:—Vi står fortsatt fast her. *iTromsø/Framtid i Nord*.

Furseth, A. (1985). Dommedagsfjellet. Tafjord 1937. Gyldendal Norsk Forlag.

Ganerød, G. V., Grøneng, G., Rønning, J. S., Dalsegg, E., Elvebakk, H., Tønnesen, J. F., Kveldsvik, V., Eiken, T., Blikra, L. H., & Braathen, A. (2008). Geological model of the Åknes rockslide, western Norway. *Engineering Geology, 102*(1), 1–18.

Giddens, A. (1990). *The consequences of modernity*. Polity Press.

Giddens, A. (1991). *Modernity and self-identity. Self and society in the late modern age*. Polity Press.

Granjou, C., Walker, J., & Salazar, J. F. (2017). The politics of anticipation: On knowing and governing environmental futures. *Futures, 92*, 5–11.

Hammer, R. (2021). *Far si historie: tek til på Åkerneset: frå oppvekst på ein fjellgard ved Storfjorden til familieliv og alderdom i bygda Langevåg*. Ragnhild Hammer.

Hamza, M., Staupe-Delgado, R., & Eriksson, K. (2024). Futureless futures. Reflections on life in doomed places in Nordic countries. In M. Cullen & M. Scott (Eds.), *Nordic approaches to climate-related human mobility*. Routledge.

Harbitz, C. B., Glimsdal, S., Løvholt, F., Kveldsvik, V., Pedersen, G. K., & Jensen, A. (2014). Rockslide tsunamis in complex fjords: From an unstable rock slope at Åkerneset to tsunami risk in western Norway. *Coastal Engineering, 88*, 101–122.

Harries, T. (2017). Ontological security and natural hazards. In *Oxford research encyclopedia of natural hazard science*. Oxford University Press.

Heidegger, M. (2010). *Being and time*. State University of New York Press (Original work published 1927).

Heidegger, M. (2013). *The question concerning technology, and other essays*. Harper Perennial Modern Classics (Original work published 1954).

Heidenreich, S., & Næss, R. (2024). Controlling the water: Citizens' place–related adaptation to landslides in mid-Norway. *Regional Environmental Change, 24*(2), 39.

Henderson, I. H. C., Saintot, A., Ganerød, G. V., & Blikra, L. H. (2007). *Fjellskredkartlegging i Troms*. NGU Norges geologiske undersøkelse.

Hepach, M. G., & Lüder, C. (2023). Sensing weather and climate: Phenomenological and ethnographic approaches. *Environment and Planning F, 2*(3), 350–368.

Hoe, M. (2023, August 28). Oppdaterte faresoner for flodbølge gir full byggestans rundt Lyngenfjorden. *iTromsø/Framtid i Nord*.

Hole, S. (2021, September 8). Slik skal dei hindre tsunamien i Geiranger. *NRK Møre og Romsdal*.

Høyer, A. B. (2024, May 19). Flodbølgefare stopper Olas planer:—Kom som en storoverraskelse. *Nordlys*.

Hungr, O., Leroueil, S., & Picarelli, L. (2014). The Varnes classification of landslide types, an update. *Landslides, 11*(2), 167–194.

Ihde, D. (1990). *Technology and the lifeworld: From garden to Earth*. Indiana University Press.

Ihde, D. (1991). *Instrumental realism: The interface between philosophy of science and philosophy of technology*. Indiana University Press.

Ihde, D. (1998). *Expanding hermeneutics: Visualism in science*. Northwestern University Press.

Ihde, D. (2009). *Postphenomenology and technoscience: The Peking University lectures*. Suny Press.

Jaboyedoff, M., Oppikofer, T., Derron, M.-H., Blikra, L. H., Böhme, M., & Saintot, A. (2011). Complex landslide behaviour and structural control: A three-dimensional conceptual model of Åknes rockslide, Norway. *Geological Society of London Special Publications, 351*(1), 147–161.

Kristensen, L., Pless, G., Blikra, L. H., & Anda, E. (2020). Management and monitoring of large rockslides in Norway. *ISRM International Symposium—EUROCK 2020*.

Kvasz, L. (2022). Instrumental realism–a new start for the philosophy of mathematics and the philosophy of science. In W. J. Gonzalez (Ed.), *Current trends in philosophy of science: A prospective for the near future* (pp. 165–188). Springer.

Kveldsvik, V., Einstein, H. H., Nilsen, B., & Blikra, L. H. (2009). Numerical analysis of the 650,000 m2 Åknes rock slope based on measured displacements and geotechnical data. *Rock Mechanics and Rock Engineering, 42*(5), 689–728.

Lacroix, P., Handwerger, A. L., & Bièvre, G. (2020). Life and death of slow-moving landslides. *Nature Reviews Earth and Environment, 1*(8), 404–419.

Latour, B., & Woolgar, S. (1986). *Laboratory life: The construction of scientific facts.* Princeton University Press.

Lie, L. B., de Korte, L., & Pursiainen, C. H. (2023). "Here, I will stay until I die"—exploring the relationship between place attachment, risk perception, and coping behavior in two small Norwegian communities. *Regional Environmental Change, 23*(3), 115.

Mathews, A. S., & Barnes, J. (2016). Prognosis: Visions of environmental futures. *Journal of the Royal Anthropological Institute, 22*(S1), 9–26.

NVE. (2024). *NVEs veileder for sikkerhet mot fjellskred.* https://veiledere.nve.no/fjellskred/

Nørskov, M. (2015). Revisiting Ihde's fourfold "technological relationships": Application and modification. *Philosophy & Technology, 28*, 189–207.

Quarantelli, E. L. (2000). Disaster planning, emergency management, and civil protection: The historical development of organized efforts to plan for and to respond to disasters. *University of Delaware Disaster Research Center Preliminary Paper #301.*

Rosenberger, R., & Verbeek, P. P. (2015). *Postphenomenological investigations: Essays on human-technology relations.* Lexington Books.

Sandersen, F., Bakkehøi, S., Hestnes, E., & Lied, K. (1996). The influence of meteorological factors on the initiation of debris flows, rockfalls, rockslides and rockmass stability. *The 7th International Symposium on Landslides*, Trondheim, Norway.

Sandvik, P., Longva, R., Behrentz, J., Kjølås, H., & Engås, T. (2015). Fjellet som trugar. *Sunnmørsposten.*

Staupe-Delgado, R. (2019). Progress, traditions and future directions in research on disasters involving slow-onset hazards. *Disaster Prevention and Management, 28*(5), 623–635.

Staupe-Delgado, R. (2021). *Disasters and life in anticipation of slow calamity: Perspectives from the Colombian Andes.* Routledge.

Stav, T. U. (2013, October 13). Lever i skyggen av Nordnesfjellet. *NRK Troms og Finnmark.*

Storrøsten, E. B., & Glimsdal, S. (2023). *Flodbølger etter skred i Lyngen. Oppdaterte skredvolumer og faresoner.* NGI Norges Geotekniske Institutt.

Sugawara, S.-E. (2023). The multistability of predictive technology in nuclear disasters. *Social Studies of Science, 53*(4), 495–521.

Taylor, C., Robinson, T. R., Dunning, S., Rachel Carr, J., & Westoby, M. (2023). Glacial lake outburst floods threaten millions globally. *Nature Communications, 14*(1), 487.

Verbeek, P. P. (2001). Don Ihde: The technological lifeworld. In H. Achterhuis (Ed.), *American philosophy of technology: The empirical turn* (pp. 119–146). Indiana University Press.

Verbeek, P. P. (2005). *What things do: Philosophical reflections on technology, agency, and design.* Penn State University Press.

Epilogue

Some after-thoughts about before-it-happens

Monika Gabriela Bartoszewicz and Reidar Staupe

Between Luhmann's assertion that 'the future cannot begin' (Luhmann, 1976) and the pop culture-wisdom that 'the future started yesterday, and we're already late,' anticipation emerges. It is in this realm of anticipation that the future takes shape, whether it surges forward on a wave of desire and excitement or advances with a tide of anxiety and fear. This volume confronts the myriad catastrophic premonitions that saturate our collective consciousness. It directly addresses how a sense of impending doom has become a central organizing principle in our perception and experience of time. However, this work is not merely a creative exercise in futuristic speculation for two reasons.

First, aligning with the insights of Cantó-Milà and Seebach (2024), our foundational premise is that anticipations reveal more about our present realities than about the future. The constellations of imagined possibilities—both plausible and implausible—do not necessarily enlighten us about what will come to pass. Instead, they primarily reflect our current perceptions and anxieties. Second, the nature of anticipation is inherently relational and communal, embedded deeply within the fabric of society. The horrendous fears that drive these foreboding visions, along with the epistemic emotions that valuate and affirm them, are never merely fidgets of individual imagination. They are collectively negotiated and amplified, feeding and informing one another, thus creating a vortex of potential futures while simultaneously shaping the ways in which we meet them. Disastrous anticipations inhabit the realm of affective ontology of future (Bartoszewicz, 2021) where future imaginaries encompass the widely shared fears that become not merely incorporated in our worldviews, but also in our responses that go far beyond personalized doomscrolling narratives. In short, institutionalized anticipations rooted in societal reciprocity become security policies.

The chapters collected here address a wide range of issues concerning how we think about the sense of impending disaster, simultaneously bringing into view many adjacent issues. We contemplate anticipation through a lens less concerned with what might happen and more focused on how these imaginaries are constructed and sustained. Of all the forms and configurations of temporality, anticipation is perhaps the most entangled with the horizon of expectations, whether reflecting human aspirations or, conversely, manifesting human fears. Given that fear is essentially the anticipation of impending evil—out of immediate temporal

DOI: 10.4324/9781003537311-12

reach yet within the realm of temporal imagination—anticipation extends human engagement beyond the tangible. Can we then propose, by sidestepping the traditional concerns about the future, that anticipation is more concerned with the politics of expectation than with the politics of fear (Furedi, 2007)? Our volume adopts the perspective of the anticipated rather than the present, focusing on what is conceived rather than what is observable.

Within the not-yet-realized, nonfactual nature of these anticipations, the volume highlights three primary dimensions of engagement. First, it examines the nature of response, exploring various frameworks for understanding. This includes positioning as Goldberg does, employing models like those proposed by Stephen and Flaherty, utilizing typologies like Bartoszewicz, or through spatial anchoring as Olofsson does, and technological contexts like Bakke Lie and Staupe. Second, it considers the direction of these anticipations, discussing concepts like chronopolitics and the formation of temporizing assemblages, as explored by Usón and Stehrenberger, or security orientations as analyzed by Gil, in conjunction with temporal agogics explored by Bartoszewicz or indeed misdirections investigated by Matejova. Last, the collection addresses the modality of response manifested on the continuum from utopian to dystopian imperatives discussed by Bartoszewicz. This is approached through different emotional and perceptual lenses—whether it be the moods highlighted by Khan and Staupe, the misconstrued perceptions demonstrated by Matejova, or the mental approximations discussed by Schabowska.

If we retain Cantó-Milà and Seebach's terminology (2024, p. 304), this volume brings together a spectrum of imaginaries that, while elusive and impossible to grasp directly, also form an assemblage of images, figures, and forms that articulate anticipated horrors. These images—concrete contents evoked by thoughts of the future—include geopolitical and health crises, climate change, displacement, and potentially techno-capitalist catastrophes. The forms that convey meaning beyond the mere content of each image include concepts such as 'apocalyptic acceleration' (Chapter 3), 'surviving in time' (Chapter 5), and 'changing mood' (Chapter 6). Our overarching framework, understood as a form, is that of a polycrisis. This framework shapes the interactions and presentations of these images and forms, illustrating that anticipation, in its relational aspect, is fundamentally a narrative exercise, which projects future events and provides orientation, not through calculating probabilities but through a sense of foreboding. Foreboding serves as a means of understanding, and awareness shapes our framing of anticipation, which becomes factual without originating as an empirical fact. This liberates anticipations from a temporal limitation of something whose impact is defined by its certainty or by its immanence and inevitability.

Anticipation is not about straining toward the future; rather, it is about the future forcefully making its presence felt in the present. Through this dynamic, the social world extends into open futures characterized by latency and immanence—realities not yet congealed into matter. In this regard, anticipation markedly differs from both forecasts and predictions, as defined by Guéguen and Jeanpierre (2024, p. 230). They differentiate forecasting, which is based on past and present data extended through logical extrapolations into the future, from predictions that aim to identify possible futures. Disastrous anticipations, however, represent the antithesis of desired futures; they are merely the offspring of the undesired, irrespective of its likelihood. Thus, anticipation does not diminish uncertainty; rather, it constitutes a collective experiment with the future. It is simultaneously imminent and distant, transcending time yet present in its effects, both possible and not. The anticipations discussed througout our volume embody all the characteristics of futures-in-the-making, which Adam (2024, p. 193) describes as futures that have not yet materialized as phenomena and symptoms, thus lacking tangibility but wielding significant potential impacts.

A place-based approach can further illuminate the nature of anticipatory experience (Hamza et al., 2024, p. 117). To anticipate is essentially to declare that the future is already here. While nebulous, anticipations are also manifestations of time and place, as the modalities of specific temporal expectations do not emerge randomly but materialize in particular loci. Expectation thus requires both temporal and spatial dimensions for its accurate articulation. Consequently, the reflections presented in this volume are inherently spatially conditioned, a perspective that would undoubtedly please Piet Strydom (2024), who developed the concept of the future as a formal cultural model that transitions from necessity to the realm of possibility. Nonetheless, through anchoring, this volume demonstrates that the true nature of catastrophe is not spatial displacement but temporal dissonance. In other words, disastrous anticipations reveal that catastrophe is not so much a matter out of place, but primarily a matter out of time.

Operating in the mode of possibility not only facilitates an immanent anticipatory orientation but also accentuates its cognitive dimension. However, disastrous anticipations often obscure the future, eclipsing alternative, potentially positive might-comes. Indeed, the concept of 'new catastrophism,' as proposed by Urry (2016, p. 91), is not entirely novel. Each era crafts its own apocalyptic visions— events that simultaneously herald suffering and promise salvation, as Mascareño (2024, p. 353) candidly observes. This sense of proximity to an endpoint aligns with the semantic notion of a katastrophe, a sudden transition or change occurring across various systemic levels—be it natural, social, economic, or political—or even across multiple systems simultaneously, as the concept of polycrisis suggests.

It is a commonplace observation that we live in an era dominated by pervasive anxiety, largely stemming from internal processes within our societies underscored by a diminishing belief in progress, characterized by incessant obsolescence. This anxiety occupies a realm filled with fears and worries, carrying with it implicit assumptions about possible threats. The crises have coalesced, leading to an amplification of impacts that makes our situation more challenging to address. Such interconnectedness of problems highlights the intersectionality and interrelatedness of challenges, adding layers of urgency and complexity in how to face them— there are no easy fixes. These are systemic and structural issues within societies that require profound engagement. Attention to crises offers additional insights into the temporal complexity of anticipation. During such times, Adam observes (2024, pp. 193–194), established methods become ineffective and begin to lose relevance, thereby opening pathways to alternatives that were previously not considered viable. It is precisely in these moments that the taken for granted is questioned; established social routines, political structures, and institutional patterns disintegrate; traditions are abandoned; and customary ways of doing things are disrupted. This upheaval leads to a categorical imperative to prepare, evolving in dystopian contexts into the idea that the future imposes an almost dictatorial immediacy, against which the present must continually contend (Andersson, 2024, p. 187). Anticipated trouble necessitates that expectations be adapted and preemptive measures be devised, all under the unease with what is to become, often coupled with accelerated tensions that spiral into further uncertainty.

But if the future is looming, what exactly is in motion? Is it us accelerating toward it, or is it speeding toward us? Which element is truly movable? And pondering further on the anticipatory dynamism: Are we paralyzed in wait, attempting to slow its approach, or trying to divert, if not even reverse, its course? To address these questions, we must acknowledge that anticipation arises from the abyss stretching between interventionist tactics and creative approaches to the future. Driven by a fear of what may come, anticipation not only imagines but also seeks to preemptively mitigate its own projections, intervening in the course of events, even those that are neither probable nor imminent. Here, anticipation benefits from a nuance introduced by Esposito (2024, pp. 215–216) who differentiates between preparedness, which equips us to handle the 'known unknowns'—the future surprises we can foresee—and readiness, which is more about an organizational state. One can be prepared for an anticipated situation without being truly ready to face it.

The hope that emerges from the apocalyptic Pandora's box is more than a mere afterthought; in an apocalyptic setting, redemption is reserved only for those who comply. This sense of future inevitability, spurred by apocalyptic premonitions regardless of their imminence, feeds anticipation with actions taken in the present. Apocalyptic thinking is inherently political in how it serves to justify beneficial interventions and delineate harmful practices. Therein lies the normative urgency to discern between detrimental inaction and beneficial interventions that are legitimized by their ability to mitigate an ominous future. In doing so, anticipations are a mirror where radical changes advocated by prefigurative politics are reflected. Prefiguration aims to embody aspects of the envisioned future society today, stemming from the belief that means and ends are inseparable (Raekstad & Gradin, 2020, pp. 19, 35). This positions anticipators as trendsetters, underscoring why the authors of chapters collected in this volume and their insights are invaluable: every widespread human idea or behavior was once prefigured by those who embraced it early.

Concluding a book on the theme of hope piercing through the veil of impending disaster might seem cliché. Yet, as Loren Goldman points out, hope is often mistakenly equated with a naive optimism that blindly expects a brighter future, ignoring the harsh realities of the present. However, throughout the chapters collected in this volume, hope embodies the aspirational essence of human endeavors, challenging the notion that it is merely an idle predisposition. Far from being a passive longing, hope acts as a dynamic catalyst for action, serving as a potent remedy against the paralysis often induced by disastrous anticipations. As opposed to fear, which is not conscious, hope is something we can opt for. Unlike fear, which often arises unconsciously, hope is a volitional. We discover we are scared, stumbling upon fear, or in some instances, it finds us—sometimes manifesting through a visceral, psychosomatic reaction, as Schabowska shows in her chapter. To hope is an act of will and may even require concerted effort; on the contrary, while fear comes instinctively, overcoming it typically demands exertion.

This is not to suggest that hope is merely wishful thinking that good will triumph over evil. Rather, it acknowledges and harnesses human agency. As Goldman articulates, hope encourages us to behave as though a better future is attainable, provided we recognize that the realization of any future largely depends on our own efforts (Goldman, 2024, p. 324). Although external circumstances inevitably shape the trajectory of events, they do not diminish our capacity to guide these events toward desired outcomes. But for this to happen, the belief in a better future, in any future possible, is crucial; it fuels our persistence even when immediate results are obscure or unforeseen. In this light, hope is not just an emotional comfort but a strategic imperative, vital for facing and overcoming the challenges that loom before us.

Neither do we want to conclude with a call for a more utopian mindset that encourages the anticipation of ideal social, political, economic, and cultural models starkly contrasting with our current systems (Featherstone, 2024, pp. 332–333). Yet, it is within this utopian paradigm that our societies exhibit a resentful, addictive, and panicked relationship with the concept of time. Society grapples with time, driven by an insatiable urge to accelerate progress, an endeavor that ultimately proves unattainable. This is crucial, as our societal identity fundamentally hinges on our relationship with time and our place within historical progress. What we hope our volume reveals is a significant omission in our collective understanding. It is not merely the eschatological failures or the inability to realize utopian visions within our lifetimes that are at stake. Rather, it is that the transformation of utopian aspirations into a pursuit of material hedonism, often masquerading as empathy, transforms ideals into selfish desires. Faustians perceive themselves on the brink of eternity, relentlessly propelled into an unknown future. Utopianists dwell in the anticipation of a world reshaped in the image of a better humanity (Andersson, 2024, p. 176). Hope enables us to view time holistically. A lifetime imbued with hope is not an end in itself, since even a failure becomes a foundation upon which future generations can build. And that is indeed something to look forward to.

References

Adam, B. (2024). Tempering the not-yet: Towards a social theory for the Anthropocene. *European Journal of Social Theory, 27*(2), 191–208.

Andersson, J. (2024). Between responsibility and escape: The future as an object of knowledge in the humanities and social sciences. *European Journal of Social Theory, 27*(2), 174–190.

Bartoszewicz, M. G. (2021). Identity and security: The affective ontology of populism. In *Political identification in Europe: Community in crisis?* (pp. 93–110). Emerald Publishing Limited.

Cantó-Milà, N., & Seebach, S. (2024). Between temporalities, imaginaries and imagination: A framework for analysing futures. *European Journal of Social Theory*, *27*(2), 298–313.

Esposito, E. (2024). Can we use the open future? Preparedness and innovation in times of self-generated uncertainty. *European Journal of Social Theory*, 13684310231224546.

Featherstone, M. (2024). The tragedy of utopia in the age of the Anthropocene: Beyond dystopia, despair and catastrophic futures. *European Journal of Social Theory*, *27*(2), 332–351.

Furedi, F. (2007). *Politics of fear*. Bloomsbury Publishing.

Goldman, L. (2024). Experimentation and the future(s) of political hope. *European Journal of Social Theory*, *27*(2), 314–331.

Guéguen, H., & Jeanpierre, L. (2024). The governance of possible futures and the regime of modern historicity: Critical theory and the modality of possibility. *European Journal of Social Theory*, *27*(2), 225–240.

Hamza, M., Staupe-Delgado, R., & Eriksson, K. (2024). Futureless futures: Reflections on life in doomed places in Nordic countries. In *Nordic approaches to climate-related human mobility* (pp. 117–133). Routledge.

Luhmann, N. (1976). The future cannot begin: Temporal structures in modern society. *Social research*, 130–152.

Mascareño, A. (2024). Contemporary visions of the next apocalypse: Climate change and artificial intelligence. *European Journal of Social Theory*, *27*(2), 352–371.

Raekstad, P., & Gradin, S. S. (2020). *Prefigurative politics: Building tomorrow today*. Polity Press.

Strydom, P. (2024). Towards a sociology of the future: An exploration in cognitive social theory. *European Journal of Social Theory*, *27*(2), 241–259.

Urry, J. (2016). *What is the future?* Polity.

Index

Note: Page numbers in *italic* indicate a figure, and page numbers in **bold** indicate a table on the corresponding page.

For Product Safety Concerns and Information please contact our EU
representative GPSR@taylorandfrancis.com Taylor & Francis Verlag GmbH,
Kaufingerstraße 24, 80331 München, Germany

Printed and bound by CPI Group (UK) Ltd, Croydon, CR0 4YY
02/06/2025
01890766-0002